HISTORICAL ECOLOGY

D1598702

Publication of the Advanced Seminar Series
is made possible by generous support
from the Brown Foundation

School of American Research
Advanced Seminar Series
Douglas W. Schwartz, General Editor

HISTORICAL ECOLOGY
Contributors

Carole L. Crumley
Department of Anthropology
University of North Carolina, Chapel Hill

Joel D. Gunn
Department of Anthropology
University of North Carolina, Chapel Hill

Fekri A. Hassan
Department of Anthropology
Washington State University, Pullman

Alice E. Ingerson
Lincoln Institute of Land Policy
Cambridge, Massachusetts

William H. Marquardt
Department of Anthropology
Florida Museum of Natural History, Gainesville

Thomas H. McGovern
Department of Anthropology
Hunter College
City University of New York

Thomas C. Patterson
Department of Anthropology
Temple University

Peter R. Schmidt
Center for African Studies
University of Florida, Gainesville

Bruce P. Winterhalder
Department of Anthropology
University of North Carolina, Chapel Hill

HISTORICAL
❦ECOLOGY❦

CULTURAL KNOWLEDGE AND
CHANGING LANDSCAPES

Edited by

CAROLE L. CRUMLEY

SCHOOL OF AMERICAN RESEARCH PRESS
SANTA FE, NEW MEXICO

SCHOOL OF AMERICAN RESEARCH PRESS
Post Office Box 2188
Santa Fe, New Mexico 87504-2188

Distributed by the University of Washington Press

Library of Congress Cataloging-in-Publication Data

Historical ecology : cultural knowledge and changing landscapes /
    edited by Carole L. Crumley.—1st ed.
        p. cm.—(School of American Research advanced seminar series)
    Includes bibliographical references and index.
    ISBN 0-933452-85-3 : $22.50
    1. Landscapes changes—History. 2. Landscape assessment—History.
3. Human ecology—History. I.   Crumley, Carole L. II.   Series.
GF90.H57   1993
304.2—dc20   93-6108
                                                                              CIP

Cover illustration: Ruins of Pecos Pueblo, 1846.
From *A Report & Map of the Examination of New Mexico in the Years 1846–'47,
Made by Lieut. J. W. Abert, of the Topographical Corps.* Washington, D.C.:
U.S. Congress, 1848. Courtesy Museum of New Mexico, neg. no. 6504.

Contents

Illustrations

Tables

HISTORICAL ECOLOGY

Preface

For two decades I have taught a course titled "Ethnohistory." The class syllabus bears signs of my classics background, our research group's ongoing work in France, and the influence of two professors from my time at the University of Wisconsin: the late North American ethnohistorian David Baerreis, and the historical climatologist Reid A. Bryson. My students and I read Vansina on oral tradition, and ethnography by Herodotus and the Jesuits; we pore over maps and photographs; we watch documentaries on the Vietnam War and grainy World War II army training films. We discuss quantitative methods and psychohistory, and the politics of archaeology and history in the marking of class, ethnicity, race, and nationality.

One would think that such a program would keep us sufficiently engaged. For the past decade, however, a lecture topic termed "Environmental Studies" has taken ever more class time. As my departmental duties expanded to include the graduate core course in ecology, it became difficult to keep the two courses' contents distinct. Finally I instituted a new course, "Historical Ecology," to address the important work of environmental historians, anthropologists, geographers, and others who seek to combine evidence of the human past with evidence about the environment by studying the evolution of landscapes.

The School of American Research advanced seminar on historical ecology, which gave rise to this volume, was held in October 1990 on the School's campus in Santa Fe, New Mexico. Participants were Carole L. Crumley (organizer), Joel D. Gunn, Fekri A. Hassan, Alice E. Ingerson, William H. Marquardt, Thomas H. McGovern, Christine Padoch, Thomas C. Patterson, Peter R. Schmidt, and Bruce P. Winterhalder.

Although the topic could prompt lively discussion among geographers, historians, natural scientists, and philosophers (to name a few), all the seminar participants are anthropologists. This choice was made so a common vocabulary would undergird the discussion of a difficult topic.

The subject's complexity stems from its intentional admixture of natural scientific and historical approaches. Our intent was to explore, in an explicitly human context, the "Great Divide" examined in C. P. Snow's *The Two Cultures and the Scientific Revolution* (1959). The subdisciplines represented among the anthropologists are ethnohistory, archaeology, evolutionary and human ecology, ethnography, physical anthropology, ethnobotany, geomorphology, and paleoclimatology.

This book concentrates on the unique contribution that anthropologists, especially those trained in diachronic approaches, can make in understanding the human-environment relation. The work of these individuals can build a conceptual bridge between the natural/physical sciences and the social sciences, and between the sciences and the humanities. The challenge will come in the practical application of particular landscape histories to regional and global issues; it is here that the responsibilities of other social scientists, humanists, and legal and medical policy specialists begin.

The final afternoon of the seminar found the participants wishing to frame a collective statement that would symbolize our unanimity of purpose and subsume differences of approach. The resulting Santa Fe Accord is found in the volume's epilogue.

In addition to thanking my students, who pressed both for more emphasis on environmental history and for praxis, I would like to thank Jonathan Haas (who was then director of programs and research at the School of American Research) and Richard Fox (then of Duke University) for encouraging me to organize the advanced seminar from which this book arose. Reid Bryson has asked me hard questions about climate and history for more than two decades, and I thank him for his persistence and far-reaching intellect. Finally, I would like to dedicate our collective work to the memory of my father, Howard M. Crumley, who could see well beyond the time and space he inhabited.

Carole L. Crumley

Chapter 1

Historical Ecology

A Multidimensional Ecological Orientation

Carole L. Crumley

Environmental change is arguably the most pressing and potentially disastrous problem facing the global community. Pollution, global warming, species extinctions, and massive disruptions of critical ecosystems have become commonplace topics, although consensus about how these problems are to be addressed continues to elude policymakers.

Although recent improvements in the quality and quantity of data documenting global environmental change have been dramatic, those who seek solutions to the problems this change will generate have, until recently, been physical scientists, engineers, or administrators with little or no training in the social and biological sciences. Global climate models (GCMs), fine-resolution remotely sensed data, and the computer-assisted manipulation of spatial information (GIS)—to name a few—have offered sophisticated means by which environments could be seen to vary through time. In conjunction with established techniques, such as geomorphology and chemical and physical dating, an impressive array of scientific tools now exists with which environmental change can be traced.

Although these developments have enabled researchers to ask complex questions about the relationships among elements affecting and affected by climate, few efforts have been made to incorporate information either about how humans have altered the environment or about how environmental change revised human activity. Changes in subsistence strategies, demography, or perception have, through time, resulted in both intentional and unintentional modification of the global environment. Although anthropologists (especially archaeologists), geographers, historians, and other social scientists have reconstructed many of these complex interactions from as long ago as the early Pleistocene (three million years ago), the data have not been incorporated into a comprehensive, interdisciplinary framework reflecting the contributions of social, physical, and biological scientists and humanists.

Even broadly trained individuals find it difficult to correlate information from a host of disciplines and extract concepts and methods applicable to contemporary problems. Only a handful of disciplines bridge natural and social sciences, the humanities, and the professions; among the most comprehensive and theoretically sophisticated is anthropology.

The advantages of using an anthropological approach to explore the human role in environmental change are considerable. Anthropology, broadly understood, is integrative and comparative; inclusive of temporal, spatial, and cultural dimensions; and dynamic. The discipline's historic focus on the dynamics of change render an anthropological perspective particularly appropriate in unraveling complex chains of mutual causation in human-environment relations.

Yet even within anthropology, contradictions that reflect contemporary industrialized societies' dualistic characterization of culture and nature are evident in the divisions within the field. In introductory anthropology classes everywhere, the field's fundamental contradiction is laid out in the course of lectures and in the structure of texts. Rarely is this contradiction examined, because its dangers are myriad and every instructor, whatever his or her intellectual orientation, sees in its discussion an invitation to disaster.

The contradiction is this: the first part of the story of the human species is couched in evolutionary and environmental terms, the second denies environment a meaningful role in human history. In examining the differences between the genus *Homo* and other species, anthropologists speak knowledgeably of the role of omnivorous diet and problem-solving abilities in the expansion of a primate niche into previously uninhabitable environments. Thus the groundwork for the essential contradiction is laid: documentation of the inexorable ascendance of culture-bearing primates begins with the exploration of tool technology and continues through intentional burial, cave decoration, animal and plant domestication, and state formation to the examination of global economics and the celebration of cultural diversity.

The environment becomes less and less important to the story: midway through the text or the term, the environment no longer figures in the narrative except as a resource to be commoditized; values, beliefs and issues, history, and culture constitute the key elements of the explanatory framework. Archaeologists and physical anthropologists rail against their sociocultural colleagues, who put issues in human adaptation, genetics, and population aside in favor of a textured analysis of contemporary human thought and action. Sociocultural anthropologists remain suspicious that their colleagues flirt with the determinisms: racial, environmental, social. Neither acknowledges (at least explicitly) their mutual reliance on elements of the tale that support their respective arguments; reflecting the values of industrial society as a whole, the story's logical flaw—that culture has triumphed over nature—remains implicit and unexamined.

Yet by the end of most introductory anthropology courses and texts, the lecturer or author takes up the single most pressing issue: rapid global environmental change at the hands of the human species. The environment, marginalized in the latter portions of the story of human evolution, becomes again the central problem for the species. To claim an integrative, holistic, and dynamic approach to human-environment relations, anthropology must transcend this fundamental contradiction.

How might this quandary be resolved? This book addresses the issue by employing a variety of approaches current within anthropology and in related natural and social science disciplines and the humanities. Although the study of ecology—the relationships among living organisms or between them and the physical environment—would seem inclusive of human-environment relations, the majority of ecologists study nonhuman relationships.

The field itself is bifurcated: macro-scale ecologists, originators of the discipline and major proponents of the global-scale ecology of the 1960s, have lost political ground (and thus funding) to micro-scale ecologists. With the exception of programs at some universities (such as New Mexico and Georgia), ecology, in the hands of microecologists, has been incorporated into schools of medicine or public health and departments of biology.

Among the macro-scale ecologies still practiced, *landscape ecology* takes up the study of ecology at the human scale and recognizes that human action modifies the habits and distributions of nonhuman species (e.g., through prescribed burning). Yet landscape ecologists persist in distinguishing human from "natural" landscapes (Ecological Society of America 1991; Forman and Godron 1986; Naveh and Lieberman 1990; see Ingerson, this volume).

Even among ecologists who explicitly study the human species, approaches cover a broad (albeit overlapping) range: *human ecology* (concentrating on systematic and evolutionary aspects), *social ecology* (emphasizing behavior), and *cultural ecology* (examining adaptive strategies). Human and social ecologists ably model human-environment relationships in the distant past or the ethnographic present. Their topics include hominid evolution in the Pleistocene and the behavior of social species (e.g., human and nonhuman primates, bees). Sociobiologists study a particular paradigm of human social ecology. Cultural ecologists and cultural geographers, while cognizant of the central role of culture in human adaptation, generally do not engage in the analysis of long-term change (but see Netting 1981; Heidenreich 1971). All lack an explicit historical component, whereby recent historical relationships, in which culture plays a significant part, are explored (see Winterhalder, this volume).

The humanities, especially history and philosophy, hold other keys. *Environmental history,* which began as an intellectual history of the environmental movement, has more recently emphasized the political and economic implications of human-environment interaction. *Environmental ethics* explores value systems as they relate to human conduct toward the environment. Although each field of study brings relevant information to bear on the study of human-environment interaction, none adopts a truly integrative approach.

In this volume we develop a multiscalar temporal and spatial frame, with an explicit focus on the role of human cognition in the human-environment dialectic. We argue that to chart sensible, sensitive policy, we must develop a comprehensive plan based on previous experimentation; following Bergson (and Marquardt, this volume), we seek to drain the past to irrigate the future.

HISTORICAL ANALOGS

The very historicity of environmental change spurs physical scientists' rejection of historical analogs. They argue that "novel circumstances"— twentieth-century chemicals, burgeoning population, scale changes in the human ability to modify the environment, and so on—render any historical analog irrelevant. Especially as regards climatic change, physical scientists consider requisite high-quality, long-term, instrumentally obtained data sets (from periods longer than 80–100 years) to be too rare to provide global baseline data, and that local conditions render proxy data (such as tree rings) insufficiently reliable except at the broadest of temporal scales. It is the rare physical scientist who is both intrigued by and able to employ information about past environmental conditions left by humans.

This attitude is due in part to dismay about the comparative messiness of "soft" social science data—the capriciousness of personal anecdote, the equifinality of material evidence—and in part to vested interests within the scientific community, which favor novel technologies and undervalue traditional solutions. Yet means do exist by which objections may be overcome and the overwhelming advantages of historical analogs can be realized.

Some benefits of historical analogs are that researchers can use a real region's air mass data, hydrology, soil, and topographic and species distributional data in their models. This is in marked contrast to the clumsy 400-mile-square, cell-based GCMs, which do not discriminate among biotic zones or at anywhere near a human scale. Through regionally documented ethnography, archaeology, and documentary evidence, researchers are able to read the results of human activities and choices and encompass the entire system, including both human and nonhuman components. Patterson (this volume) refers to these systems as totalities. The more varied the sources of data—ice cores, pollen, written accounts, and so on—the more effectively they can be used to cross-check conclusions independently.

Most important, the long-term understanding of global change is facilitated by documenting multiple regional environmental changes; in turn, these regional environmental histories can identify sensitive geographic locations for both human and other living populations (e.g., Bryson and Murray 1977). Interregional relationships may then be established and integrated with global data (Crumley and Marquardt 1990; Gunn 1991; Gunn and Crumley 1991). Thus, patterns of drought or flooding or the movement of ecotones through time can be mapped and a variety of impacts assessed.

This approach fosters creative thinking about the mitigation of contemporary problems and encourages the development of local and regional answers to global situations in which sensitive cultural issues play an important part.

HISTORICAL ANALOGS AND LANDSCAPES

The two types of historical analogs in current use are either strictly environmental (not inclusive of human agency; e.g., the global effects of the eruption of El Chichon in 1982 are like those of Krakatoa in 1883) or environmental/cultural, where causation is interactive (rather than deterministic) and the operant relationship between humans and the environment is assumed to be interactive (dialectical). The latter genre of historical analog, which traces sequences of mutual causation (e.g., a volcanic eruption

induces a period of crop failure, which is offset by reserves in some regions but not in others) is the subject of this book.

These interactive long-term sequences may be traced through the
study of changing *landscapes,* defined as the material manifestation of the
relation between humans and the environment (Crumley and Marquardt
1987). *Landscape ecology* is the study of the structure, function, and change
of a heterogeneous land area composed of interacting ecosystems (Forman
and Godron 1986). *Historical ecology* or *landscape history* is the study of
past ecosystems by charting the change in landscapes over time. Humans
are mobile, observant, and communicative; humans have adapted to—
and have been the periodic instigators of—ecosystemic change for at least
a million years. Circumstances in which human action may be seen as
pivotal vary with time, space, and culture.

Reliable and widely available evidence for the historical interrelat-
edness of humans and the environment may be read in the landscape.
Through several traditions in anthropology and related disciplines, landscape's changing spatial and temporal aspects are investigated. By infer-
ence, changing human attitudes toward the environment may also be
identified and their effects studied; it is, after all, decisions—both conscious and unconscious—and their effects that impact human lives and
livelihood and change the face of the earth. These complex cause-and-
effect relations must be patiently untangled.

For example, astronomically driven regional climate is modified by
latitude and topography, and by the nonuniform distribution of population and human activity; thus the existence of a forest is the result of both
location, which determines temperature and rainfall patterns, and previous and current human management practices. Regional climates both
affect and are affected by local (microclimatic) meteorological conditions,
many of which are also caused by humans (anthropogenic effects).

The introduction of historically informed environmental analysis
into regional studies offers an important opportunity for anthropologists,
archaeologists, historians, and geographers to demonstrate the relevance
of work in which they have been engaged for a century. Such a multidisciplinary approach is traditional for archaeologists, who employ both
natural and physical sciences (biology, geology, physics, chemistry) and
the humanities (history, classics, philosophy, linguistics). Despite what
sometimes appear to be rather parochial interests, archaeologists routinely
consult colleagues in the sciences and humanities or are trained in these
disciplines themselves. Most important, archaeology offers the temporal
and spatial breadth required for long-term ecological analysis.

Although the public perceives sites and artifacts to be the units of archaeological analysis, professional archaeologists have long sought to understand changes through time in regional populations, their distribution, and their economies. Requisite data include evidence for changing human-environment relationships in the form of remains of human manufacture and elements of the environment related to human activities. It seems evident that archaeology (*sensu lato*) is in an excellent position to render service to a number of fields by proposing a *rapprochement*.

Along with archaeology, ethnohistory is particularly suited to this formidable integrative task. Ethnohistorians are anthropologists who critically examine documents for evidence of human actions, relations, and attitudes. Ethnohistorians have a variety of historical evidence about past ecosystems at their disposal. Briefly, they may be divided into written (e.g., diaries, government documents), oral (stories about storms or pest invasions), and visual (dated drawings of Alpine glaciers documenting advances and retreats). Such information provides an important cross-check on environmental (varves in lake sediments, bubbles of air trapped in ice cores) and instrumental (LANDSAT scenes, weather balloons) records.

The memories and opinions living peoples have about their region are a rich and relatively untapped resource in contemporary environmental impact studies. Ethnographers study customs based on observations and understandings that guide indigenous peoples' adaptive strategies. This information is transferred—whether in complex ritual behavior or casual conversation—between and across generations; in addition to patterns of material relations with the environment, this transmittal of information constitutes *culture*.

Among a majority of the world's peoples, the decision to change practices or livelihood, or to relocate, is made on the basis of culturally transmitted information rather than scientists' projections and policymakers' edicts. Collectively, ethnography, ethnohistory, and archaeology—in conjunction with history, geography, and environmental sciences—offer a laboratory of past human choice and response in which the effects of environmental change can be palpably understood. Consultation with indigenous peoples can serve both as a practical basis for regionally appropriate adaptive solutions and as a means of increasing cooperation with eventual policies.

The practice of globally relevant archaeology, ethnohistory, ethnography, and related disciplines can be termed *historical ecology*. While the practical integration of spatial structures—such as habitations, river drainages, soils—may be accomplished with sophisticated information systems (e.g., GIS), the practical understanding of past and current *relationships* among these environmental and human systems requires a culturally specific temporal and spatial perspective applied at the regional scale.

This approach can be expected to identify (1) extant environmental and cultural evidence for the region in question (baseline data); (2) the range of current practices likely to be impacted by environmental change (impacts); (3) traditional and innovative adaptive strategies appropriate to the region, to the culture(s) affected, and to the nature and magnitude of the anticipated change (effective responses); and (4) the means by which such adaptations might be fostered (policy).

By making explicit contemporaneous and diachronic comparisons among regions, this approach may be expected to chart future course(s) of global action by addressing questions such as the following:

1. What was the duration and frequency of air mass patterns that characterized earlier warm episodes (e.g., middle Holocene, Roman Empire Climatic Optimum, Medieval Climatic Optimum), what region(s) were affected, and how did biotic and human communities respond to these conditions?

2. What spatial patterns are characteristic of biotic communities (species diversity and distribution, etc.) and human communities (settlement and land use, population agglomeration, etc.) in the earlier warm episodes?

3. How might these patterns be mapped in advance of contemporary global warming?

4. What measures could contemporary societies employ to cope with supra-annual (years, decades, centuries) cycles?

5. What human behaviors, attitudes, beliefs, economic strategies, and forms of governance are associated with periods of stable or unstable climate?

6. What measures could contemporary societies employ to cope with a marked increase in climatic instability (e.g., more hurricanes, more unseasonable weather)?

7. What values ensure the greatest flexibility in adapting to changed or unstable conditions?

8. Can environmental flexibility be taught?

9. How can a global environmental ethic also be culturally sensitive?

10. Are some governmental structures better able than others to employ the necessary strategies of adaptation?

INTEGRATIVE THEMES AND CONSIDERATIONS

Historical ecology traces the ongoing dialectical relations between human acts and acts of nature, made manifest in the *landscape*. Practices are maintained or modified, decisions are made, and ideas are given shape; a landscape retains the physical evidence of these mental activities. Past and present human use of the earth must be understood in order to frame effective environmental policies for the future; this necessitates deft integration of both environmental and cultural information at a variety of temporal and spatial scales. Landscape provides practitioners of many disciplines— from ecology and geography to architecture and philosophy—with a common and useful concept (Crumley and Marquardt 1990).

Even though people share many understandings about the real world, they participate to greater or lesser degrees in the production and application of perceptions of their environments. Inevitably, when decisions must be made, contradictions present themselves to both individuals and groups owing to the variety of roles and interests represented. Contradictions emerge between human groups because people occupying particular localities develop models of their environments based on their specific needs and experiences; these models may be at variance with those of other groups, leading to competition over scarce resources, religious conflicts, or wholesale disaster (see McGovern, this volume).

For example, an individual may wish to see a redwood forest preserved for future generations but also needs to be employed to ensure the survival of the present generation. If alternate employment is impossible because of educational or mobility restrictions, the person is forced to make an uncomfortable decision that leaves its mark on the face of the earth. Contradictions constitute the raw material of change, which occurs in the resolution of conflicts and tensions within individuals and among human groups, and between humans and their physical environment. Landscapes manifest the resolution(s) of these contradictions.

As abstractions whose components vary between individuals and among groups, landscapes cannot be studied in their totalities. The concept of scale is important in everyday human-environment relations and also in the study of those relations. Just as specific models of reality are conceived, negotiated among human groups, and applied at specific scales, so are investigations of landscapes undertaken—and the results of studies applied—at specific spatial and temporal scales. When a particular scale is chosen during one moment of analysis, it is because at that effective scale one can comprehend patterns (Marquardt and Crumley 1987:7).

The scale at which human action becomes a major factor in environmental change varies with time, space, and culture. In broad evolutionary terms, humans have indeed played an increasingly larger role in forming and modifying the environment, due both to the increasing size of the human population on the planet and to the increasingly formidable tools of modification that are available. Beyond this generalization, it is necessary to examine factors of duration, intensity, and periodicity at specific temporal and spatial scales, which cannot be defined in simply arithmetic terms. These parameters must be considered relative to a particular environment, because a small change in one environment could be perceived as a major change in another.

Each disturbance parameter has a threshold or crisis level that, if reached, triggers some cultural response. Thresholds are determined by, transmitted through, and vary with the corpus of cultural knowledge possessed by a given society (see Gunn, this volume). Determining both the threshold at which a response will be generated and also the particular response itself, cultural knowledge frames a society's resilience in the face of environmental (and other) disturbances. Transgenerational transmission of this knowledge ensures that risk acceptability remains dynamic and responsive to new experiences.

Thus, severe earthquakes in California are thought to occur only every hundred years or so; milder earthquakes are considered much more frequent. Yet, as the San Francisco earthquake early in this century demonstrated, severity (measured seismically) is an issue apart from the ability of structures to withstand both mild and severe quakes. California residents know that unreinforced buildings can sustain severe damage and cause loss of life as a result of even mild seismic events. Although this knowledge has resulted in stringent building codes, neither it—nor scientists' warnings of a large impending quake—has stemmed a steady increase in the state's population. The risk of being near the epicenter of a severe earthquake is considered by residents to be acceptably low, so long as the frequency of severe disturbances remains low and structures are rendered "earthquake-proof." Even living directly on the San Andreas fault is deemed by many to be an acceptable risk (Fallows 1981). Californians' decisions are based on both scientific and cultural information about the disturbance parameters of intensity, duration, and periodicity, coupled with a comparatively sophisticated understanding of West Coast geology. In contrast, residents of other areas of the country consider living anywhere in California to be courting unacceptable risk; the entire state is considered a dangerous region.

Any area of the earth may be termed a region for purposes of the study of human-environment relationships, so long as demonstrable homogeneity can be recognized. But any such region is inadequately conceptualized unless both its temporal relations (connections with the past and the future) and its spatial relations (connections with other areas at the same scale and at larger and smaller scales) are specified. This deficiency, prevalent in spatial approaches ranging from traditional culture-area studies to modern regional marketing analyses, can be rectified by using a multi-scalar (hence, multiregional) and multitemporal analytical strategy. A region, then, is a unit that can be recognized at a certain scale because of its distinctiveness from and interrelations with other such units, both spatially and temporally. The recognition of pattern and distinctiveness at one scale simply begins the analysis, uncovering contradictions whose resolution leads us to other scales, elements, and structures. Regional history constitutes an accessible account of choice and experiment as regards plant and animal species. Human choices that seem undeniably efficacious and correct in one context or period may prove disastrous in another; it is also true that cultural or biological connections between historic and contemporary populations of a region may be remote or nonexistent (e.g., the Maori of New Zealand and New Zealanders of European ancestry), but lessons learned by an indigenous group about a region often prove invaluable to newcomers.

Boundaries are of substantive interest because of their inherent duality, from the point of view both of the researcher and the communities under study (Crumley 1979; Crumley and Marquardt 1987; Green and Perlman 1985; Melko and Scott 1987; Renfrew and Cherry 1986). In general, arbitrary boundaries around an area of study are to be avoided, except in the initial stages of investigation. Instead, a research area defined at a number of different scales, from observation of a multiplicity of not necessarily coincident boundaries, offers a fertile ground for discovering the contradictions those divisions manifest.

One of the most attractive aspects of boundaries is that researchers in both the social and natural sciences are able to explore their characteristics in relation to living populations: ecologists refer to the boundaries between biomes (macro-scale) and communities of organisms (meso- and micro-scale) as ecotones. Throughout their history, human populations have actively positioned their communities to take advantage of animal and plant populations on either side of and within ecotones. The ecotone itself has species and communities peculiar to it. Perhaps most advantageous is the high correlation between the position of biomes (and their ecotones) and the position of climate-driven air mass activity (Beug 1982; Daget 1980; Denizot and Sauvage 1980; LaFontaine, Bryson, and Wendland 1990).

Administrative boundaries do not nest with but overlap environmental, social, and economic boundaries. For example, the Temperate-Mediterranean ecotone and the long spine of the Alps bifurcate southwest Europe, often rendering the politics of southern regions strongly divergent from national interests. Reflecting (among others) European Economic Community threats to the Mediterranean-oriented Provençal economy and the complex history that region and France share with Algeria, the rise of Jean-Marie LePen's ultra–right wing party in Provence has increased national sympathy for LePen's ideas and hampered Paris's negotiations within the European Community. The enduring power of Provence to influence the affairs of the European continent is in no small measure due to its historic mediation between temperate Europe and North Africa (see Crumley, this volume).

Another concept, especially relevant for both natural and social sciences, is *diversity*. Biological diversity, usually expressed in terms of genetic variation, has been proven critical to the maintenance of a variety of ecosystems. Similarly, the richness and innovative potential of cultural diversity can also be seen as a potent tool in the mitigation of human-environment relationships. Human activities must not always be seen as deleterious to a reified "Nature"; on the contrary, human ingenuity and husbandry have maintained natural resources as often as they have destroyed them (see Hassan, this volume).

For example, Christine Padoch (who joined us in Santa Fe) and Wil de Jong contrast "large" and "small" history in their research among Amazon basin peasants (Padoch and de Jong 1991). They argue the utility of ethnography in efforts to document extreme variation in the river, agricultural forms, domesticates, and ethnic admixture. They underscore the importance of great diversity—both biological and ethnic—in a dynamic environment, one in which the difference between the high water and the low water stages is eleven meters and the river's course changes overnight.

Finally, and of central importance, is the concept of *heterarchy* and its distinction from the more familiar notion of hierarchy. Heterarchies are complex systems in which elements have "the potential of being unranked (relative to other elements) or ranked in a number of ways, depending on systemic requirements" (Crumley 1979:144; Marquardt and Crumley 1987:11). In contrast, hierarchies are those in which some elements, on the basis of certain factors, are subordinate to others.

A common error, not just in settlement archaeology but in ecology, biology, and elsewhere, is that researchers uncritically "nest" levels of analysis, confusing scalar with control hierarchies and leading to the misinterpretation of chains of causation. Global-regional-local climate is an example of a scalar hierarchy; any level can affect any other. The American court system is an example of a control hierarchy; decisions at higher levels affect the operation of lower levels. Hierarchies are generally understood in a commonsense way, but scalar hierarchies are routinely mistaken for control hierarchies; in essence, the position of an element in a hierarchy is invariably given value.

Although hierarchies are of considerable utility in the organization of data at a variety of scales, the researcher risks forgetting that hierarchy is an analytic strategy imposed on the heterarchical face of nature. These hierarchical links, whether programmed or conceptual or both, hobble the understanding of complexity, bias analysis, and render inoperable a dynamic concept of region. It is quite possible (perhaps even probable) that events that occur at "subordinate" levels have major systemic effects: they can change parameters (boundaries) or "control levels" (center-periphery shifts, scale changes) or the ranking of various elements. For example, defense becomes more important than commerce, which causes elevation to be a more significant factor in explaining changes in settlement patterns than proximity to commercial routes.

Similarly, a single organism—not even necessarily high on the food chain—can change the ecology of a stream (as lamprey eels did in the Great Lakes) or the economy of entire regions (see also Schmidt, this volume). Hierarchies, although eminently worthy of study, are only one version of the ways in which elements might be ranked. If we are to study change in human perceptions of structure through time and across space we must include other, more flexible concepts of organizational structure. The concept of heterarchy reminds us of a natural, multidimensional fluctuation in the importance of elements. This flexibility is essential to a dynamic approach.

In summary, the concepts of landscape, scale, region, boundary, diversity, and organizational structure (hierarchy/heterarchy) encourage the development of language that bridges the social and natural sciences and facilitates the analysis of complex human-environment relations.

STRUCTURE OF THE VOLUME

The first three papers in this volume facilitate multidisciplinary thinking through exegesis of ideas that are often taken for granted (such as the utility of the ecosystem concept or the distinction between "Culture" and "Nature") and by forging links among global- and human-scale phenomena. The four papers that follow employ the concepts outlined above in detailed analyses of sustained human-environment relations in particular regions. The final two papers explore historical ecology in theory and practice.

Winterhalder's paper examines the intellectual context and customary use of the following terms and concepts: ecology, system, ecosystem, homeostasis, and equilibrium, as well as living-physical and human-living systems distinctions, causation, and environmental history. He also offers a working distinction between environmental historians and historical ecologists based on identification with their respective "home" disciplines (history and anthropology/ecology, respectively).

Ingerson elaborates this distinction, which may be termed the "nature-culture debate," and explores its poisonous effects in academia and elsewhere. Although scientists and environmental historians would seem to share a field of interest, these scholars' broader disciplinary affiliations exert centrifugal forces on collaborative efforts. Environmental historians have a perspective distinct from those of other historians; their predominant interest is the intellectual history of environmentalism. As a rule, natural scientists test hypotheses about the environment. Scientists dismiss as egotistical and polemical the historians' narrative style; historians find the scientists' work trivial and programmatic. Much of this mutual animosity is vented in the review process, posing a threat to interdisciplinary projects.

Gunn introduces the reader to the body of scientific evidence for historical global environmental change. He demonstrates how teleconnections can be used to ascertain the regional effects of global climatic change. This important technique enables both retrodiction (the modeling of past environments) and prediction at human spatial (regional and local) and temporal (seasons, years, decades) scales. This regionalization of our understanding of global environmental change is critical to the success of any mitigation.

Schmidt offers a cognitive blueprint of landscape use through time in a moist forest environment (equatorial Africa). His paper draws together population, early industrialization (Iron Age technology), environmental degradation, out-migration, social relations of production, and ideology in a convincing argument for their collective and cumulative epidemiological effect (AIDS) on contemporary Tanzanian society.

McGovern emphasizes the importance of high resource variability in the initial success of Norse agricultural colonization of Greenland and documents subsequent climatic change. Yet it was not deteriorating conditions but cultural beliefs and practices that led to the colony's demise from starvation despite bountiful available resources. Norse and Inuit alike refused to see the other as human, which in the Norse case was fatal: Inuit food (ringed seal) was excluded as a potential protein resource and colonists starved—not froze—to death.

Hassan explores long-term processes: the continuity of the past into the present through the study of structures' transformation through time. Using the flood history of the Nile ("time *as* the river"), he examines the role of elites in mediating attitudes toward the environment, and he attributes the durability of Egyptian life to a weak coupling between food production and central administration.

Crumley presents a case study from an ostensibly familiar period of European history in a new light, examining the role of climatic change in the capitulation of continental Celtic peoples to Roman domination. She concludes that a flawed understanding of what constitutes cultural complexity has led to a dangerous undervaluation of economic and social diversity in adapting to environmental change.

In Marquardt's paper, the analytic strategy outlined above finds practical application in south Florida. Marquardt explores the role of archaeology in contemporary environmental awareness. Using his research on the vanished Native American Calusa polity, he promotes public understanding of historic environmental conditions at the regional scale. He argues that conservation problems in Florida should be addressed with attention to social, demographic, and economic characteristics of current residents. Marquardt notes that since fourth graders can understand the intricate relations among mangrove swamps, fishes, and Indians, there is reason to attempt to disseminate a more complex and more accurate understanding of human-environment relations to the public as a whole. Marquardt's quote from Henri Bergson, "the present drains the past to irrigate the future," seems a particularly apt aphorism. Public education, as well as guidelines to aid administrators, policymakers, tourism, and historic preservation, can be constructed on such an analytic base.

At a broader scale, Patterson offers a review of the sociopolitical context of major environmental and ecological movements, chronicling their effect in shaping current attitudes toward the environment. He reviews the neo-Malthusian, expansionist, eco-development, and radical ecology movements and then argues that all fail to conceptualize humans and the environment as a single totality. He outlines the means by which deepening awareness of the complex nature of the relation, necessarily precursive to appropriate action, can be fostered.

Chapter 2

Concepts in Historical Ecology

The View from Evolutionary Ecology

Bruce Winterhalder

Our charge in this volume is to identify or, more boldly, to create concepts to guide an endeavor we call "historical ecology." Some things seem to me critical in such an undertaking. First, we must know what we mean by the term; clear definition will be essential. Second, we must be aware that concepts have a particular role in scientific analysis. They are important but they are not theory or methods, even though these three aspects of scientific investigation are always entangled. Third, although it will be important to enlist concepts supportive of this endeavor, we also must identify and try to understand how existing, sometimes implicit ideas may impede or thwart it. Finally, our deliberations occur in a context of heightened concern about the health of the environment. We have assumed practical as well as scholarly obligations to think in ways that entail pragmatic and ethical issues of remedy. This imposes urgency and groundedness on our discussions.

I shall try to address all of these considerations at least to some degree. Effective interdisciplinary cooperation will require that each gets our collective attention. My thoughts on this subject arise from the perspective of evolutionary ecology more than from population, community, or ecosystem ecology. I conduct most of my research in terms of the behavior of individuals in populations. My theoretical commitments are neo-Darwinian and my methodology primarily is that of microeconomics. Most of my empirical studies are in the form of ethnographic and simulation analyses. I work broadly within the tradition of ecological anthropology, studying both hunter-gatherers (Cree speakers, in northern Ontario) and peasant agriculturalists (Quechua speakers, in the Peruvian Andes). This orientation itself has a history (Winterhalder and Smith 1992), which assures it biases and limitations plus a few merits that I hope will be apparent.

HISTORICAL ECOLOGY

Historical ecology might mean several things: a commitment to certain theoretical principles, a methodology or form of investigation, a predilection to certain topics, or investigation within a framework provided by a certain set of concepts. At this early stage, probably any definition will be provisional. Nonetheless, the cross-disciplinary ambiguity, breadth, and nuance associated with the terms "history" and "ecology" beg explicit attention.

Ecology is the easier term. I take it to refer to the holistic study of relationships among living organisms or between them and the physical environment. The relationships may be dyadic (a predator and prey) or more complex (a community food web); explicit (parasite and host) or implicit (community stability); biophysical (ecotypic variation along a climatic gradient) or purely biological (competition). This definition encompasses a variety of more specific types of ecology—autecology, synecology, chemical ecology, population ecology, community ecology, ecosystems ecology, human ecology and so forth—most of which refer to self-evident topical specialities.

History is the more difficult term. History itself is the descriptive, chronological account of selected events given coherence and boundedness by reference to some theoretical proposition, analytical problem, or limitation of space or time. Adjectival uses of the word—as in our subject, "historical ecology"—are problematic and for our purposes perhaps meaningless. Strictly speaking, historical factors, causes, processes and the like do not exist. We can isolate such things as sociocultural or environmental causal factors or processes. Important properties of these may depend on their location in time, that is, they may have a *temporal dimension*. But we cannot define or isolate time itself as a causal variable or process. The same is true of (so-called) spatial variables or processes.

This fine distinction matters in at least two senses, one weak and one strong. In the weak sense it is slipshod usage, because it hides the fact that we are actually referring to the historical dimension of some unidentified type of variable or process. And in the strong sense, the adjectival form necessarily draws attention to a possibility that we wish to deny: that there is an ahistorical ecology.

What then are we to make of historical ecology, which for reasons just stated is a suspect combination of adjective and noun? I think we should mean the historical dimension in ecology and should use the reference not to distinguish a subset of ecological subject matter but rather to draw attention to a strong epistemological assertion: *a complete explanation of ecological structure and function must involve reference to the actual sequence and the timing of the causal events that produced them.* This assertion is a claim about the nature of ecological investigation, equivalent to the belief that it cannot be reduced to statements that might qualify as "laws" (Hull 1974:45–50). It is a claim with implications for theory and methodology, and for the kind of knowledge that we seek. It is a claim that is controversial in the philosophy of science (Hull 1974). Any explanation that cites only the type, number, and cumulative value of the independent variables is incomplete. It also must acknowledge their possible novelty and give attention to the actual order and timing of their impacts.

This raises the question, are all complex assemblages of linked and interacting parts historical? What properties make a system historical for purposes of analysis and management?

I will try to develop an answer from a simple beginning. Most everything has a narrative past, even a cobble. Obviously the same can be said for physical systems (a lightning storm) and mechanical systems, and for natural and anthropogenic ecosystems. Further, most things bear traces of this history. The cobble has a composition identifying certain parent materials, a structure that indicates its conditions of formation, and surface features that indicate its erosional exposure. This record may be highly imperfect, but it is directly observable, and the evidence, to the extent it is preserved, is usually interpreted by an expert with few uncertainties. On this much, historians and scientists might agree. Each also might find that past intrinsically worthy of study. A more difficult question follows: Does that history matter to our ability to explain the present or predict the future? What kinds of knowledge about an entity are dependent on the specifics of that narrative history? Are there important properties not discernible from present observation and analysis?

For the cobble we might do well without the narrative. We could reconstruct something of its origins, explain much about its present state, and in principle could predict its response to future conditions using data only from contemporary observation and experiment. The geologist who undertook this task might seek evidence of the cobble's history and might include it in his or her description, but strictly speaking the key scientific objective of explanation and prediction can be met without it. The cobble

has a history and bears traces of it, but its narrative past is largely inconsequential to what we can learn and might want to predict about it. The
cobble bares its soul; its extant "phenotype" is the full and direct expression of its essential properties. Without elaboration, I will claim that in
principle the same is true of any physical system.[1]

This is not the case for living systems—for simplicity, exemplified
here by an individual organism. The phenotype of an organism is a partial
and indirect manifestation of a special kind of history, a functional history
recorded by natural selection in its underlying genotype. The genotype
thus is both a record of a species' past and a program for its current adaptive interactions with the environment. It is especially important that this
historical record cannot be determined directly from the genotype, nor
can it be fully discerned from the organism's present phenotype, which
is observable only after the transformations occurring during a particular
ontogeny.

For this reason, the full set of functional relationships that would
enable us to predict the phenotype for each genotype in all possible environments (technically, the norm of reaction) is effectively "hidden" to analytical view (Lewontin 1974). The history that matters to living organisms,
the one they carry into their future interactions with their environment, is
a single, somewhat *opaque* layer beneath the entity we observe. Unless we
recover it as history, through knowing the temporal past of the organism,
this information is not directly accessible. Evolved beings do not bare their
souls; their phenotypes only partially and indirectly reveal their essential
properties.

Using an analogy, this is much like the "hiddenness" of the dynamic
properties of ecosystems (technically, the phase or domain of attraction
map; see below).[2] Functional ecosystem properties that we need to understand (e.g., resilience) reflect an equally deep and obscured history. As
in the case of genotype-environment interactions, these properties remain
potent but are incompletely and only indirectly revealed in the manifest
form and behavior (phenotype) of the extant system. As with phenotypes,
feasible manipulation of extant ecosystem processes provides only a limited ability to explain and predict. An ecosystem is an indirect manifestation of its own special kind of history, a functional history arising from the
partial coevolution and adjustments of the species composing it. Without
knowledge about the system's actual history, our understanding is quite
limited.

The inability of biologists to decipher the properties of evolved creatures fully, or those of the ecological systems composed of their inter-

actions, by studying their extant form gives substance to the claim that their full understanding requires historical analysis.

ENVIRONMENTAL HISTORY

Historical ecologists and environmental historians ought to be natural allies. For this reason, it may be instructive to compare the evolutionary view of history developed above with that of the latter group, especially the essays of Bailes (1985), White (1985), and Worster (1984, 1988a). This group has its intellectual origins in the work of Walter Prescott Webb and James Malin, but it has flourished recently with studies of the relationships among the natural (physical) environment and American society and social institutions. Environmental historians initially focused on leaders of the conservationist and preservationist movements, and on the relationship of the frontier and wilderness to American culture and politics. Specific topics include the history of the dust bowl, the development and impact of western lands irrigation, the creation of national parks, the relationship between environmentalism and scientific ecology, and the emergence of governmental regulation of environmentally sensitive activities.

Although environmental history began as a form of intellectual or institutional history, it more recently has turned to examinations of the political and economic implications of the topic. The reciprocal relationship between culture and nature has been revealed in several dominant themes: the European expansion and colonization of the New World (by people, weeds and animal pests, domesticates, and diseases), the expansion of market capitalism as the dominant global mode of economic action, and the expansion of science as a disciplined basis for pursuing mastery over nature. Worster (1988a:289) describes this self-consciously "revisionist effort" as one dedicated to writing historical narratives that recognize and document the role of the "earth as agent and presence in history," as a source of "fundamental forces." He adds, environmental "damage had itself become an historical force, threatening to bring down political regimes, disrupt social patterns, and force fundamental economic and technological change." (Worster 1988b:17).

Worster recognizes three levels for the analysis of human ecology: the organization and functioning of nature (which he allocates to the discipline of biological ecology and paleoecology); the realm of material culture, that "age-old dialogue between ecology and economy" (1988a:301) (where ecological anthropology holds sway); and the realm of mental culture, of perception, meanings, and values (where environmental historians and anthropologists divide duties along the axes of Western and non-Western peoples, history, and archaeology). Worster especially looks to ecological anthropologists for guidance and inspiration, because they "are among the most wide-ranging and theory-conscious observers of human behavior" (1988a:299). The contrast between his evaluation of anthropology, and geography and history, is instructive:

> Geographers, like historians, have tended to be more descriptive than analytical. Taking place rather than time as their focus, they have mapped the distribution of things, just as historians have narrated the sequence of events. Geographers have liked a good landscape just as historians have liked a good story. Both have shown a love of the particular and a reluctance to easy generalizing. (Worster 1988a:306)

Worster (1984) identifies ecological anthropology with the work of Julian Steward and his students, noting the influence on Steward of Karl Wittfogel and their joint commitment, historian and ecological anthropologist alike, to historical, comparative environmental studies. "So far has this study [of ecological anthropology] progressed that now it is the historian's turn to become learner and follower, seeking to apply the anthropologist's approach to the investigation of past societies" (1984:6).

When Worster comes to examine the "specific ways in which an ecological approach to history can be pursued, to ask what it can seek to do, what its limits are, and why its time at last has come" (1984:16), however, the results are disappointing. There is the admonishment that history itself has no theory to contribute to this task, being instead more a "clustering of interests." There is advice that "all generalizations must be rooted in specific times and places." There is acknowledgment of differences of subject matter (historians deal with written records of the modern era, etc.), and a short list of potential topics for interdisciplinary study.[3] But there is little about theory or methods, or even a clearly enunciated sense of the potential interdisciplinary meaning(s) of history in analyses that would combine natural science, social science, and humanism. Whatever its potential, the possible alliance of human ecologists and environmental historians is not yet set within an analytical framework that can encompass them both.

Because they are evolved creatures or aggregates of evolved creatures, biological entities—from individuals to systems—have properties that make them historical in ways that are central to their *scientific* analysis. Ecologists thus have special reasons to pay attention to history. Historians have recently discovered the importance of ecological variables to their (more humanistic and socially oriented) analyses of American landscape, culture, and institutions. It is encouraging and a little daunting that historical ecology, as pursued by anthropologists, might provide a meeting ground for these endeavors.

It may be useful to recall that ecology began in the nineteenth century, fresh on the vivid discovery that the geological and biological realms imperfectly preserved, and were the product of, an actual (evolutionary) record of past events. The earth and natural worlds had history; the scholars who studied these realms thought of themselves as "natural historians." It is an important endeavor of this volume that we produce a concept of history that is congenial to scientific endeavor and a concept of ecology that is congenial to the historian. Nothing less will sustain our sense (based in experience and practical concern) that an undertaking called "historical ecology" is essential; nothing less will inspire the interdisciplinary collaboration it requires.

A beginning definition that is rooted in the natural science component of our subject would include the following: historical ecology undertakes the temporal (diachronic) analysis of living ecological systems that in principle is necessary to analyze their structural and functional properties fully.

CONCEPTS

Some of the most powerful contributions of the natural historians were temporal concepts (e.g., descent with modification, gradualism). This volume is about concepts, of which ecosystem is an example. We might ask then, what is a concept? What kind of scientific work do we mean it to do? A cursory sampling of philosophy of science books indicates that three (Hull 1974; Thomas 1979; Toulmin 1953) have no explicit reference in the index or table of contents to the idea of a concept. Two (Hempel 1966; Schleffer 1967) contain index entries for the term but no explicit definition.

Neglect of the scientific status of concepts is widespread even in biology, which thrives on them. The evolutionist Ernst Mayr notes that important changes in concepts are seldom recorded or explicitly discussed in publications (1982:18) and have received little attention from the philosophy of science (1982:43). Mayr has repeatedly emphasized the "overwhelming importance" (1982:43) of concepts in the history of biology,

arguing that the greater part of progress in the discipline and the reputa-
tion of leading figures has turned on the development and refinement of
concepts:

> One can take almost any advance, either in evolutionary biology
> or in systematics, and show that it did not depend as much on
> discoveries as on the introduction of improved concepts. . . .
> Those are not far wrong who insist that the progress of science
> consists principally in the progress of scientific concepts. (Mayr
> 1982:24)

He argues that concepts have a place and significance in biology comparable to that of laws in physics. Among his list of eight propositions
forming the basis of a philosophy of biology are "that the historical nature
of organisms must be fully considered . . . [and] that the history of biology
has been dominated by the establishment of concepts and by their maturation, modification, and—occasionally—their rejection" (1982:76).

Despite his attention to concepts, I have not found an explicit definition of concept in Mayr's (1982, 1988) writing. He does provide examples
(population thinking, meiosis, natural selection, phenotype). He mentions
that concepts are refined and articulated primarily by definition, and he
refers to their flexibility and heuristic usefulness. He observes that they
constitute a framework for organizing generalizations.

I propose this definition: *A concept is a statement that isolates and systematically defines relationships or processes thought to be especially worthy of
analytic attention* (see Winterhalder 1984:303). A concept provides a framework for viewing facts selectively, with heed to certain of their attributes or
relationships. Niche, surplus, and ecosystem are examples. Concepts are
most useful when joined to appropriate theory, hypotheses, and methods.
The ecosystem concept, for instance, "cannot substitute for theory that is
coherent and that can yield testable hypotheses" (Gross 1984:254).

Concepts are not facts or theories (Rigler 1975) as they are commonly
understood. Neither are they principles, which are statements of "a general
or fundamental truth: a comprehensive and fundamental law, doctrine, or
assumption on which others are based or from which others are derived"
(*Webster's Third New International Dictionary* 1971). For instance, foremost
among the principles of the natural historians is that of uniformitarianism
(Simpson 1970); central to this volume is the claim that history is in principle important to ecological study. In one of the earliest attempts to list
the generalizations of ecology systematically, in 1939 Allee and Park set
out a list of nine "principles" (law of the minimum, adaptation, commu-

nity, succession, etc.; see McIntosh 1976:358–59). All of them would be termed *concepts* according to the present definition.

If we can take the history and philosophy of evolutionary biology as a reliable guide, concepts are likely to be important components in the science of historical ecology. They fully merit the explicit attention assigned them in the organization of this volume; they provide a meeting ground for the interaction of environmental historians and human- and bioecologists.

The Ecosystem Concept

Ecology as a professionally organized and self-conscious discipline postdates the beginning of the twentieth century.[4] The explicit formulation and expansion of what we know as ecosystem ecology occurred only after World War II (McIntosh 1976, 1985). It was propelled by scientific advances in nonbiological fields during the war, although it had antecedents much earlier. It rested especially in the holistic practices of the natural historians and their vision of an integrated and "balanced" nature. Reference to three "milestone" studies will provide a highly schematic sense of this complex history.

The entomologist-limnologist Stephen A. Forbes, chief of the Illinois Natural History Survey, provides an early and influential example of an ecosystem view. His 1887 study, "The Lake as a Microcosm" (Forbes 1925), articulated a holistic vision of a lake as a complex of interacting physical and biotic processes. Forbes (1925:537) wrote:

> [A lake] forms a little world within itself. . . . Nowhere can one see more clearly illustrated what may be called the sensibility of such an organic complex, expressed by the fact that whatever affects any species belonging to it, must have its influence of some sort upon the whole assemblage. . . . a comprehensive survey of the whole [is] . . . a condition to a satisfactory understanding of any part.

Forbes detailed the life forms found in the lakes of Illinois, gave examples of their manifold interconnections through predation and competition (what he called "remote and unsuspected rivalries" [Forbes 1925:548]), and went on to describe the remarkable "steady balance of organic nature, which holds each species within the limits of a uniform average number, year after year . . . the little community secluded here is as prosperous as if its state were one of profound and perpetual peace" (1925:549). To explain this stability, Forbes argued:

> Two ideas are thus seen to be sufficient to explain the order evolved from this seeming chaos; the first that of a general community of interests among all the classes of organic beings here assembled, and the second that of the beneficent power of natural selection which compels such adjustments of the rates of destruction and of multiplication of the various species as shall best promote this common interest . . . even here, out of these hard conditions, an order has been evolved which is the best conceivable. (Forbes 1925:550)

According to Forbes, this "beneficent order" is maintained by natural selection, competition, and predation, all "laws of life" that determine an equilibrium, a state that is "steadily maintained and that actually accomplished for all the parties involved the greatest good which the circumstances will at all permit" (quoted in McIntosh 1985:59). Forbes's vision of the balance of nature sounds as if it were inspired as much by Adam Smith as by Linneaus.[5] Developed by pioneering limnologists such as E. A. Birge and C. Juday, this approach became influential in the community ecology studies that occupied the early days of the discipline (1920s to 1950s). It focused on photosynthesis, respiration, decay, and processes controlling lake productivity.

A second important event in the development of ecosystem ecology was Lindeman's 1942 paper, "The Trophic-Dynamic Aspect of Ecology." Also a limnologist, Lindeman added a theoretical emphasis to the holistic, biophysical view by emphasizing quantitative study of trophic function, energy and materials flows and transfers, and the relation of these processes to seasonal and longer-term changes in the community of organisms. The period immediately following World War II saw a great expansion of funding for ecosystem studies based on Lindeman's work, from the National Science Foundation (founded in 1950) and the Atomic Energy Commission. The field developed around a trophic-functional orientation, through studies of productivity and nutrient cycling. The emphasis was often on the abiotic components and processes of ecosystems, on large-scale computer models, and on application of ideas from cybernetics, general systems theory, and operational research. By 1964 Eugene Odum could state:

The new ecology is thus a systems ecology—or, to put it in other words, the new ecology deals with the structure and function of levels of organization beyond that of the individual and species. (Odum 1964:15; emphasis original)

In fact, the third highlight may well be the epitome of this approach: Odum's (1969) *Science* article, "The Strategy of Ecosystem Development." In this influential article, Odum presented a successional model of the components and stages of ecosystem development. The process was presented as one of orderly, directional, and predictable development, culminating in the maximization (or minimization) of various structural and functional properties of the community. Among the twenty-four different attributes listed in the model were such things as biomass, productivity, diversity, and homeostasis. According to Odum, these trends were based on fundamental evolutionary principles related to energy dynamics, which have "parallels in the developmental biology of organisms, and also in the development of human society" (Odum 1969:262). The paper was rich in generalizations that proved attractive to natural and social scientists (Winterhalder 1984): as an example, "quantity production characterizes the young ecosystem while quality production and feedback control are the trademarks of the mature system" (Odum 1969:266). Citing these and other generalizations, Odum argued that "the framework of successional theory needs to be examined as a basis for resolving man's present environmental crisis" (1969:262).

Although not all ecosystem studies are systems ecology (see discussion in McIntosh 1985:202–7), a systems approach drawing theoretical inspiration from engineering and the physical sciences has been dominant (Golley 1984). Proponents of an ecosystem approach emphasize its holistic orientation to a degree that recalls the organismic analogy of Clements (see below). Odum described the ecosystem as "the *basic unit* of structure and function" for ecological analysis (1964:15; emphasis added). Woodwell and Botkin (1970:73) note that "There is something rejuvenating in the tacit but progressive acceptance of Clements's classical assertion that the community is an organism." In debates provoked by the creation and evaluation of the International Biological Program (IBP 1964–74), proponents made an impassioned defense of the holistic, systems approach: "Although systems analysis is most commonly encountered in ecology as a method, principally the mathematics model, it has overtones of a philosophy . . . or even . . . an ideology" (McIntosh 1985:232).

The influence of the ecosystem concept is pervasive in human as well as biological ecology (Moran 1984).

Community and Succession

The other guiding concepts of ecology prior to World War II were those of succession and community, developed primarily in the work of F. E. Clements (McIntosh 1985). Clements made his first systematic statements on the concept of succession as early as 1905; the classic description is his 1916 book, *Plant Succession,* and the 1936 paper, "Nature and Structure of the Climax." In Clements's view, succession is the regular process of development of a plant community after a disturbance. The species composition and physiognomy (three-dimensional form) of the community pass through a regular sequence of changes until they reach a stable, self-replicating climax determined by external climatic factors (typically temperature and moisture). These climatic factors are themselves stable, so the climax persists unchanging for a long period over large regions. Disturbance is external and rare. Whatever the character and impact of a perturbation, hence whatever the state from which succession is initiated, it will converge to a pathway of development that leads again to the climax.

Clements was the "premier American plant ecologist" (McIntosh 1985:354), and his ideas dominated the subject during the decades of the twenties, thirties, and forties. They exerted considerable influence even after the focus had shifted to ecosystem questions (see citation of Woodwell and Botkin, above). The climax community was a stable equilibrium, its structural and functional integrity like that of an organism. Systems ecologists adopted large parts of this conception, merely shifting its application from the biotic components of the community to more inclusive energy and geochemical relationships, and from analysis of structure to that of function.

The past two decades have seen strong critiques of both systems ecology and the concept of succession developed and promoted by Clements. Before summarizing them, I want to note an influence common to both approaches: Herbert Spencer. McIntosh (1985:43) observes that Clements's ideas had their origins in German idealism and in "Herbert Spencer, a source he shared with the premier American animal ecologist S. A. Forbes." McIntosh (1985:254, citing Tobey 1981) notes that "Clements's holistic organismic views were influenced by reading Herbert Spencer and his association with social scientists of similar persuasion":

> Clements's theories were extremely controversial, and the persistence, intensity, and inconclusiveness of much of the controversy suggest a philosophical as well as an empirical problem. . . . Clements . . . formalized ideas about the holistic nature of communities as organisms which were widespread, if not universal, among other progenitors of animal ecology, oceanography, and limnology. (McIntosh 1985:43)

Forbes himself attributed certain of his ideas to Spencer (McIntosh 1985:65). Spencer's influence is evident in the emphasis on organismic analogy, ontogeny (succession), equilibrium, and system determination of directional change.

Spencer of course had a direct but much more apparent impact on anthropology. As a consequence there is a long and incomplete but very public struggle to escape from his legacy of determinism, evolutionism, and ontogenetic and organismic analogies. Spencer's similar influence on ecological concepts in the biological sciences is less well appreciated, and it would be an especially ironic twist to intellectual history if human ecologists inadvertently gave Spencer new influence by adopting a bioecology influenced by his ideas.

I want to focus on one particular problem with the ecosystem concept produced within the Spencerian legacy: the claim that ecosystems function as organisms. It is an important claim because if ecosystems are cybernetic in this manner then a sufficient explanation can end when the equilibrium has been characterized. Deviations are due to incidental, exogenous factors, typically of limited duration and impact. System history is of little or no consequence. But the cybernetic characterization is not uniformly accepted (cf. Engelberg and Boyarsky 1979; Patten and Odum 1981) and not that clearly manifested in empirical studies. The information circuits that could provide negative feedback are not evident. Most important, the only theory that we have to account for design in nature, neo-Darwinism, does not give us reason to expect homeostatic design of functional relationships *at the level of ecosystems* (see below).

The description of ecosystems as balanced, cybernetic entities has also suffered from revised views of succession and community (Drury and Nisbet 1973; Horn 1974). There are multiple inconsistencies between Clements' view and empirical studies. The sequence of changes during succession is not so regular as once was thought, nor is sequential replacement of species always the case. Disturbance is more pervasive in its effects and more common than was originally realized; it is often endogenous in origin and character, resulting from properties of the community itself (recurrent disease or parasitic outbreaks, cycles of senescence, predator-prey cycles, etc.). Rather than one climatically determined climax, alternative stable-state communities may be possible in a given locale, also determined in part by endogenous factors (Holling 1986:298–300). Many of the generalized structural-functional patterns thought to be associated with succession (Odum 1969) are riddled with exceptions.

In an alternative view, succession can be explained in terms of statistical patterns of replacement rather than the organismal development (ontogeny) of a cybernetic community (Horn 1974). Ecologists now speak of "blurred successional patchworks," "gap phases," and "moving mosaics" as ways of characterizing the highly localized dynamics of ecological disturbance and succession (Picket and White 1985). If they speak of an equilibrium, it is a statistical statement referring to a stabilized distribution of vegetational patches taken over a region large enough to even out the local dynamics and irregularities. Even the descriptive sense of a community as a distinctive, bounded, and nonarbitrary assemblage of biota has been replaced to some extent by a more individualistic view. Species respond somewhat independently to environmental gradients and in their collective distribution meld together and replace one another in a more continuous fashion than the community concept implies.[6]

The ecosystem and community concepts with their embedded organismic analogy have had a tremendous influence on social scientists pursuing interdisciplinary analyses of human ecology (Winterhalder 1984:302). But we ought to be wary of these ideas. They yet are imbued with Spencerian ideas based in organismic analogy and equilibrium, and their most potent contemporary theoretical expression is a form of systems theory that likewise places its emphasis on cybernetics and homeostasis. In either case, they grant little or no analytical room to history. Furthermore, the ecosystem concept offered us by the biologists is a curiously *social* construct: its origins were strongly influenced by the social evolutionary theories of Spencer, and its current theoretical interpretation is fixed to cybernetic devices engineered by human beings. We should worry (and I take this to be the substance of much recent critique), however, about whether or not it is also an appropriate *natural* construct. Without being aware of it, human ecologists may be borrowing back from the biologists disguised versions of some of our own outdated and less salutary ideas.

EVOLUTION, ECOLOGY, AND HISTORY

Throughout the development of ecology there has been a tension over the appropriate level of analysis: individual, population, community, or ecosystem. While system ecologists have sometimes insisted that the ecosystem itself has functional integrity as an evolutionary unit (for example, "the ecosystem can be taken to consist of biotic and abiotic components that change and evolve together, and the term ecosystem implies a unit of coevolution" [Patten 1975; quoted in McIntosh 1985:239]), others disagree ("There is in the community no center of control and organization . . . and no evolution toward a central control system. . . . Community organization is a result of species evolution and species behavior" [Whittaker and Woodwell 1972:150; also quoted in McIntosh 1985:239]).

Advances in evolutionary theory in the past twenty years support Whittaker and Woodwell. Neo-Darwinian mechanisms of evolution lead us to expect that adaptive design is a routine property of individuals, a less common property of kin or unrelated intraspecies groups, and occasionally a property of very limited sets of coevolved organisms (as in cases of interspecific mutualism). Beyond these levels, unless we can interpret the properties of more complex aggregates as emergent and thus incidental results of adaptive design at lower levels, we ought to be skeptical. Further, if there are emergent properties, we are obliged to be quite cautious in appraising them using cybernetic, homeostatic, organismic models. Forbes's appeal to Darwinism as the source of harmony and balance in natural systems (cited above) and all of the like appeals subsequent to him must grapple with the trenchant hostility of neo-Darwinian theory to such interpretations.

Evolutionary theory adds to the doubts expressed about the concepts of community and ecosystem ecology. It is more supportive of the historical endeavor proposed in this volume. For instance, Lewontin (1966) has identified two properties which generate what he calls the "historicity" of evolution. First, the extent to which organisms incorporate and retain experience with past environments in their adaptive repertoire influences whether they will experience recurring environmental challenges as predictable or capricious. Most genetic systems have a limited memory, and the organism will experience even recurring events as capricious if they occur at intervals longer than the retention of the relevant adaptive information. Second, adaptations are a response to an exact historical sequence of environmental conditions. It is relatively easy to show through computer simulation that selective regimes with like normative qualities but

differing in their exact sequences of environmental perturbations will produce different evolutionary pathways and outcomes. This occurs because
a gene system with allele frequencies approaching fixation (i.e., approaching 0.00 or 1.00) is less responsive to selection of a certain intensity than
is one with more equal allelic distributions (say, 0.45 and 0.55 for a two-
allele locus).[7] If subjected to the same selection pressures, they will behave
differently. The "historical accident of the order in which the environments occur necessarily changes the long-time life history of a population"
(Lewontin 1967:86). The key to this result is a nonlinear relationship between perturbation and response—one in which the magnitude of the
response is sensitive to the preexisting state of the organism. It is likely to
be a widespread feature of natural and sociocultural systems.

Building on these evolutionary ideas, Lewontin (1969) analyzes the
claim that the history of an ecosystem is unimportant to its present state.
At least three assumptions are implicit in this view—the system has one
stable configuration, it is in that state, and how it got there is dispens-
able to analysis. Each assumption can be questioned. Multiple stable states
are empirically known; the claim that a system is at a stable state already
presumes we know something about its history; and finally, analysis at a
stable state cannot provide information about how the system will evolve
or respond to stress or perturbation. Lewontin's observations are among
the reasons that extant phenotypes of evolved beings cannot fully reveal
their origins or future behavior (see above).

Advances in evolutionary ecology have also drawn attention to the
importance for adaptation of spatial heterogeneity and temporal dynamics in natural environments. Unfortunately, normative description and
averaging statistics (e.g., mean temperature, average biomass of resource
species) characterize most studies of environment found in the human
ecology literature. Ecological factors typically enter the analyses as static
and predictable variables, shorn of their dynamic, discontinuous, unpredictable, and especially their historical qualities. This has been the case
even though virtually all of the various analytical approaches guiding ecological anthropology studies suggest that temporal variance and spatial
heterogeneity drive ecological adaptation (Winterhalder 1980:136).

The adaptive content of human-ecological systems is a response to
the extremes of environmental variability they have experienced; virtually
all of their adaptive crises occur at these extremes. Thus, it is important
to come to an understanding of what constitutes an analytically sufficient
environmental description, one more cognizant of history, and to find
the concepts that will produce it. Here we must delve into what Worster

(1988a:290) calls, one hopes with some bemused respect, the "outlandish language" of the natural scientist.

Patchiness

The distribution in space of ecological communities is locally heterogeneous and quite labile. In the place of succession and climax, ecologists are developing a more differentiated and dynamic vision of the spatial qualities of communities. Disturbance is seen as a regular element of the system itself, and although there are patterned responses to perturbations, it is the processes of adjustment that are taken to be fundamental.

The set of ideas mobilized around the concepts of *patch* and *patchiness* (Pickett and White 1985; Wiens 1976) is an important component of this shift. A patch is an ecologically distinct locality in the landscape; it is problem- and organism-defined, relative to the behavior, size, mobility, habits, and perceptive capabilities of the population being studied. For an herbivorous insect, individual leaves may operate as patches; for an ungulate, isolated mountain meadows or localized areas of fire-regenerating brush might represent patches. In general, patches are localized discontinuities in the landscape which affect behavior; they are assessed in terms of properties like the number of patch types and their size, quality, turnover and developmental dynamics (e.g., succession), and distribution.

A related concept is *grain*. Grain is established by the mobility of the organism relative to the scale of patchiness and by the ways in which the organism responds to environmental heterogeneity. A coarse-grained environment is one in which patches either are much larger than the typical range of the organism or are utilized very selectively. In either case, the organism uses selected portions of the landscape disproportionately. A fine-grained environment has a small scale relative to the organism's mobility, or patches are utilized generally. In this case, the organism encounters and uses patches more or less in proportion to their representation in the habitat. Patchiness has become a basic feature of analyses of such evolutionary ecology topics as habitat selection, foraging behavior, life-history strategies, and population dynamics (see Southwood 1977; Wiens 1976, 1985); it also has become a basic feature of ecological management practices (Pickett and White 1985).

The boreal forest of northern Canada is a particularly good example of a patchy environment (see Winterhalder 1983a). Edaphic differences associated with low-relief landforms (uplands of kames and eskers; basement

shield; rivers and kettle-lake depressions) coupled with recurrent disturbances (fires; animal activities, such as flooding from beaver dams; and
toppling of trees by wind and snow) create a dynamic and highly heterogeneous landscape. Each patch type has a set of associated resource species
and dynamics; each presents unique subsistence opportunities and im-
pediments. Knowledge of this spatial variation is essential to studies of the
productivity and dynamics of boreal forest resources and to analysis of
the tactics of the Cree foragers who harvest and live from them (Winterhalder 1983b).

Persistence and Predictability

Patterns of temporal variation and long-term change are also important. If
patchiness summarizes the state of environmental heterogeneity in space,
the concepts of persistence (Botkin and Sobel 1975) and predictability
(Colwell 1974) help to characterize the range and regularity of variation in
environmental states in time. An organism's experience mingles the space
and time dimensions, but it is analytically difficult to treat them simultaneously and their effects are often different.

   Persistence (Botkin and Sobel 1975) is a term meant to characterize
the natural dynamics of time-varying ecosystems without assuming that
they have a static equilibrium (a condition to which they will always return
following a disturbance, the classical definition of succession to a climax
being an example). Persistence implies that the system characteristics of
central interest fluctuate within defined boundaries, which may be more
or less "stringent" (i.e., encompass fluctuations of lesser or greater magni-
tudes). Within a certain time interval, the fluctuations may be either "recurrent" (a repetition of a particular state of the system) or "transient" (the
state does not repeat). In this view, a perturbation alters the future states
that otherwise would have occurred by changing boundaries of persistence
or the likelihood and frequency of recurrent or transient states of a particular type. Persistence and the related terms have the important advantage
that they can characterize regular or irregular fluctuations without implying that the system possesses qualities of homeostasis or static equilibrium.

   Persistence describes the expected magnitude of fluctuations, but it
says nothing about the regularity or patterning of recurrent states. Colwell's
(1974) concept of predictability fills this gap by providing a quantitative
characterization of periodic phenomena with a simple measure based on
information theory. Seasonal amounts of rainfall over a period of years will
serve as an example. To simplify we consider four seasons (spring, sum-

mer, fall, and winter) and rainfall in three categories (low, medium, and high). If knowledge of the season (time) is enough to determine with complete confidence the quantity of precipitation (state), then rainfall is maximally "predictable." Conversely, if any category of precipitation amount is equally likely in each season, predictability is at a minimum. Predictability can arise from "constancy" (the same state category obtains for all time seasons for all years), from "contingency" (a different state category pertains for each season, but in exactly the same pattern for all years), or some combination of the two. In practice, Colwell's measure is easily calculated, with predictability being the simple sum of constancy and contingency, measured on a scale of 0 to 1 (i.e., $[0 \leq P \leq 1]$; $P = C + M$).

An example of an analysis that uses the concept of predictability can be drawn from human ecology studies in southern Peru (see Winterhalder in press). The data are monthly precipitation records from weather stations located on the eastern escarpment of the Andes, an area of intensive, dry-farming peasant agriculture. In this case the study objective is an analysis of the roles and relative importance of production, storage, and exchange decisions in mitigating subsistence risk arising from drought and frost. Both for the local analysis and for regional comparisons, it is important to know the degree and regularity of fluctuations in seasonal precipitation. In this case the relationship between altitude and the predictability, constancy, and contingency of monthly precipitation is quite regular. Although predictability owing to contingency (seasonality) increases with elevation, the increase is not sufficient to offset the large drop in predictability owing to constancy. Overall the predictability of the monthly distribution of rainfall declines at the higher altitudes, indicating that subsistence risk increases with elevation.

Ecological studies have demonstrated regularities of ecosystem structure and function, but most of these regularities are empirical generalizations that have not been set within a solidly established theoretical framework. Commitment to "benign" system-level functionalism (homeostasis, balance, harmony, etc.) is a matter of much faith and very limited experience. Emergent properties like stability and resilience may characterize an ecosystem, even though they are not an (organismic) adaptation of an assemblage of species (in the sense of a quality designed by natural selection). Evolutionary theory suggests that we should be skeptical of attributing cybernetic properties to high-level entities like ecosystems, and it gives us additional reason to believe that history itself is important in the scientific analysis of ecological questions. Here is a natural collaboration, in which the natural and social scientist can profit from the methods and attentions of environmental historians.

In pursuit of historical ecology, we might be tempted to produce chronologies of highly detailed environmental information. But narrative ecohistory is not the entire answer. For some scientific goals, we also need theoretically sensitive means of summarizing the descriptive detail of environmental variability without succumbing to it. This is precisely the kind of scientific work for which concepts like patch, persistence, and predictability are suited. Although none of these concepts fully captures history in its narrative sense of sequence, timing, and uniqueness, they do generalize some of the key effects of this history on properties of ecological systems.

ADAPTIVE MANAGEMENT

By claiming that our subject is historical in principle, we place certain limits on our confidence in prediction, whether it is based on theory, empirical generalization, simulation, or analogy. Quite beyond our considerable present-day ignorance about the structure and function of complex human-ecological systems—ignorance that we can hope to diminish—these systems will always contain the possibility of novelty and capriciousness. Their specific histories, which may be only partially known to us, contain implications for their future development. All of this reduces our certainty about how these natural and anthropogenic ecosystems will function, especially when exposed to stress. History compels us to allow for the unexpected.

Adaptive management is Holling's term for the research and policy consequences that follow from acknowledging these sources of uncertainty (Holling and Goldberg 1981; Holling ed. 1978; Holling 1986). Holling begins by stating four basic properties of ecological systems (Holling and Goldberg 1981:83): (1) they have systemic qualities (there are complex interactions or connections among parts); (2) they are historical (current behavior is shaped by past events); (3) they are spatial (local behavior is shaped by surrounding events); and (4) they are nonlinear (key interactions may be characterized by lags and thresholds). These qualities are important, but they also are sometimes exaggerated or misunderstood (Holling ed. 1978). For instance, only certain of the connections within an ecosystem matter (we need not study everything to understand the behavior of the system); the effects of events are localized and heterogeneous across space (we cannot assume that the impact of an event gradually diminishes with distance); abrupt shifts in system behavior are always possible and are difficult to anticipate; and variability, not constancy, is fundamental.

Linked to these properties is a distinction between two ways of conceptualizing the structural properties of ecosystems: *stability* and *resilience*.

> Stability . . . is the propensity of a system to attain or retain an equilibrium condition of steady state or stable oscillation . . . resist any departure from that condition and, if perturbed, return rapidly to it . . . a classic equilibrium-centered definition. . . . Resilience . . . is the ability of a system to maintain its structure and patterns of behavior in the face of disturbance. (Holling 1986:296)

The difference between these terms can be visualized in terms of a simple diagram (technically, a "phase portrait") representing the behavior of two ecosystem variables (fig. 2.1). In a simple system the axes might be the population sizes of two interacting species. So long as the two variables remain in central portions of the *domain of attraction,* small disturbances are absorbed with modest and perhaps temporary quantitative changes in the system. However, if the variables move across the boundary or the boundary shifts so that it passes over their position, unstable, qualitative changes can result.

Stability focuses on maintenance of an equilibrium and ecosystem conditions near it. It might refer to a stable equilibrium point, cycle, or trajectory. As an analytical or policy concept it emphasizes low variability and resistance to change. It contains the presumption that incremental change will have a predictable, incremental effect, and that the relationship between the variables will reliably signal this effect. In contrast, resilience focuses on the size and form of the domain of attraction, on the behavior of the variables near its boundary, and on the susceptibility of the domain to contract under differing ecological or management conditions. It emphasizes nonequilibrium events and processes, variability, and adaptive flexibility. From a resilience perspective, incremental change may not reliably signal its effect. If a boundary is reached, the effect will be abrupt, unpredicted, and disproportionate to the cause—a surprise.

System resilience is determined by history and is linked to properties like diversity and complexity, although these relationships are only partially understood and they provide generalizations of limited reliability. For

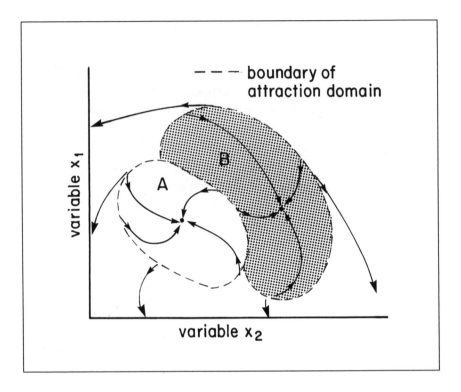

Figure 2.1. Domains of attraction for a system of two variables and two alternate stable states (A and B). A perturbation that displaces the variables to a point within their present domain of attraction will be followed by a regular return to the equilibrium. However, if the position of the variables crosses a boundary, either because they are perturbed or because the boundaries of the domain shift or contract, then the system will abruptly make a qualitative shift from one to the other domain of attraction or from an attraction domain to extinction. (After Holling 1973)

instance, complexity, measured as connectedness, seems to reduce system resilience; homogenization of systems spatially increases their connectedness, etc. The descriptive properties of ecosystems may not provide reliable or highly generalized clues about their functional responses to change.

A resilience-oriented view draws attention to important properties of ecosystems. Multiple domains of attraction can characterize a set of interacting elements; system behavior becomes discontinuous at the boundaries of these domains; the boundaries themselves can shift. The combination of complex interactions, hidden functions and the limited reliability of extrapolation from the effects of observed changes make prediction difficult. Experimentally we might be able to make localized measurements of the effect on x_2 of varying x_1 (see fig. 2.1), but except in a few exceptionally well documented cases, we cannot "see" the underlying phase map. Like the norm of reaction (see above), it is effectively hidden to us in the cases that matter, those that are complex and not amenable to laboratory or experimental manipulation. The effect of a disturbance can be measured only by observing its actual impact, a prohibitive and in some circumstances risky experimental procedure, or by attempts to simulate the response. Thus it is especially important that we examine the consequences of past impacts to try to assess system resilience. And that returns us to history: "All the facets of the problem of stability of ecosystems are pervaded by history" (Margalef 1969:29).[8]

Holling's approach relies on a generally accepted principle of ecosystem studies: systems that have experienced variation, that are spatially heterogeneous, and that are more complex (but lack high degrees of connectedness) are likely to be more resilient. Nonetheless, as Holling puts it, we should expect surprises from ecosystems-qualitative departures from our expectations about causes, system behavior, and the consequences of intervention. We should analyze and plan based on a "presumption of ignorance" (Holling and Goldberg 1981:79) and the "inevitability of uncertainties" (Holling 1978:5). We should minimize risk by focusing on boundaries rather than equilibria. These actions would acknowledge that "what a complex system *is doing* seldom gives any indication of what it *would do* under changed conditions" (Holling 1978:4; emphasis in original). Management objectives consistent with this view would include recommendations such as the following:

> Actions [should be] limited in scope and diverse in nature . . . [C]omplexity is a worthwhile goal in its own right . . . [We should] adopt a more boundary oriented view of the world. (Holling and Goldberg 1981:91)

In the terminology of Botkin and Sobel (1975), it would be better to manage for the recurrence of desirable states than constantly try to force an ecosystem to maintain a particular state.

The methodological specifics of Holling's ecosystem models are beyond the scope of this paper, as are the details of his policy recommendations, especially those related to institutions and development. It is enough to note here that current approaches to policy almost universally adopt an equilibrium view; thus much environmental and developmental policy attempts to suppress temporal variation (e.g., fire control), homogenize spatial heterogeneity (monocrop tree planting), and introduce connectedness (industrial-scale timber harvesting), all of which promote constancy and stability at the expense of variability and resilience. As a consequence, environmental systems become ever more liable to surprise us, unpleasantly.

The concept of adaptive management captures some of the policy implications of a scientific commitment to historical ecology. It is an attempt to formulate development and policy tactics that recognize (1) the importance of ecosystem history, (2) uncertainties in our ability to predict ecosystem behavior, and (3) the desirability of focusing on change and resilience rather than attempting to guarantee stability.

CONCLUSIONS

Historical ecology (historical factor, historical process) is a misnomer, unless we take it to represent an epistemological commitment to the temporal dimension in ecological analysis. This commitment rests in part on the claim that knowledge of the history of natural systems is an indispensable part of their *scientific* analysis. The structural and functional properties of organisms, communities, and ecosystems must be sought in their history because they are only partly revealed in their extant form. It is evident from the history of biology that concepts are an appropriate focus of our endeavor, so long as we are sensitive to the theory and methods that accompany them. It will be a prime challenge of historical ecology to find or to generate concepts that will promote collaborative work among social and natural scientists, especially environmental historians, anthropologists, and geographers.

To succeed in being historical, however, practitioners of ecological analyses must be wary of concepts like succession or ecosystem, which derive from or continue to rely heavily on organismic analogies or cybernetic theory. They trace a record of deep ambivalence about the place of history in ecological analysis. More promising are concepts like patch, persistence, predictability, stability, and resilience, which direct attention to the spatial and temporal dynamics of ecosystems and to the effects of history on their current and future functioning. From a policy and planning perspective, the uncertainties inherent in predicting ecosystem behavior argue for an approach like that of adaptive management.

-------- *Notes* --------

1. In practice, however, the scientist may find it expedient to look to the past for information in order to replace current knowledge that is incomplete or not easily supplied by experimentation.

2. The analogy is useful, but it should not be pushed too far. Ecosystems are not individuals (superorganisms), and they do not have adaptive, information-preserving capacity comparable to the genotypes produced by natural selection.

3. These are "the rise and evolution of industrialism and . . . capitalism" (Worster 1984:17), "the frontier" (p. 18), and the "regulation of exploitative behavior" (p. 18).

4. In 1902, a letter published in the journal *Science* complained about an article that had used the word "ecology" without explanation, noting that it was not an entry in the standard dictionaries of the era (McIntosh 1985:354).

5. Humans were seen as elements with qualities foreign to this formulation, as intruders and a source of disturbance: "There is a general consent that primeval nature, as in the uninhabited forest or the untilled plain, presents a settled harmony of interaction among organic groups which is in strong contrast with the many serious maladjustments of plants and animals found in countries occupied by man" (cited in McIntosh 1985:74).

6. Anthropologists will be familiar with an instructive parallel: the breakdown of the typological description of human races with empirical evidence that the different measures of human variation were clinal and to a large degree expressed independently of one another.

7. This has the curious consequence that the highly imbalanced allelic systems contain more information about selection pressures in their remote than their immediate past (because they are relatively insensitive to recent selection pressures), whereas the reverse is true of gene systems with more equal allelic frequencies (they are very sensitive to selection, hence contain information mainly about the immediate past; Lewontin 1967:87). The same cannot be said of the cobble mentioned earlier. This capability for historical acquisition or loss of buffering is a key difference between living and nonliving entities.

8. A particularly interesting example of such an analysis, combining information from the disciplines of marine population biology and archaeology, is Simenstad, Estes, and Kenyon's (1978) demonstration of alternate stable states in the prehistoric Aleut subsistence system.

Chapter 3

Tracking and Testing the Nature-Culture Dichotomy

ALICE E. INGERSON

The case studies in this book illustrate for various parts of the world and times in world history that it is possible to chip away at the nature-culture dichotomy empirically, even while using that dichotomy to communicate. Each of these inherently interdisciplinary studies deliberately pursues the flow of cause and effect back and forth across the nature-culture boundary, from adaptation (humans adapt to nature) to impact (humans have an impact on nature) and back again. Thus Schmidt explains "how the exploitative economy and the cultural system have changed and adapted to a transformed landscape" in eastern Africa (chapter 5). McGovern examines ecological and cultural factors behind "Norse Greenlanders' failure to adapt successfully to a changing climate" (chapter 6). Hassan compares the effects of "dire ecological events" and "oppressive regimes" in producing the highs and lows of the Nile Valley's population curve (chapter 7). Crumley considers the relationship between "environmental uncertainty" and "economic, social, and political flexibility" in Burgundy (chapter 8). And Marquardt considers theoretical and practical ways of bringing together "historical preservation" and "habitat conservation"—in other words, to use the "social, and not merely natural science" of "anthropological archaeology" to foster a joint understanding by both scholars and the public of culture and nature in southwestern Florida (chapter 9). Prepositions and conjunctions sit at the center of each case study: "changed *and* adapted" (Schmidt); "adapt successfully *to*" (McGovern); "ecological disasters *or* the demands of a top-heavy economy" (Hassan); the "social structure, ecology, *and* political economy of Celtic society" (Crumley); "to educate the public about the relations *between* themselves and their environments" (Marquardt).

This essay proposes two additional strategies to supplement these and future case studies of this type, in hopes of helping to create a vocabulary that could eventually describe this subject matter without so many prepositions and conjunctions. The first additional strategy suggested here is "tracking" the nature-culture dichotomy as a piece of sociolinguistic data through direct observation, rather than treating it as a background assumption. The second is "testing" that dichotomy empirically, looking on both sides of the boundary between nature and culture for characteristics commonly associated with only one side. Tool making and language use, for example, have long been associated only with culture and not with nature, but recent studies of animal behavior have begun to break down this association. This essay focuses especially on the implications of finding history—defined as unique sequences of contingent events that shape entire social and ecological systems—within both nature and culture.

FROM LANGUAGE TO REALITY AND BACK AGAIN

To some extent, the second strategy explored here depends on the first. Until we recognize and articulate the assumptions that structure our discussions of the similarities and differences, and therefore the relations, between nature and culture, we cannot test those assumptions empirically. But the first strategy also depends on the second. The nature-culture dichotomy is not "merely" a language problem. We cannot abolish or revise that dichotomy simply by redefining words. As Alice discovered in *Through the Looking Glass,* Humpty Dumpty could not, in fact, "make words mean whatever I want them to mean, neither more nor less." New definitions imposed by fiat simply create a new, smaller "speech community" of people who accept those peculiar definitions, within an otherwise unchanged larger community of speech and action.

Criticizing and finding ways to test the language that we normally take for granted is far more difficult and uncomfortable than accepting that language and using it to analyze the "mutual causality" across the nature-culture boundary that is explored by most of the chapters in this book. The nature-culture dichotomy may not be a universal structure of the human mind, as Claude Lévi-Strauss suggested, but it is so deeply ingrained in our everyday language that anyone trying to work around that dichotomy sounds at best idiosyncratic and at worst mystical. Yet in the long run, our capacity to manage nature and culture as a single system depends on our finding a way to see, and discuss, nature and culture as quantitative varia-tions along a single spectrum rather than as an either/or dichotomy. And describing that spectrum requires us to disassociate qualities and charac-teristics that are closely and even unquestionably associated in our every-day language.

Recognizing that language reflects social reality, however, does not mean that language cannot be a significant tool for social change. By analogy, the use of such constructions as "s/he," "he or she," and the gender-neutral plural ("everybody . . . they") might not erase gender discrimina-tion. But the studies of gender-biased language motivated by demands for greater gender equality in economics, politics, and society at large have surely made it more difficult for most speakers of everyday English to leave their own assumptions about gender unquestioned. It is hard to see how the ultimate goal of social equality between women and men would have been better served by assuming that change in the language of gender would "naturally" follow social change and could not precede or accompany it.

This essay draws data about the interpenetration of scholarly and everyday language about nature and culture from several sources. One such source is academic writing in environmental history and historical ecology. But two other sources used here are seldom treated as sources of data by either environmental scholars or reformers: the reports of peer reviewers in scholarly publishing, and classroom comments by undergraduate students. Referees' comments are especially powerful shapers of scholarly behavior because they are hedged about with taboos. Few authors or editors ever discuss these comments with anyone. As a result, the regularities and rules of referees' reports are effectively invisible and off-limits to critical analysis.

Students' classroom comments fall under some of the same taboos that govern peer reviewers' comments. More often than not, scholars simply "correct" students in classroom discussions, thereby enforcing scholarly definitions and styles of argument. But the same comments that are de-fined as "errors" by the smaller, scholarly speech community may be seen as critical data about the language and reasoning of the broader commu-nity of speech and action outside universities. Students who have not yet accepted their professors' specialized vocabulary and rules of argument represent the otherwise elusive "general public" that many scholars say they want to reach, and that the project described by Marquardt elsewhere in this volume clearly does reach. A professor may fail a student who re-fuses to abide by that professor's definitions, but scholars do not have such authority over the general public. To influence public policy and public debate, we must work from within the implicit assumptions and reasoning by analogy that characterize public speech and action, to make those assumptions and analogies visible and thus subject to explicit discussion.

TRACKING THE NATURE-CULTURE DICHOTOMY

Case 1: A Theoretical Debate in Environmental History

Assumptions about the differences between nature and culture clearly shape scholarly communication, even as scholars attempt to straddle the boundary between the two realms. Ecological anthropology, for example, is defined as the branch of anthropology that focuses specifically on the interactions between nature and culture. The materialism-idealism debate in ecological anthropology dealt with whether to view cultural practices as adaptations to particular natural environments or instead as actively shaping environmental perception and resource use. The first approach was defined as materialist, the second as idealist (a good summary of this debate is in Jamieson and Lovelace 1985:27–54).

Environmental historians recently recapitulated and extended that debate. In the historians' discussions, Donald Worster's work served as a touchstone for arguments over whether environmental history is, should be, or can be consistently materialist. At one point, Worster distanced himself from self-declared anthropological materialists such as Marvin Harris by accusing them of "an oversimplified, mechanical determinism" (Worster 1984:14). Worster has similarly argued that "[as] Henry David Thoreau told his elders, 'There are a thousand hacking at the branches of evil to one who is striking at the root.' The branches are class, race, and gender discrimination, industrial hubris, and colonialism[, but] the root is the human drive to dominate the earth" (1986:46–47).

Yet Worster (1984:12) had earlier recommended that environmental historians adopt the perspective defended by Harris. And since that recommendation was published, Worster has been accused of underestimating the role of ideology or culture in shaping relations between human beings and natural resources. According to Nash (1989:198), "Worster [implies] that cultural factors play a very minor role in historical development, except as they reflect an economic mode of production." In a *Journal of American History* (1990) environmental history round table Richard White argues that Worster's recommendations for environmental history as a field suffer from a "failure to recognize the role of value judgments and beliefs" and are "in danger" of turning "culture [into] superstructure in the old vulgar Marxist sense" (1990:1113). Worster apparently accepted this accusation when he decided to title his reply to these commentaries "Seeing Beyond Culture."

Despite his choice to stand defiantly on the materialist high ground in this instance, Worster has insisted more generally that critics who charge him with "failing to recognize the role of value judgments and beliefs" are perpetrating "heavy distortions, almost perverse misreadings" (personal communication). Ultimately, Worster's position is simply ambiguous, as some of his critics have pointed out and as he himself has admitted. An editorial query about his review of a Marxist history of ecological ideas (Pepper 1984) for *Forest & Conservation History* (at the time, the *Journal of Forest History*) elicited the response that he had "not meant to have disposed of either the . . . book or Marxism. As one who has been called a 'neo-Marxist' and a 'pseudo-Marxist' both, I have mixed feelings" about Marxism (letter in *Forest & Conservation History* files). William Cronon has pointed out this persistent ambiguity throughout Worster's work between a theoretical commitment "to a materialist ecological and political-economic analysis" and case studies grounded "not on a capitalist mode of production but [on] a capitalist ethos, which he essentially defines in terms of idealist ethical imperatives rather than materialist relations of production" (*Journal of American History* 1990:1124–25).

In short, as Cronon has observed, even sophisticated scholars read most case studies in environmental history as leaning *either* toward materialism *or* toward idealism: "Studies that do a good job at the materialist end of the spectrum, linking ecosystems and economies, often are less successful at integrating belief systems into their [economic] arguments, and vice versa" (*Journal of American History* 1990:1123). The readers of these studies, sometimes in spite of the authors' intentions, emphasize either the adaptiveness of culture, and thus nature as cause, or the transformation of nature, and thus culture as cause.

Both in the original debate over materialism and idealism in ecological anthropology and in the subsequent debate among environmental historians, scholars who wanted to avoid or overcome the nature-culture dichotomy tried consistently to distinguish those scholars who agreed with them from those who did not. Often they failed, not because they were bad scholars but because they could not define their own positions or communicate with their potential allies and enemies alike except through a language in which the nature-culture dichotomy was deeply embedded. In that language, nature and those human activities most closely tied to

nature differ qualitatively from human ideas, which reflect other causes—
usually other ideas. These associations are perfectly functional in many
contexts, but they entangle in apparent contradiction any attempt to assign
an active, causal role to nature in history (which means taking up a materialist position in some sense) while still trying to reform current human
behavior toward nature. The axiomatic contrast between nature and culture makes it logically awkward to pursue both goals simultaneously. The
material laws of nature cannot be reformed, they can only be understood.
Thus using nature, or material forces rooted in nature, to explain human
behavior makes that behavior—including the abuse of nature—seem un-
reformable. To the extent that human ideas, independent of natural or
material forces, explain human abuse of nature, however, nature seems
merely an inert, passive receiver of human "impacts." In short, it seems
impossible for an environmental reformer to be a consistent materialist,
but equally impossible for anyone who wants to give nature some causal
power to be a consistent idealist.

Case 2: Interdisciplinary Peer Review

The unintended or implicit power of the nature-culture dichotomy to
shape interdisciplinary communication was especially clear in the process
of scholarly peer review for *Forest & Conservation History,* a journal I edited
from 1984 through 1991. The relatively small group of scholars who wrote
and reviewed for the journal apparently had strong common interests. Yet
these reviewers frequently disagreed over whether papers were based on
original research, whether they were well written, and even whether they
explained anything at all.

For purposes of this summary, the positions that emerged in these
disagreements can be identified as Science and the Humanities. Most social
scientists allied in practice, if not in declared intention, with the Scientists
rather than the Humanists. (The capitalization of the two positions in this
summary indicates that the summary is, to some extent, a caricature of
any one referee's position.) Just as individual authors complained of being
misread by their opponents in the debate over materialism and idealism
summarized above, peer reviewers subjected any case studies located even
slightly to the Humanist or Scientific side of the nature-culture boundary
to criticisms that their authors could also claim were misreadings. In both
cases, trying to assign any one individual definitively to one camp or the
other is ultimately a distraction from the critical challenge of uncovering

the fundamental influence of the opposition and mutual dependence of the two positions on the work of all individual scholars.

Humanists who served as referees, usually historians, made the following complaints about work submitted by Scientists, including some social scientists:

> I find this paper to be exemplary of a particular genre—which I do not think should continue to be published. It begins from the implicit assumption that local human activity has . . . been responsible for the ecological degradation of a particular area, and proceeds to assemble as much information as possible as illustration. . . . It does not demonstrate anything and it does not investigate anything. . . . It has no progressive argument—only implicit assumptions and innuendo. . . . The introduction [tells] the reader nothing about the aims of the author in writing the paper.

> I suspect that there really is a *story* to be told here but it simply doesn't materialize in the current manuscript. [This article's] introduction was ineffective almost to the point of not being an introduction. In fact one didn't know entirely what the authors were doing until the conclusion.

> The introduction does not really establish a purpose, although one is implied. . . . The author addresses the importance of this species by seemingly discussing a list of topics that have some association with the species, but the reason for the list is not evident.

> [This manuscript] lacks a focus. . . . It needs to start some place and logically move the story along some clear path. . . . It lacks any sense of historical development.

> The author has adopted a style—a variant of standard scientific literature—that makes it simple to fashion a composite essay. . . . Personally, I find the genre . . . intrinsically flawed when applied to synthesis or to historical review. [It produces] an illusion of comprehensiveness that does not in fact exist.

> In its present form [this manuscript is] unsuited to publication in [this journal]. . . . [It is] too much a technical contribution to forest ecology and too little a historical account. . . . [The journal] should not accept jargon like "anthropogenic forces" where "human action" is intended.

Scientists, including social scientists, had fundamentally different complaints about manuscripts by Humanists, who in this case were usually historians. One referee (an archaeologist) condemned one manuscript precisely because it relied heavily on unpublished reports by a university research project. To the historian, this criticism was puzzling—a paper based on unpublished data would be more original and therefore more valuable than one based on published sources. An economist who was making a good-faith effort to include historical materials in his courses on natural resource management and policy complained that history's "fuzzy" reliance on example and anecdote, rather than on statistical patterns and testable generalizations, frustrated students seeking general principles to apply in making policy. Another social scientist, when refereeing a manuscript by a historian, complained that

> The hypothesis is unclear. The cause or causes for the change in . . . attitudes [described in the paper] is ambiguously stated if it is stated at all. The author(s) write(s) in the first sentence [that] "environmental objectives . . . emerged . . . to reshape . . . public attitudes." This cause and effect is unlikely. Public attitudes can change public objectives, but I doubt that public objectives can change public attitudes. The author writes three sentences later that new people came to [the region] and their different attitudes changed the collective public attitude toward the environment. This is a plausible—however in my judgment, doubtful—hypothesis, but the author does not test it.

The historian author rebutted this criticism by arguing that

> [The cause-and-effect criticism] seems a bit of a quibble. The article obviously argues that changes in attitudes changed public policies and the wording can be changed to avoid other implications. . . . I'm not sure it would be possible to "test" either of the two possibilities as the commenter [sic] seems to wish. . . . The main point of the article was to describe the changed attitude and its consequences.

In this case the Scientist and the Humanist finally agreed on the actual sequence of cause and effect. Very few Scientists, however, would have agreed with the Humanist author in this case that criticizing an apparently accidental reversal of cause and effect was a "quibble." The author's response to the referees also offered other evidence of these two very different attitudes toward explanation itself. The author first explicitly stated that the article's purpose was "to describe" a historical process, then insisted that the article was analytical rather than merely descriptive, and finally concluded that addressing the causes of the changes documented would therefore—but to a Scientific reader paradoxically—dilute rather than strengthen the article as history.

In the end these most characteristic divergences between Humanists and Scientists had less to do with particular papers than with assumptions about natural and cultural causality, and therefore about the proper relationships between purpose and method in research and writing. Scientists put method first, and Humanists put purposes first. As a result, Humanists often found Scientists' purposes trivial, and Scientists often found Humanists' methods opaque. Humanists were interested not only in finding new sources but in devising new interpretations of those sources. Scientists were more concerned to show that anyone using their methods would arrive at the same conclusions. Humanists usually avoided detailed discussions of methodology, but Scientists provided detailed methodological recipes. Humanists often stated an opinion about their subjects' admirable or despicable behavior at the very start of their narratives. Scientists usually relegated such comments to brief asides, footnotes, or a loosely appended "discussion" section. Given these preferences, it was hardly surprising that Science was read as bad Humanities research, and work in the Humanities as bad Science.

Certainly the first, and undoubtedly all subsequent versions of even this essay have reproduced these differences and assigned an implicit hierarchy to the relationship between Science and the Humanities, with predictable results for interdisciplinary communication. When I wrote the first draft I saw myself as a Humanist, at least in contrast to the majority of other seminar participants who were clearly Scientists (ecologists and archaeologists). Yet unconsciously I used a Scientific style of organization, piling up observations and stating my own interpretations and preferences as afterthoughts. In response, historians Donald Worster and Richard White asked for Humanist corrections: "more of a program from Ingerson" and more detail on "what exactly you want" (personal communications).

Finally, the very same kinds of misreading and disagreement surfaced during the peer review of this book, and particularly this chapter. One Scientist treated the entire book as a failed attempt to bring together "disparate approaches to ecology," recommended that the very word "historical" be removed from the title and replaced with "processual," and argued that peer review reports were simply not a legitimate form of data. A Humanist, in contrast, saw this data as providing "substantial behind-the-scenes

insights into research in the field" and argued that the book as a whole supported increased attention to specifically "historical/contingent causality."
A third reader echoed the Humanists' earlier complaints about this chapter,
that "the author's own position remains hidden," then agreed that "careful
comparison and analysis of praxis is often a good way to escape the paralysis of old philosophical dichotomies," and finally noted that "here my comments read like the excerpts from reviewers' comments cited, don't they?!"

Case 3: Classroom Discussions

The failures of interdisciplinary communication in environmental history
and historical ecology cited above are not just academic, in either sense of
that word. They are in fact the tip of a linguistic, and therefore a social and
political, iceberg. The first level of that iceberg below the waterline of consciousness was revealed frequently in a seminar I taught on "History and
Ecology in Anthropology."

Many if not all of the students in the course were committed environmentalists who hoped the class would teach them about ancient or exotic
societies that lived in harmony with nature and that could provide positive
models to be imitated. When those hopes were disappointed by classroom
readings and discussions, one class leaped to the apparently nonsensical
conclusion that "capitalism is universal." Since that statement is not literally true, as the students themselves acknowledged, what did they mean by
it? I think my students differed from the scholars whose linguistic behavior
has been discussed above primarily in accepting the self-presentation of
capitalism as a system that gives free reign to a human nature centered on
narrow self-interest and dedicated to unlimited consumption and growth.
In short, what the students identified as "universal capitalism" was simply
and exactly what Worster identified as "the human drive to dominate the
earth." The students' tendency to read the work I assigned them as evidence of a panhistorical, cross-cultural, and ultimately destructive human
"nature" was, for me, equivalent to the "heavy distortions" and "almost perverse misreadings" that Worster saw in critics who accused him of being
too materialist. In neither case did the problem originate with either the
"speaker" (in these two cases, me as the aggrieved teacher or Worster as
the aggrieved author) or the "hearer" (my students or Worster's critics). It
originated, and thrived, below the waterline of consciousness in the language each party had to use to communicate with the other.

Like those of the referees for *Forest & Conservation History,* my students' comments thus made visible a logic that invisibly structures most debates, scholarly and unscholarly, over environmental reform. First, students usually assumed that any human behavior or institution, from the degradation of natural resources to long-term population growth to social stratification, must be natural or innate if it occurs in many historical periods and many different societies. Behavior that is determined primarily by culture, they believed (as many cultural anthropologists have themselves argued), necessarily varies significantly over time and across cultures. The students were not satisfied with conclusions that any given interaction between human beings and the nonhuman environment reflects a perfect balance or "a little of both" innate human nature and variable culture, or that the relative importance of the two causes "varies from case to case." They wanted to know whether, in the aggregate of global history, unsustainable human exploitation of nature was due more to variable, cultural causes or to invariant, natural ones.

In many of my classes, students phrased their demands historically— that is, they assumed that the most critical cause of environmental destruction by human beings must necessarily be the cause that appeared first, and persisted the longest, in human history. This "search for origins" was never an organizing principle of the formal syllabus. In fact, I usually assigned readings from archaeology only in one of the last two or three sessions. Yet well before those sessions, students began asking each week when and where human beings first became alienated from nature, when and where we as a species stepped out of adaptation and deterministic, cyclical time into transformation and contingent, linear time. Each case history showing that linear change had occurred in a nonindustrial or precapitalist setting pushed the date of the "original sin" of escape from nature back in time and farther across the geographical horizon.

In the end, for the same reasons that make it difficult for ecological anthropologists and environmental historians to write studies that can be read as neither materialist nor idealist, or for authors who submitted manuscripts to *Forest & Conservation History* to construct manuscripts that were invulnerable to misreading by either Humanists or Scientists, I found it difficult to find literature that students could not interpret as evidence of original environmental sin. Clearly the many case studies of capitalism's adverse impact on the land only reinforced the students' assumptions. In practice, however, so did studies of precapitalist systems' benign relationships with nature, which the students read inevitably as suggesting that the advent of capitalism was the occasion of the original environmental sin. The few available studies of precapitalist systems' destructive effects on ecosystems were simply grist for the argument that the original sin was the emergence of culture itself. In this interpretive framework, in fact, any study that acknowledged the overuse or abuse of natural resources under *both* precapitalist systems and capitalism was read as evidence of universal human depravity no matter how strongly those same studies emphasized the quantitative differences between the two kinds of systems.

"Ecoethnographic romanticism"—which buttresses the conclusion that the Industrial Revolution was the original environmental sin—now abounds in both the popular environmental literature and in public policy statements by environmental and development organizations responding to (or incorporating) their anthropologist critics. I assigned my students some of this literature, in an attempt to get some culture into their view of "pure" nature, a view they shared with the American wilderness preservation movement. Thus I assigned some readings from Nelson (1983), several articles in Denslow and Padoch (1988), and Anderson and Huber (1988).

This stance certainly had its political uses. Nelson, for example, astutely emphasized an ahistorical tradition because he was working for a Native American group that had to justify its resource uses within a federally protected area (the Gates of the Arctic National Monument), for which the critical legislation limited the Koyukon to preserving "their traditional lifeway on ancestral lands" (Nelson 1983:xv). The legislation itself did not give the Koyukon within the national monument's boundaries the right to develop in any direction they might choose; rather it required them to "adapt" to their environment as the legislators assumed the group's "ancestors" had.

A few of the contributors to the volume edited by Denslow and Padoch clearly hoped to encourage the application of some similar principle to international interventions, if not national policies, in rain forest management. In that volume Carneiro argues that slash-and-burn agriculture as practiced by Amazonian Indians "proved to be a long-term system" and supported "a distinctive and successful culture that, wherever it has been left untrampled by the outside world, continues to flourish" (Carneiro 1988:86). In the same book, Posey writes that "native peoples have had much time to discover uses for the natural resources around them and to develop strategies to exploit and manage them," strategies that could serve as models for "a socially and ecologically viable alternative for the humid tropics" (Posey 1988:90). And Wilkie argues that the "traditional system of land tenure" in the Ituri forest of Zaire "promote[d] conservative use of the rain forest, as individuals would not degrade a resource that their children and children's children will inherit and upon which they will depend for subsistence" (Wilkie 1988:115).

Anderson and Huber attempt to describe the history of the so-called Gonds in India and criticize their displacement by a World Bank project. Yet these authors see history, defined as process of social change, at work only in the contact between the Gonds and groups conventionally assumed to have their own histories, such as Hindu kingdoms or and British colonialists. Anderson and Huber (1988:28–30) often lapse into the ethnographic present tense when describing the Gonds' forest-based subsistence economy, thus reinforcing the notion that the Gonds, if left to themselves, would have no internal "history" or evolution.

Yet this literature often suggested to my students that any people who adapted to rather than transformed their natural environment had lived, as the students often assumed plants and animals did, outside of history altogether. I therefore tried to criticize this literature from the perspective defended by such anthropologists as Eric Wolf (1982), and to assign as many readings as possible that would show how non-Western peoples transformed nature in major ways prior to contact with Europeans. At least until recently, such works were much rarer than the romantic ones mentioned above, but they do exist. Harms (1987) uses game theory, following in the footsteps of anthropologist Bailey (1970), to explain Nunu transformations of the Zaire River and its wetlands since the seventeenth century. Perdue (1987) plays a more-or-less spiral vision of expanding and collapsing settlement and political frontiers off against theories of oriental despotism and economic stagnation in China. And White (1983) portrays Native Americans before European contact as evolving, as involved in social conflict and inequality, and as transforming their natural environments. Ultimately, White blames the defeat and eviction of Native Americans on a combination of natural and cultural causes: the indigenous peoples' biological susceptibility to alcohol dependence, on the one hand, and European or Euroamerican military force, on the other.

My students accepted these authors' arguments that precolonial African lineages, classical Chinese agriculture, or Native American combinations of hunting, herding, and farming were not timeless adaptations to stable natural environments. The students, however, often took these authors' evidence a step further than the authors themselves do, to argue that if societies as different as these three all altered nature rather than adapted to it, then economic growth and transformation, rather than adaptation or coexistence, must be the tap roots of human nature. Richard White, for example, insisted that the Choctaws, Pawnees, and Navajos were culturally self-determining, that they were not mere pawns in European hands but active shapers of their own history. The students therefore concluded that these Native Americans must in some sense have *chosen* to adopt European economics (including participation in the fur trade) and religion because they saw something desirable in that system. The students argued that something in frontier capitalism, probably associated with material wealth and a more efficient exploitation of nature, appealed to the human nature Indians shared with the European interlopers.

The ways in which the nature-culture dichotomy is embedded in our language and reasoning make it difficult to argue effectively to the general public, including students, that noncapitalist societies or non-European peoples were or are rational, creative, and historical without encouraging such an audience to see those societies and peoples as "capitalist," because "capitalism" in my students' discourse simply means continuous change and exploitation of nature. Of course no professional anthropologist or historian, least of all Richard White, directly suggests that "capitalism is universal" (as he himself has pointed out with some indignation; personal communication). But White himself has admitted that this kind of conclusion may be unavoidable when we try to construct strong causal arguments. The "simple determinisms that lurk within the base/structure/superstructure model," he noted, "may be inevitable [in] hierarchical models" (*Journal of American History* 1990:1114). Scholars may be able to avoid such hierarchical models in communicating among themselves. The term *heterarchy,* as Carole Crumley deploys it in this volume, is one tool for avoiding determinism. But causal hierarchies inevitably reappear in public demands to know which of the multiple causes of environmental problems is ultimately the most critical and thus should be addressed first. In the context of public policy, advice to address all causes simultaneously because they are all equally important often has the same effect as advice to do nothing at all.

TESTING THE NATURE-CULTURE DICHOTOMY: FINDING HISTORY IN NATURE

The disagreements and misreadings outlined above were not over "mere style." They can be patched over, as we did when editing some manuscripts for publication in *Forest & Conservation History,* or as I did in leading classroom discussions beyond the despairing conclusion that "capitalism is universal" or that all human beings have a "drive to dominate the earth." But such misreadings cannot be *prevented* by careful speaking or writing, simply because in all our speaking and writing we depend for intelligibility on associations and meanings created by previous speaking and writing.

Once we have raised our own consciousness about how our normally implicit assumptions about the nature-culture dichotomy affect our reading and hearing of each other's arguments, we may be able actually to begin studying the dichotomy itself. Seeing it as an object is another critical step toward breaking it down. Earlier definitions of the border between culture and nature centered on the creation of tools intended to manipulate the environment, or the use of language to transmit knowledge from one generation to another without face-to-face contact. A number of primatologists and other students of animal behavior have already begun to undermine the notion that tool making, or even language use, bifurcates humans from the rest of nature.

History, defined as unique sequences of events that are nonrandom without being perfectly predictable, is another such border post between nature and culture. Some scientists are now questioning whether history also occurs on both sides of the border. Alvin Toffler, for example, lauds a work in which two physical chemists recommend that scientists pay more attention to "disorder, instability, diversity, disequilibrium, nonlinear relationships . . . and temporality—a heightened sensitivity to the flows of time" (in the foreword to Prigogine and Stengers 1984). Those two authors attempt to describe "a nature that might be called 'historical'—that is, capable of development and innovation," by moving their focus of study "from equilibrium to far-from-equilibrium conditions" and therefore "away from the repetitive and the universal to the specific and the unique" (Prigogine and Stengers 1984:152–53, 13). Many ecologists would agree with biologist Daniel Botkin, who recently announced that "wherever we seek to find constancy we discover change. . . . [N]ature undisturbed is not constant in form, structure, or proportion, but changes at every scale of time and space" (Botkin 1990:62).

We have often collected utterly incomparable kinds of information about processes of change in nature and in culture precisely because we have assumed that change in nature occurs through predictable or cyclical events in which conscious intention plays no part, and that change in human social life occurs through unique events and deliberate decisions. To some extent these assumptions are so deeply embedded in most of our data that we must start from scratch to collect information that will actually let us test these assumptions. Botkin, for example, points out that "few scientists have maintained an interest in one population for more than a decade. And in the cases where they might have, it has been rare that any government or private organization has been willing to fund such long projects" (1990:43–44).

Imagine the effect on social or economic policy of assuming that human experience is adequately described through methods that consider all individual human "subjects" to be interchangeable and that document their behavior for at most a few months at a time. Yet we have routinely based environmental policy on data limited in just this way. How can we judge other organisms' adaptiveness, let alone tell how destructive or adaptive our own actions are, if none of our data about plants' or animals' activities cover more than a single generation of a single species? Or if we never observe the full process of adaptation, from initial habitat change through final morphological or genetic changes?

For longer than a century anthropology has held pride of place in upholding the barrier between natural and cultural evolution. Radcliffe-Brown justified that barrier by explaining that "a pig does not become sick and recover as a hippopotamus; but that is what a society does" (1957:83). To Radcliffe-Brown's credit, intentionally sustaining life on the earth probably does require distinguishing the time scale of individual or even social sickness and recovery from the time scale of evolution, both social and biological. But achieving that purpose also requires understanding the relationships between the two scales. Here my argument and Radcliffe-Brown's definition both converge with Crumley's suggestion in the original outline for this book, that "effective environmental policies for the future" will depend on "deft integration of both environmental and cultural information at a variety of temporal and spatial scales."

As a hypothesis rather than an axiom, Radcliffe-Brown's statement offers an important advantage over definitions of culture that set human beings apart from the rest of nature as tool-making or language-using animals. A focus on change and time draws our attention not to the abilities of individuals but to the general relationship between unique events and system transformations. We have often defined change in opposition to system, within nature (evolution vs. ecosystems) and culture (evolution vs. world views) as well as between the two.

Theoretical frameworks for such research already exist in the cultural disciplines. Braudel's schemes contrasting the *conjoncture* of events with the *longue durée* of system, or distinguishing individuals and events from social trends and those in turn from the time scales of geography and geology (1972–73[1]:21, [2]:1242) are rooted in culture history, but they are compatible with images of evolution as a series of "punctuated equilibria" (see Stanley 1984 and Gould 1980, especially p. 184). Chemists Ilya Prigogine and Isabelle Stengers argue that "bifurcation points" in purely physical systems bear a strong resemblance to the punctuation marks in biological evolution and to human social revolutions: physical and chemical systems sometimes "seem to 'hesitate' among various possible directions of evolution. . . . A small fluctuation may start an entirely new evolution that will drastically change the whole behavior of the macroscopic system. The analogy with social phenomena, even with history, is inescapable" (1984:14). New research in the physical sciences has made the image of fixed natural laws recede and has brought forward images of "biological, ecological, or social evolution" in all of which "the definition of the system is . . . liable to be modified by its evolution" (1984:189). Biologist Daniel Botkin lists several fundamentally new dynamics that have emerged in the earth's history, from the evolution of life to the successive appearance of large continents, angiosperms, and human beings (1990:148).

A few scientific field studies have already begun to fill the gap between single-system or single-generation studies and studies of biological evolution. Science conducted on this intermediate, "historical" time scale has already provided some revealing results. Botkin reports that a study of moose and wolf populations on Isle Royale in Lake Superior since the late 1960s revealed "complex patterns, which show great variations over time . . . in which the individuality of the wolves and moose seemed to play an important role" (1990:31). Jane Goodall's observations of wild chimpanzees in Tanzania are one spectacular example in which generational differences and cumulative learning become visible in a supposedly noncultural population (1990). Elizabeth Marshall Thomas (1990) recently offered evidence of a very similar sort for the lions of the Kalahari. Thomas has seen these lions radically change their behavior toward human beings as a result of interruptions in the nongenetic transmission of information across generations since the 1950s. The Kalahari lions, she argues, show that "cultural diversity—brought about by experience, thought, feelings, education—as well as genetic diversity accounts for the different customs found in different populations of many living things" in addition to human beings (Thomas 1990:78). It is significant that both specialists and the public are beginning to refer to the "chimpanzees of Gombe" and "Kalahari lions" rather than simply to generic chimpanzees and lions. The collection of historical data in these two cases has begun to modify our perceptions of the culture-nature border.

Even the resolutely synchronic and functional science of cell biology has recently "gone historical" in some ways. Many biologists now see the structures of cell nuclei as the contingent results of unique or irreversible events, such as the capture of smaller organisms by larger ones, or the co-operation of smaller ones to form "superorganisms" (see Margulis 1970; Margulis and Bermudes 1985; Botkin 1990:113–14). A cell history of that type is far more likely than any purely functional or structural analysis to discover and acknowledge nonfunctional vestiges, accidents, and contra-dictions within biological systems. As this inherently historical biology gains further acceptance, it surely will force biologists to begin to distin-guish more clearly between the *systemic* functions of a structure and the *historical* reasons for its existence-introducing unique, contingent connec-tions between cause and effect.

THE CRITIQUE OF HISTORY IN NATURE

The scientists cited in the preceding section seem to have accepted a world view and methods more conventionally championed by historians. Yet en-vironmental historians have not embraced these converts. On the contrary, Donald Worster, speaking probably for many of his colleagues, has argued vehemently against seeing nature as historical. As he did in 1977, and along with environmentalist Edward Goldsmith (1985), Worster insists that the shift in ecology from a focus on climax systems and homeostasis to an inter-est in stochastic processes and disturbance or chaos is at bottom a means of removing the economically and politically inconvenient but emotion-ally powerful image of nature as self-balancing and self-limiting. He argues strongly that "a nature characterized by highly individualistic associations, constant disturbance, and incessant change may be more ideologically sat-isfying than . . . [the previous] stress on cooperation, social organization, and environmentalism" (1990:11). Although Worster admits that a focus on disturbance and change in nature *could* lead to greater "respect [for nature's] baffling complexity, its inherent unpredictability, its daily tur-bulence" (1990:14), he suggests that this is unlikely. Instead, he warns both that "there will no longer be any science if all faith in order vanishes" (Worster 1990:15) and that "science . . . promotes . . . a few of our darker ambitions toward nature and therefore itself needs to be morally examined and critiqued" (1990:2). He insists that "scientific analysis cannot take the place of moral reasoning" (1990:2). Therefore, "we should take up and practice history as a form of moral reasoning, and not as some appendage to the sciences with their data-collecting" (personal communication).

Which is more likely to promote environmentally responsible action

—finding history in nature, or upholding the nature-culture dichotomy as a critical tool of "moral reasoning"? The proponents of a contingent or historical science have acknowledged that too celebratory an attitude toward change in nature could justify destructive human behavior. Prigogine and Stengers admit that " 'order through fluctuations' models introduce an unstable world where small causes can have large effects" (1984:206). Botkin makes similar admissions: "Clearly, to abandon a belief in the constancy of undisturbed nature is psychologically uncomfortable [because that belief] provided . . . a simple standard against which to judge our actions, a reflection from a windless pond in which our place was both apparent and fixed. . . . Abandoning these beliefs leaves us in an extreme existential position" (1990:188–90).

Worster is surely correct that some of the scientists who enthusiastically adopt this existentialist position are promoting their own ambitions, however dark or light. Botkin, for example, acknowledges that his "new perspective does not give the same simple answers to all questions, but requires that our management be specific. . . . Knowing what to do in each case requires considerable information, surveys, monitoring, knowledge, and understanding, which . . . [are] not amateur activit[ies] and will require considerable sums of money" (1990:190, 197). Botkin does not make clear how scientists would be held accountable for the results of this additional funding.

Prigogine and Stengers, on the other hand, do explore that question. With Botkin, they insist that "this world is not arbitrary. On the contrary, the reasons for the amplification of a small event are a legitimate matter for rational inquiry" (1984:206). But they also acknowledge that scientists must accept new, fundamentally ethical responsibilities, and therefore moral as well as factual critiques of their work, if they adopt historical methods: "We can no longer accept the old a priori distinction between scientific and ethical values. . . . Today we know that time is a construction and therefore carries an ethical responsibility" (1984:312).

NATURE AND CULTURE IN FUTURE PRACTICE: FROM DICHOTOMY TO DIALOGUE

If further research on the culturelike qualities of nature breaks down even more the "old a priori distinction between scientific and ethical values" defended by Worster and attacked by Prigogine and Stengers, what will replace Nature with a capital "N" as a moral beacon? What should we seek to preserve or create, if change in nature is no more self-justifying and automatically progressive than change in culture has proven to be, in most cases? If nature is not governed by unchanging laws, then how can we know what nature, and therefore ultimately we ourselves as part of nature, "needs" or "wants" over the long term?

One possible answer to this question emerges from another border post between nature and culture, the one with which this essay began: language in its complex role as both reflector and shaper of social, and possibly natural, reality. Linguist Benjamin Lee Whorf (1978, originally 1956) suggested that science, materialism, and this essentially spatial use of language were all bound up together with the development of markets—in short, of capitalism (see also Crosby 1990):

> [Our language embodies] our whole scheme of OBJECTIFYING— imaginatively spatializing qualities and potentials that are quite nonspatial. (Whorf 1978:145)

> Monistic, holistic, and relativistic views of reality . . . are badly handicapped in appealing to the "common sense" of the Western average man—not because nature herself refutes them . . . but because they must be talked about in what amounts to a new language. . . . Our objectified view of time is . . . favorable . . . to the building up of a commercial structure based on time-prorata values: time wages . . . rent, credit, interest, depreciation . . . and insurance premiums. . . . The need for measurement in industry and trade . . . standardizing of measure and weight units, invention of clocks . . . keeping of records, accounts, chronicles, histories, . . . and the partnership of mathematics and science. (Whorf 1978:152–57)

It is very nearly impossible to bring such a language to bear on the nature-culture dichotomy in a critical way, no matter how carefully we redefine words in that language, because this type of language forces attention onto spatial or descriptive accuracy and away from both mutual responsibility and change through time. One theory of accountability or democracy that does without the fixed moral beacon of a law-governed nature is that of Jürgen Habermas. Habermas has argued that nonauthoritarian politics—the kind of politics that is required to manage human action as part of an evolving rather than equilibrated ecosystem—must be based on the development through time of an "unconstrained consensus" (1971:314; and see Alford 1985 as cited in Fayter 1990, especially the latter's pp. 88–89). This standard of accountability is essentially horizontal and temporal, based on communication between equals rather than description of a passive object (nature) by an active subject (culture, including science).

To envision a new, inherently ethical science as a tool for building a more egalitarian relationship between culture and nature, it may also help to see language less as a means of picturing the world and more as a kind of cooperative work *in* the world (see Pitkin [1974:24–49] on Wittgenstein; Rossi-Landi 1983). The political and ecological "heterarchy" of Celtic Burgundy, as Crumley describes it in chapter 8, illustrates that kind of working cooperation on a regional scale. Our daily experience of work in the late twentieth century is not often very egalitarian. Still, most of us can imagine cooperative work over time, and we can more easily associate mutual accountability and responsibility with that image than we can with images of science as dissection or vivisection.

Such metaphorical proposals to reinvent science are, as Whorf predicted, "badly handicapped in appealing to 'common sense' because they must themselves be talked about in a new language." Yet some scientists have already adopted this new language. Prigogine and Stengers, for example, have argued that "science [is] a poetical interrogation of nature, in the etymological sense that the poet is a 'maker'—active, manipulating, and exploring. Moreover, science is now capable of respecting the nature it investigates. Out of the dialogue with nature initiated by classical science, with its view of nature as an automaton, has grown a quite different view in which the activity of questioning nature is part of its [own] intrinsic activity" (1984:301).

This kind of proposal, in early drafts of this essay, was far from universally accepted. It elicited the same polarized responses from historians and scientists as the very notion that history might exist within nature, as well as in the relations between nature and culture. Historians considered these metaphors "a little obscure and yet a little utopian (a tone of 'New Age dawning' . . .)" (Worster, personal communication) and as exemplifying a kind of "left mysticism, which I am sympathetic with but not particularly convinced by" or as implying the "heavily idealistic proposition that reforming language is the first step to reforming the world" (Richard White, personal communication). Ecologist Frank Golley, in contrast, "really liked [the] . . . comments on language" (personal communication).

No argument, no matter how logical or elegant, can make such metaphors sound like common sense, just as the redefinition of terms by fiat

cannot change the habits of an established speech community. Even if reforming language is one step among others toward reforming the world,
it is not an easy step. New metaphors for science and new definitions of
nature are far more likely to isolate their users from any broad, public environmental debate than they are to change the vocabulary, let alone the
outcome, of that debate. The metaphors suggested here will have served
their purpose if they encourage some scientists and historians first to notice
and discuss the usually unexamined barriers to interdisciplinary understanding tracked in the "case histories" of the nature-culture dichotomy
presented above, and second to borrow and test each other's research
methods and ways of judging research results.

AFTERWORD: FROM DIALOGUE TO DIALECTICS

Prigogine and Stengers point out that, "to a certain extent, there is an
analogy between this conflict [over historicism in science] and the one that
gave rise to dialectical materialism. We have described . . . a nature that
might be called 'historical'—that is, capable of development and innovation. The idea of a history of nature as an integral part of materialism was
asserted by Marx and, in greater detail, by Engels. Contemporary developments in physics, the discovery of the constructive role played by irreversi-
bility, have thus raised within the natural sciences a question that has
long been asked by materialists. For them, understanding nature meant
understanding it as being capable of producing man and his societies"
(1984:252–53).

The analogy between recent attempts to historicize natural science
and Marx's attempt to historicize political economy may not be exact, but
it may at least be politically instructive. The environmentalist's dilemma
is explaining nature so as to change our way of understanding nature,
which of course shapes the way the environmentalist explains nature in
the first place. This bears a strong logical resemblance to Marx's dilemma
of explaining social evolution in order to change our way of understanding
social change, which of course shaped Marx's own view of social evolution
in the first place. Marx saw his central challenge as eliminating capitalism. Environmental reformers may see theirs as eliminating the human
exploitation of nature. But both reformers want to change a system that
shapes their definitions of and their desire for change in the first place.
Environmentalists must try to preserve nature at least partly by applying
the methods of a science they believe has been instrumental in damaging

nature. Marx sought to accelerate the demise of capitalism by applying the methods of "political economy," a discipline he believed had been instrumental in helping capitalism to thrive.

Envisioning any alternative to the present system necessarily seems "utopian" or "mystical," in part because that alternative must be formulated in a vocabulary that relies for its meanings on associations drawn from the social or environmental status quo. Yet insisting that we cannot use language to envision alternatives to the status quo, because language is strictly a reflector and not an active shaper of current conditions, seems a cowardly way of insuring against failure in practice by making change theoretically impossible. The only way to prove that truly unprecedented change is possible—that history is not the playing out of fully predetermined ("natural"?) processes, and that the present system is not "the end of history"— is to make such change actually happen, which requires imagining alternatives and probing for weaknesses and contradictions from inside the existing system. In short, scientific prediction that challenges rather than accepts the conventional nature-culture dichotomy will fit the definition of "prediction" by Antonio Gramsci as "the abstract expression of the effort made, the practical way of creating a collective will" (Gramsci 1975:438).

The argument in this essay is in essence an argument for doing what we can to make Gramsci's definition of prediction begin to sound like common sense, instead of absurd. In a final Marxist translation, then, I have argued: Reconceiving the relationship between nature and culture as a dialogue (translation: "dialectic," or even as the kind of "totality" recommended by Patterson in chapter 10) rather than as a dichotomy is a necessary but insufficient step toward reforming that relationship. Without new kinds of practice (translation: "praxis"), including but not confined to scientific research and writing, any new definitions we promote will remain hollow and theoretical. One powerful way to understand nature and culture as points on a quantitative spectrum (translation: "dialectically") rather than as qualitative opposites is to make those differences topics of empirical study. In a world altered by these new kinds of knowledge, we may gradually stop posing questions about the hierarchy of causality between nature and culture, and begin to pose questions about heterarchies that are both and neither natural nor cultural as we now understand those terms. We may even begin to take seriously our responsibilities as the most vocal, and potentially the most consciously destructive or constructive, group of voices on a planet that expresses itself through many other voices as well.

——— *Note* ———

I would like to thank Donald Worster, Richard White, and Frank Golley for permission to quote their comments on earlier drafts of this paper. Along with comments from my students and colleagues at the Forest History Society and in the School of the Environment at Duke University, their criticisms have helped me to understand why proposals that are hard to accept are nevertheless useful. I owe a special debt to the students who took my course on history and ecology in anthropology, offered through Duke's anthropology department, for their courageous decision in the hierarchical setting of a university classroom not just to imitate my academic vocabulary and agenda but to make me listen to their version of our "common sense."

Chapter 4

Global Climate and Regional Biocultural Diversity

Joel D. Gunn

This chapter undertakes to study methods of investigation at the interface between culture and physical environment. Culture is the body of knowledge that a people amass and pass from generation to generation, and physical environment is geology and climate. Biological systems, soils, and hydrology are so completely interactive with humans and culture, and appear to have been so for at least a million years (Pope 1989), that they should be treated as a richly networked analytical unit. Geology and climate, on the other hand, are relatively independent of the biocultural network and can be treated as somewhat independent of life systems. Of course, we now suspect that the geosphere and biocultural domains are interdependent (Lovelock 1979), which is in part the justification for this volume, but for purposes of analysis and understanding they can be, in a limited fashion, teased apart.

Climate emanates from astronomical forces of great power, and geology from lesser but equally formidable origins within the earth. That which separates this age from others is the feeble but persistent assertion of human agency at critical nodes in the network of geophysical and life-system relationships that regulate the habitability of the earth. Climate and geology tend to bump biocultural systems around heavy-handedly, but they do not totally escape the recoil of self-organizing life systems (Adams 1988), so human agency has become a fourth and presumably ill-tempered player. Humans have appropriated, rather than a place in the sun, a place with the sun in world affairs in the broadest ecological and political sense.

This book undertakes to understand both human agency and global habitat. The purpose is to provide a baseline for responsible policy which will mitigate the impact of human agency on global ecology. In this chapter I initially examine the somewhat more predictable and mechanistic physical side of the geosphere-biosphere question and then venture into the cultural interface between the physical and biosocial domains. At its most practical level, this paper is concerned with cultural diversity relative to global climate. The questions it attempts to address are, what is the relationship between biocultural diversity and global climate, and how much biocultural diversity can be expected to exist in the world? The opportunities and responsibilities that biocultural diversity offer policymakers are akin to those of species diversity: the potential to heal or further disrupt human social ills consequent from global climatic change.

My objectives are as follows:

1. to suggest a workable causal perspective that is suited to multiple cause-and-effect relationships among cultures, climates, geology, geomorphology (topography, soils, hydrology), and individuals;
2. to negotiate a working model of atmospheric circulation that physical scientists will regard as being adequate, but with which social scientists and humanistic scholars will feel comfortable;
3. to show how to manipulate the atmospheric model relative to global average temperature to explain regional climatic changes, in order to provide a forum for cooperation among the various disciplines;
4. to describe how the model is projected into the past and future;
5. to provide a plausible link between cultural knowledge retention and global climate;
6. to outline some of the biocultural diversity that has resulted from this link; and
7. to outline a means of distinguishing climatic and cultural causes and effects through parallel events.

THE RELEVANCE AND PRIORITY OF CAUSATION

With the advent of global ecology as a paradigm, the need for an explicit and workable multicausal methodology that addresses the relationships of the physical environment to cultural life has become imperative. Examinations of so-called systems—social, biological, atmospheric, oceanic— perhaps illuminate the internal structure of global network components, but they reveal little about the biosphere as a whole. An approach is needed that will provide an interdisciplinary, multicausal methodology to study the structure as a whole. I address factors that have a true external, and therefore causal, component that emanates from ultimate astronomical and geological forces. My colleagues investigate issues of the richly networked, and therefore highly interactive, internal biocultural factors in other chapters of this book.

The perspective I use assumes that effects are apportioned among causes, which are all *by definition* regarded as contributing to an event of cultural change. Students of cultural change have posed their arguments for various regions of the world in terms of primary causes, or "prime movers." An example is the debate over the origin of civilization. Among the suggested prime movers have been climate, hydraulic agriculture, diffusion of cultural traits, innovation by individuals, geographic circumscription, hierarchical organization, and population. Although a single cause may pose a best explanation of cultural change in a specific region, such as hydraulic agriculture in Mesopotamia, it is most likely that all of the listed causes were active in all regions. Rather than reject these monocausal treatises as irrelevant, I take them to be thorough examinations of some factors relevant to cultural change, each factor being examined in the world region where it was most evident, and presumably most powerful. It has been recognized since the 1930s that these studies, though illuminating, are limited by lack of attention to context. Multicausal models to address these shortcomings have been much discussed, and hardly a book on culture change begins without alluding to the question. However, there has been little development, beyond numeric description, of multicausal methodologies to advance understanding of the processes involved.

If one presumes that all factors are active, it is more productive to think in terms of the portion of contribution of each factor in a given regional situation than to examine the factors one at a time. One might suppose, for example, that hydraulic agriculture gave little impetus to the rise of agrarian social organization in the Fremont culture around the Great Salt Lake of Utah, but rather that climate and cultural diffusion provided the more powerful conditioning factors. This is not to suggest that the invention of small water impoundments in the Southwest proper did not provide some portion of the milieu that brought forth Fremont agriculture (Gunn 1975). By comparison, powerful cultural traditions focusing on information control (Chang 1986:366), the locations of copper mines (Chang 1986:367), and to some extent climate (Chang 1986:76) played a role in cultural location and form in China.

There are several alternative approaches to presenting the results of an apportioned analysis. One is ranking causes accompanied by a causal account (Salmon 1982), such as the parallel events analysis presented below. Other approaches are available depending on one's taste, discipline, and data resources. A set of logical relations may provide a convincing vehicle in which information on scale and relative power can be found. If quantitative measures are available, portions can be defined as percentages by multiple regression. The unpretentious pie chart provides an effective graphical vehicle for visualization of this type of analysis, which approximates Clarke's (1968:103–4) conception of multicausality.

To be sure, an important component of this chapter is to investigate the means by which climatic effects on cultures can be assessed. In my view, determining potential climatic causation should precede attempts to delimit the contributions of innovation and culture history (Gunn and Adams 1981). This is because climate is the most easily and precisely assessed of the three causes of culture change: it is the only factor with origins clearly outside the biosphere. Unmasking environmental causes benefits subsequent analysis by delimiting that portion of cultural change interfaced with environment, and it leaves the investigator with the expectation that what remains is attributable to culture history and innovation. Of course, the usual caveat applies that these factors are interlinked and interactive with environment, so the investigator must never resort to uncritical reductionism.

CLIMATE IN BIOCULTURAL PERSPECTIVE

Defining climate to assist our attempts to understand cultural change requires a modified approach from that used by meteorologists, who aspire to understand weather, or even that used by climatologists, whose goal is to comprehend atmospheric and oceanic processes. For purposes of understanding cultural change, climate should be defined at a spatial and temporal scale that is meaningful in terms of human social organization and adaptation. Emphasis should be given to those aspects of climate that impact most directly on human activity. This involves reemphasizing pieces of the atmospheric puzzle, and giving careful attention to the accuracy of the data on the emphasized pieces. I will first attend to the important pieces of the puzzle, global average temperatures and regional hydrology. Then I will discuss appropriate data.

Climate is defined by the National Academy of Sciences (1965) as weather phenomena lasting more than two weeks. For a number of reasons this definition of climate is useful from a cultural perspective, but only as a point of departure. Most important is that it distinguishes climate from weather. Weather is a short-term phenomenon at the scale of a few days. As such its description and forecasting are based on secondary causes—fronts, clouds, and air mass movements. Climate, on the other hand, is a long-term phenomenon that is investigated at the scale of weeks to billions of years. As such it requires the invocation of primary astronomical and global causes, quantity of solar radiation, orbital configurations, global-scale volcanism, and atmospheric chemistry. At the same time, to be relevant to social processes it must be understood at the spatial scale of social units. Occasionally these units may be relatively large, such as the Roman Empire, but the building block of society is the region (Crumley and Marquardt 1987). As we shall see, the global and regional aspects of climate are related to each other. I will first discuss global climate and then its regional effects.

Global Climate

Understanding the link between global climate and regional conditions comes from generally understood atmospheric circulation principles. The rudiments of atmospheric circulation theory have been known since early in the century. Dines (1917, 1923; cited in Brooks 1949) conceptualized the atmosphere as a thermodynamic system whose pattern of flow at any given time was a result of its overall temperature. Budyko (1956, 1980; Webster 1981) popularized the thermodynamic system concept and extended it into an explanation of how global climate and ecology vary through time. The temperature of the atmosphere, or global energy balance (GEB), is composed of solar insolation, plus sensible and latent heat, minus radiation. If any of these contributors to the GEB changes, then the atmospheric temperature changes and the location and direction of atmospheric flow patterns change; life systems change along with them. Since any change in the GEB affects patterns of flow everywhere, the atmosphere is said to be "teleconnected." Thus, if a change in atmospheric conditions is observed in any region in the world, it implies some sort of change in all regions.

In addition to being directed by thermodynamics, atmospheric circulation is deflected about by mountain ranges, pools of ocean waters of varying temperature, basins, seasons, and other factors, which include chaotic elements (Reinhold 1987). In principle, the flow of atmosphere and oceans is not very complicated (Broecker and Denton 1990; Webster 1981). It follows broadly definable patterns. Probably the most illuminating experiment ever performed to understand atmospheric circulation consisted of contaminating a spinning pan of water with white specks and then heating it. The result revealed currents and eddies, which varied with the temperature (Rieter 1961). The pan appeared much like what we see on satellite weather reports. Similar experiments are still performed (James 1988), and sophisticated studies of short-term chaotic properties of the atmosphere are essentially variations on the heated-pan theme.

The details of atmospheric circulation are complex, and creating mathematical models of the atmosphere has been daunting (Schneider 1987); nevertheless, the important point for the nonspecialist who needs a working model of atmospheric thermodynamics is that the shape of atmospheric circulation can be measured very simply by determining how hot the atmosphere is. As happened in the experimental pan, atmospheric structure assumes different characteristic shapes at different temperatures. The most important structure in the atmosphere from the perspective of temperate-zone humans is the boundary between polar and equatorial air masses (fig. 4.1). This boundary is marked by a distinct change in temperature (Barry and Chorley 1968). It is notable at the surface as fronts, and the change in temperature with the passage of a front is the difference between the temperatures of the polar and equatorial air masses. The jet stream follows the upper edge of the boundary and flows from west to east at about one hundred miles an hour. The utility of the jet stream global air-mass boundary in a working climate model will become apparent when I address regional effects.

The position of the air mass boundary controls weather and climate at a given location. At the seasonal scale, if one is located north of it, it is winter; to the south, it is summer.[1] We follow the passage of this boundary each year as the seasons change; the polar air mass shrinks and swells. At the annual scale, climate, like seasons, reflects the location of the air mass boundary; it is, however, the average location of the boundary over the year that makes climate, rather than its annual movement. When the perspective is one of tens of thousands of years, during some years the boundary remains south all year around, and the poles experience glaciation. In other periods it remains far to the north year-round, and even the most resilient polar glaciers disappear. As a result, there are three basic mid-latitude climates in any location: hot and dry, warm and wet, cool and dry. Variations of these basic climates are generated by variations in the monthly distribution of seasonal precipitation. Trewartha (1961) has made

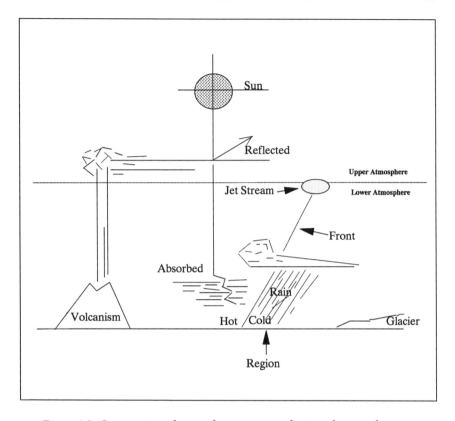

Figure 4.1. Cross-section of atmospheric structure showing elements that contribute to changes in the global energy balance and surface distribution of precipitation.

extensive studies of seasonal precipitation. Most regions experience about a dozen types of precipitation. During much of the past 10,000 years, the boundary has made annual transgressions, so climate has varied between winter and summer. A helpful definition of "a climate" is a ten-year period when the average position of the air mass boundary (and global average temperature) remains at about the same latitude (Gunn 1991). Ten years is adequate duration for a culture to adjust to the conditions imposed by an atmosphere-ocean circulation pattern.

The location of the average position of the air mass boundary is controlled by the average temperature of the atmosphere (and oceans), or global average temperature. The global average temperature depends on the amount of solar energy retained by the atmosphere as sensible or stored heat. When a volcano injects debris into the upper atmosphere, as El Chichon did in 1982 (Rampino and Self 1983), it reflects sunlight into space and cools the atmosphere. As a result, the air mass boundary will move south and a larger proportion of the world will experience cooler average temperatures (Angell and Korshover 1983). If the upper atmosphere is clear, and energy-absorbing trace gases are made abundant in the lower atmosphere, the atmosphere warms. As a result, the air mass boundary will move north and a larger proportion of the world will experience year-round warm climate. Thus, from the perspective of an organism or society on the ground, climate is related to global average temperature.

Since the International Geophysical Year in 1957–58, careful attention has been paid to the measurement of global average temperature. From these measurements have come a growing understanding of global climatic processes (Angell 1991; Angell and Korshover 1983). Global average temperatures have been found to respond to solar energy variation, El Niño–Southern Oscillation cycles, global volcanism, and anthropogenic trace gases (Gunn 1991).

Regional Climate

Regional climate is the scale at which atmospheric phenomena impact biocultural systems. It is clear from the foregoing discussion of global average temperatures and atmospheric circulation that systematic relationships will exist between climates characteristic of the globe and the region. A number of individuals and agencies have suggested in the past few years that the global average temperature is likely to rise in the next decades because of emissions of trace gases, such as carbon dioxide, CFCs, and nitrous oxide, mostly from automobiles. We would expect, therefore, that a larger proportion of the world will experience warmer climate year-round. People and societies, however, do not live in a "larger proportion of the world." They live and perform economic and life functions in regions. The next focus of our interests, then, turns to the causes of regional climate.

Although we are concerned with temperature at the global scale because of thermodynamics, temperature is not of primary importance at the regional scale. Temperature is only marginally useful in defining regional life systems, but water is eminently important as regards quantity and spatial and seasonal distribution of living entities.

If we assume one more atmospheric circulation principle, it will be possible to link global average temperature and local water supply. This principle is something we all basically understand from watching television weather: it rains under the jet stream (Barry and Chorley 1968:221). The flow of the jet stream from west to east along the top of the lower atmosphere (the troposphere; see fig. 4.1) tends to carry the rest of the atmosphere along with it, and moist air and clouds follow. Frontal turbulence under the jet stream stirs the air and triggers rainfall. Thus, the amount of rainfall in a given region is controlled by its relationship to the average annual position of the jet stream, which is, in turn, regulated by the average annual global temperature.

Thanks to the relationship between global temperature and regional moisture, the water supply in most regions can be estimated as a function of global average temperature (Gunn and Crumley 1989; Boer and DeGroot 1990:36). An important question is, what is the best measure of local moisture? I have found for a number of reasons that stream discharge is a holistic, reliable, and accurate measure of regional hydrological balance. It simultaneously reflects precipitation, evaporation (local temperature and humidity), land use, vegetation, soils, and geology (see also Jongman and Sour 1990). Furthermore, stream basins can be selected that are spatially equivalent to communities. They thus provide direct links between population or cultural trends and hydrological climate.

As an example, data were collected for Mechet Creek, which heads on Mont Beuvray, the mountaintop capital of the Celtic Aedui, and ends at Autun, the Gallo-Roman capital of the region (Crumley and Marquardt 1987). Correlation of discharge from Mechet Creek with global average temperatures shows that in the past thirty years global temperatures had great influence on local runoff (fig. 4.2). In years when the atmosphere was of a medium average temperature (about 3.9–4.2°C), the Mechet experienced maximum discharge. In years when the atmosphere was exceptionally hot or cold the discharge tended to be less. When the correlation was used to reconstruct discharge for the past 10,000 years, it reproduced observed hydrological conditions (Gunn and Crumley 1989).

A parallel analysis was made of the discharge of the Candelaria River in Campeche, Mexico (fig. 4.3) (Gunn, Folan, and Robichaux 1990). The Candelaria River heads near the great abandoned Preclassic and Classic period cities of Calakmul (in Campeche) and El Mirador (in Guatemala). The Candelaria River is in a tropical circulation system, so one would anticipate that the relationship between rainfall and global average temperature would differ from that of middle-latitude France. In the case of this tropical system, precipitation shifts from spring to fall as the world warms. At medium global temperatures, rainfall is evenly spread over the summer, providing ideal conditions for cultivation of Indian corn, or maize. In

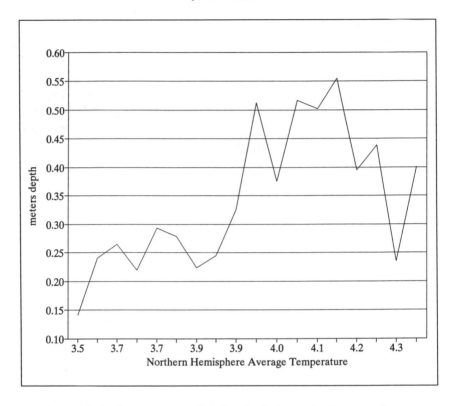

Figure 4.2. Discharge response of Mechet Creek, Burgundy, France, to changes in global average temperature during the years 1968–1986.

years in which the atmosphere was hot, the rainy season tended to come later in the summer, or even in the fall. This produced a less abundant harvest of maize.

Some additional facts can help to refine our understanding of global and regional climate. The transformation of global temperature to local moisture may produce a direct or inverse effect. The magnitude of the effect also varies with each region, ranging from very pronounced to virtually inconsequential (Bryson 1986).

The transformation of global temperature to local moisture is usually a curvilinear function because of the jet stream rain effect and the relationship of the jet stream to global average temperature. If the average position of the jet stream is over the region, it will rain frequently. It will rain less frequently when the globe warms or cools, moving the average position of the jet stream north or south. An interesting example is the Southern

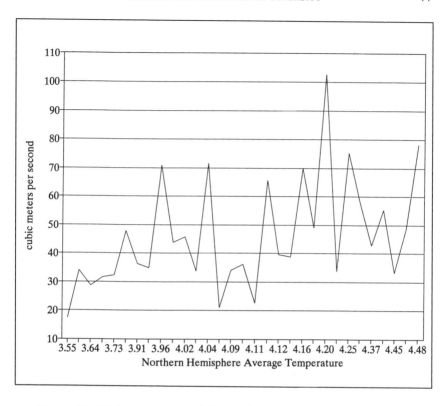

Figure 4.3. Discharge response of the Candelaria River, Campeche, Mexico, to changes in global average temperature during the years 1958–1990.

Plains. Since 1976 global average temperatures have increased from record lows to record highs (Angell and Korshover 1983; Houghton, Jenkins, and Ephraums 1990). During that time winter precipitation has cycled from low to high and back to low again (fig. 4.4).

Regional climatic changes are punctuated by thresholds controlled by local conditions. Such events occur when the jet stream suddenly shifts to accommodate mountain ranges, as when it "jumps" over the Himalayas, or when the number of loops in the jet stream changes (Bryson and Murray 1977), the latter also being a function of global average temperature. Thus, a region will tend to have a few well-defined climates separated by jumps rather than continually varying climate precisely correlated with the global energy balance.

Events in the Medieval Climatic Optimum (AD 900–1250) and the middle Holocene (4500–7500 BP, Altithermal) suggest that there is a global

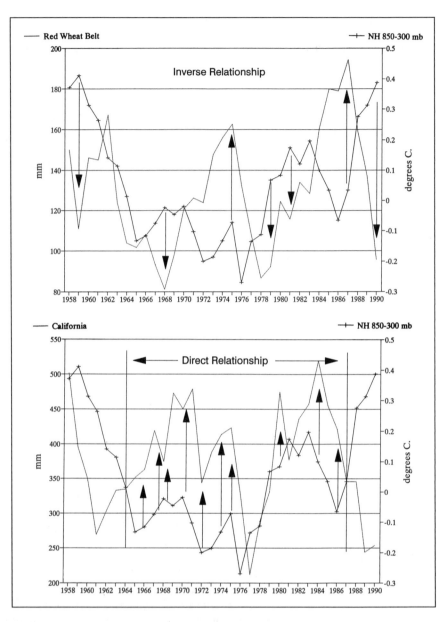

Figure 4.4. Winter precipitation on the Southern Plains (top) follows an inverse function relative to global average temperatures, whereas the relationship between California
precipitation and global temperature (bottom) is direct (after the Weekly Weather and
Crop Bulletin 1991). Data for the Southern Plains (Red Wheat Belt) and California are
three-point running averages of precipitation from October to February. NH 850–300
mb: the average annual temperature anomaly of the atmosphere ranges from 850 millibars (at about 5000 feet) to 300 millibars (at about 30,000 feet). These values are being
used as proxy measures of global average temperature.

threshold at about 16–17°C, 1–2°C above present global average tempera-ture. This threshold has not been studied to my knowledge, and in fact it is only a suggestion resulting from my own investigations (Gunn 1991). Once this postulated threshold is passed, there may be a critical jump to another global climatic regime resembling the last interglacial (120,000 BP) or the Mesozoic. It has recently been discovered that the very con-siderable sea-level rise during the last interglacial was due to the melting of the Greenland glaciers. Several forecasts of increases in global aver-age temperatures caused by anthropogenic trace gases suggest increases as large as 3 to 5°C. If the 17°C threshold exists, the dislocation of climatic zones could be pronounced. Simulations of Mesozoic climate with a dif-ferent continental configuration, but with global average temperatures 5 to 15°C higher (Kutzbach 1985:169), show continental centers to be extreme deserts, with some coasts being very moist (Kutzbach and Gallimore 1989).

Locally, precipitation may occur because of topographic uplift, such as on the side of hills or mountains, or where surface texture promotes disturbances (Gunn 1982).

Scales of Global-Regional Impacts

The spatial scale of climatic impacts is an important consideration in any attempt to understand global climate's effects on biological and social sys-tems. In the previous examples, the discharge of drainages encompassing hundreds of square miles was observed to be modified by global climatic changes. I have focused on stream basins because human regions are often bounded by, and intimately related to, stream basins. Similar measures could be made at other scales with equally important implications for dif-ferent scales of biocultural systems. Occasionally I have found that ring sequences from individual trees reflect influences from global average tem-perature. A tree is a point on the surface of the earth, a microenvironment, and is appropriate for investigations at the finest scales. As with a stream basin, the growth rings of a tree reflect its hydrological context, geology, soils environment, elevation, slope, and aspect. Rivers perform at inter-mediate spatial scales comparable to those of territories, counties, states, and small countries. Occasionally it is of interest to perform areal and con-tinental analyses: for example, in studies of empires, interaction spheres, alliances, and modern trade networks linked by rail, ship, air, pipelines, and electrical transmission wires.

The temporal scale is also important, and the major emphasis of this chapter. An interesting consensus has arisen in the past twenty years to

TABLE 4.1.
Global-scale climatic episodes

Episode Name (Abbrev.)	Period	Duration
Little Ice Age (LIA)	AD 1250–1910	660
Medieval Climatic Optimum (MCO)	AD 900–1250	350
Vandic	AD 400–900	500
Roman Climatic Optimum (RCO)	500 BC–AD 400	600
Homeric Minimum	900–600 BC	300

the effect that the global climates are episodic, and a vocabulary has developed around this consensus (table 4.1). Important articles by Wendland and Bryson (1974) and Denton and Karlen (1973) established the episodic character of global-scale Holocene biological and glacial data. These terms represent only the broad outlines of global climatic change during the Holocene (10,000 BP–present), and the culturally important 300–600 year episodes are by no means internally homogeneous. They should be thought of as middle-level analytical units between the Holocene interglacial (which has lasted 10,000 years) and, for purposes of adaptive studies, the more important climatic variations at the scale of years and decades. The naming of global climatic episodes after events and societies in Europe is perhaps a questionable practice, but the North Atlantic sector is thought to be more than usually sensitive, as a region, to global climatic changes (Kutzbach and Bryson 1974:1962), so it is not entirely inappropriate.

Global Average Temperature Measurement

Once a global-regional model of climatic change is formulated, it can be tested and used in a number of ways. Suppose that a local climate is projected into the past for 10,000 years (the Holocene climatic era). When the projection is compared to the regional paleoclimatic sequence reconstructed from geological, paleohydrological, and paleobotanical means, the paleoclimate becomes a test of the global-regional climatic model.

Alternatively, the climatic model may enhance and extend the empirically gathered data. The model can be projected at any time scale with which the researcher feels confident, and to any time depth. The projected climatic sequence therefore provides information on climatic change at time resolutions that are inaccessible through labor- and cost-intensive empirical approaches. These more costly approaches should be used, however, to test the model during critical transitional climatic intervals, and then the model can be projected over broad time intervals.

The following paragraphs discuss some of the data sets that are available for the study of global-regional climatic problems. The shorter series are used for developing models, the longer ones for testing models.

1958–90 Trajectory (Seasons). By far the most comprehensive data on global average temperatures have been collected since the International Geophysical Year (1957–58). Angell and Korshover (1983; Angell 1991) work with a data set collected by the release of balloons each day all around the world. The data measure atmospheric conditions from the surface to about 100,000 feet. The data are available in seasonal (three-month) time increments. This is the best scale with which to build global-regional climatic models because of the precision of the data. Fortuitously, there has been a remarkable amount of global climatic change in the past thirty years, from near-ice-age conditions in the 1970s to near-Mesozoic conditions in the 1980s and 1950s. I have referred to this interval elsewhere as the period of intensive instrumental observation (Gunn 1991).

1865–1990 Trajectory (Years). Several attempts have been made to construct global average temperature back in time as far as the 1860s. Jones and Wigley (1990) review these efforts. When Hanson and colleagues' (1981) reconstruction of terrestrial global temperature is combined with Parker and Folland's (1989) nighttime marine air temperatures, the trajectory essentially duplicates the 1958–present balloon measurements but at a lower amplitude. This scale provides vistas on the globally colder conditions of the late 1800s, particularly the 1880s when Krakatoa (Indonesia, 1883) and several other large volcanic eruptions cooled the atmosphere.

Millennial Trajectory (Decades). Reconstructions of climate over the past one thousand years resort to more indirect means. Pfister (1988) uses diary citations. Bergthorsson (1969) depends on ten-year (decade) reports of sea ice flows around Iceland. In some regions tree rings are available: for example, conifers in the southwestern United States (Dean et al. 1985) and bald cypress in the Southeast (Stahle, Cook, and Hehr 1985). High-resolution pollen studies include that of Bernabo (1981) in the Great Lakes region. Williams and Wigley (1983) review numerous sources of data from the last millennium. This period spans the several episodes of the Little Ice Age (AD 1250–1910), which was about a degree centigrade colder than the twentieth century, and the Medieval Climatic Optimum (AD 900–1250), a period when the world was about a degree centigrade warmer than it is now. An important contribution to global climate studies will be the conversion of the proxy data into an accurate estimate of global average temperature for the past one thousand years.

Holocene Trajectory (Centuries). Chronologies of global climate for the past 10,000 years are currently at coarser scales. Bryson and Goodman's (1980) volcanism chronology, for example, is at 100-year intervals and can be used to reconstruct some portion of Holocene global climate (Gunn and Crumley 1989). Annual measures from ice cores, corals, and cave deposits are in prospect. Landscheidt (1987, 1988) has calculated solar output as far back as the middle Holocene (7500–4500 BP).

BIOCULTURAL DIVERSITY AND GLOBAL CLIMATE

Let us now shift our attention away from the physical environment and consider the interface between the physical environment, society, and the individual. I will first discuss some conceptual limitations and anthropological and archaeological perspectives that need to be adjusted. This will be followed with a framework for modeling the human engagement of global climatic change. This model will be built around a concept called "capturing" or "encoding," as Richard Lee calls it. I prefer the more active term, but encoding alludes to information theory, which is also pertinent. Finally, some brief case studies will be offered to provide illustrations of key elements of capturing, and also the "parallel events" concept, which is an attempt to provide a nonteleological, nontrivial assessment of global impact on regional cultures. More detailed case studies appear in other chapters in this book, but it seems useful to formulate some case studies that target the pivotal concepts of this culture-change model.

Biocultural Systems

When the effects of climate on culture are being studied, it is important to consider the causal relations among biological, cultural, and physical subsystems. Biological species are not primary indicators of climatic change and should not be treated as causes of cultural change, for a number of reasons.

Uniformitarianism cannot be assumed. Looking at climate uncritically through pollen analysis has led to a reconstruction of only slight warming and drying through the Holocene in many areas of the southern United States. However, global temperature has been cooling toward glacial conditions since the Middle Holocene (7500–4500 BP), and the world has become cyclically more glacial (Williams and Wigley 1983). A reasonable alternative explanation of the apparent pollen-inferred climatic stasis is that the pollen record reflects vegetational adaptation to Holocene variation (J. Schoenwetter, personal communication) and human manipulation. Thus, biological organisms should be studied *with* culture rather than in opposition to it.

Rather than being determinants of human systems, biological organisms have been interactive with humans for millions of years. Culture is the more adaptable system, so it will retard or hurry the biological systems at its pace. This pace is regulated by the partially unpredictable element of human agency. Cultures may have been the dominant or codominant players in the biocultural mix through CO_2 release for some time, perhaps millennia (see Schmidt, this volume, for discussion of deforestation during the period of the Roman Empire) or even tens of millennia by controlling vegetation with fire (e.g., Patterson and Sassaman 1988).

With regard to time involved in adaptation, biological systems, particularly vegetation, are slow to colonize and change. Colonization by trees may lag behind climate by hundreds of years (Gaudreau 1988). On the other hand, to address temperate and polar zone cultural adaptations, measures must be annual to be meaningful. This principle applies to any large mobile animal. The more intelligent and mobile the biological organism, the closer it will come to isomorphy with its preferred regional climate. Bison and elephants migrate hundreds of miles each year to follow annual seasonal temperatures and rainfall (Churcher 1978; Gunn 1987; Guthrie 1978; Turpin 1987). For elephants, bison, humans, and most creatures of the higher latitudes, adaptation to these interannual changes is necessary for survival. Even today, many human groups follow seasonal rounds that are isomorphic with temperature or hydrological cycles, both annual and nonannual. Of course, other human groups appear to have gone beyond adaptation and become independent of annual cycles and even predatory on the total global system, thus divorcing themselves from adaptation.

Physical systems provide potentially and variably independent measures of climate. Measures of solar output can be presumed to be entirely free of human effects. Glacial varves and icebergs in Icelandic waters are independent of immediate human activity, although the question of the time depth of codominant anthropogenic effects on global climate through

CO_2 release must again be raised. River geomorphology responds at the appropriate time scales to enable measurement of climate, but it may be influenced by cultural actions like burning of vegetation and thus must be treated in the context of human activity. Since cultural systems are able to respond directly to changes in the physical environment without delay, their activities are potentially better indicators of changes in climate than biological systems.

The Theoretical Limits of Capturing

Understanding the temporal limits of capture is a high priority, if not the highest priority, in this study because time depth distinguishes capture from adaptation, its conceptual relative. The time of origin of the capacity to capture and the duration of utility of captured information are both important time-related issues. The origin certainly dates to the Paleolithic. Straus (1991) suggests that Paleolithic cave paintings in Europe were part of a cultural custom that was designed to carry complex and/or rarely used information forward in time. This perfect example of capture suggests that Paleolithic cave painting opens the first clearly recognizable cognitive window on the phenomenon. Regionalization and rapid phasing of cultures are additional hallmarks of Upper Paleolithic technology that distinguish it from the antecedent Middle Paleolithic. The evidence strongly suggests that these cultural phenomena appeared with the Upper Paleolithic 30–50,000 years ago, and they are propelled by the emergence of capturing as a human capability.

It is reasonable to think that multigenerational capturing had its origin, at least in its broadest definition, with the advent of the capacity for fully modern language. The origin of language is currently as controversial as the origins of *Homo sapiens*. Convincing arguments are being made for pre-*Homo sapiens* with and without fully modern communication skills (Frayer 1992 and Krantz 1980, respectively). Important implications for the duration of capturing await resolution of this pivotal question.

The theoretical limits of cultural information capture of global climate regimes can be defined in terms of these human evolution issues and global-regional climate. To capture a full range of cultural experience in some region of the world, a culture would have had to be in place for the past 35,000 years (fig. 4.5, horizontal axis): the duration of the present *sapiens* regime (Krantz 1980; Wolpoff 1989) and the span of a full range of glacial and interglacial climates. The culture would have to have perfect

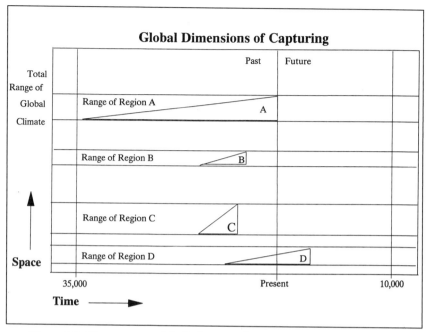

Figure 4.5. Time-space model of adaptive information capture potential during the past 35,000 years.

retention of the range of experience over that time period (fig. 4.5, A). Presumably no culture retains the maximum potential information; however, it is potentially useful to understand where long-lasting and short-lived cultures are dispersed. Some regions of the globe (fig. 4.5, vertical axis) could foster very old traditions; others are unlikely to do so because of extreme instability inherent in the region's geographical location.

Of particular relevance to the issue of global warming are middle Holocene adaptations. The middle Holocene was globally warmer than any other period during the span of *sapiens'* existence. Even if only subliminal and verbal elements of ancient traditions could date to this period, they could be a significant adaptive advantage for current residents. Egypt, China, Southeast Asia, and the lower subcontinent of India have exhibited relatively unbroken cultural continuity since the Pleistocene, and the native cultures may contain packages of information that were useful adaptations to the hot global conditions of the middle Holocene. The non-indigenous cultures of the Western Hemisphere are likely limited in terms of experience because of their relatively late arrival from the Old World.

Nevertheless, many cultures of Mexico, Middle America, the Andes, and Amazonia date from early episodes of the Holocene, including the globally hot middle Holocene.

In theory, Old World cultures in relatively stable environments could most closely approach the information retention maximum. However, some regions are clearly climatically unstable and undoubtedly possess attenuated retention of past information. Europe is one such area in the Old World, and Yucatan in the New World. They appear to have regularly undergone interruptions of continuity because of migration and population reduction and increase.

Cultural Change and Global Temperature Trajectory

A culture's breadth of comprehension of its regional climates, or its repertoire of captured information, depends on the duration of the culture in that location. As global average temperature varies, cultures experience climates and capture packages of information on appropriate survival measures for each. Captured knowledge is "packaged" when it has been formulated into folk tales, ritual, calendrical ceremonies, and other religious practices in a manner appropriate to each culture. The breadth of this repertoire is as wide as the global average temperature variations (or more specifically the regional transformation of them) during the culture's duration in the region. Therefore, the breadth of a culture's climate repertoire can be measured in global temperature degrees since the time of initial settlement. Its existence presumes its survival of past climates and acquisition of knowledge from them. Whether or not a culture has knowledge of an impending climate depends on whether the culture was in place during the previous occurrence of that climate in its region. Since information decays with time, also important is whether knowledge of the impending climate is viable in its repertoire or has decayed below the threshold of utility.

A culture's tolerance of changes will grow with time as it experiences more episodes of regional climate and accumulates a broader repertoire of climate experiences. Knowledge of frequently reoccurring climates will be reinforced and expanded with the passage of time.

Several factors modulate the range of climatic variation a culture will experience over time. The range of the regional climatic trace reflects the climatic sensitivity of the region. Some regions will be much more sensitive to changes in global temperature and circulation than others (Gunn 1979). The type of culture may reflect the breadth (amplitude) and frequency (duration) of climatic variation in its region. Regions with precise

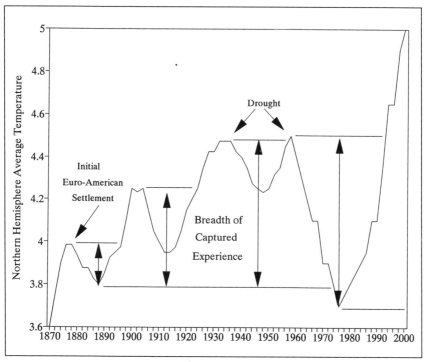

Figure 4.6. Climatic trajectory and cultural experience on the High Plains.

annual cycles of moisture may exhibit complex cultures based on a relatively narrow range of climates and adaptations (fig. 4.5, B). Regions with irregular seasonal variations of less than or more than a year will require a wide range of adaptive alternatives (fig. 4.5, C). They will be confined to less complex cultures in the absence of an interregional transportation network capable of transporting adequate quantities of food for their populations. Cultures will be more or less sensitive to climatic variations depending on the sensitivity of preferred crops.

Global climatic sensitivity itself varies with the level of the global average temperature. Around 15.5°C, global circulation mechanisms respond strongly to an enhanced El Niño–Southern Oscillation and act to destabilize atmospheric processes. Atmospheric processes appear to be annually more stable above or below 15.5°C (Gunn 1991).

The modern agricultural adaptation to the High Plains of North America is an example of climate and human interaction, and we have good climatic and documentary records of its development. Tree rings are available from the 1600s to the present to serve as measurements of growing-season precipitation and drought (Mitchell, Stockton, and Meko 1979; Stockton, Boggess, and Meko 1985). Since the mid-1800s the Plains have experienced settlement by Euroamerican agriculturalists (Bennett 1969). Except in areas such as South Dakota with extensive Native American populations, there was very little transmission of knowledge from previously adapted groups, so the Plains are a good region in which to observe initial adaptation to regional climates. Following settlement, regional climates lurched through a number of moderate episodes punctuated by crippling droughts (fig. 4.6). Beginning with little or no knowledge of the region's climate in the late 1800s, Plains dwellers captured more than one hundred years of climatic types and responses. I will return to these adaptations for illustrative material in the following discussion of the capturing process.

The Parameters of Global Temperature Adaptation

The fact that cultures use bits of information to ensure survival is well established in the anthropological literature, where it appears under the term "adaptation." Perpetuation of packages of information that pertain to an existing set of circumstances is implied by the term "tradition" in the Caldwell (1958) and Willey and Phillips (1958) terminology. It suggests a sustained effort to adapt to regional conditions across several cultural phases, which frequently imply climatic episodes. Clay (1976) suggests that predictable patterns may exist in regional adaptations, progressing from tactics to strategies to operations. It follows from the implications of capturing noted above, however, that realizing this three-part progression is contingent on there being periods of stable environmental conditions of sufficient duration to achieve all three steps. As an example, the long and globally relatively stable Roman Empire Climatic Optimum (500 BC–AD 300) provided sufficient time for the Roman Empire to evolve through all three stages.

Recent efforts to incorporate elements of cognition into landscape models are also relevant to the coevolution of cultures, biota, and terrain or landscapes (Crumley and Marquardt 1987).

It is useful to distinguish adaptation from events that mark information capture because captured, packaged knowledge can be passed across times when it is not useful or adaptive and saved for times when it will again be adaptive. To use a biological analogy, it provides the means for punctuated equilibrium-like changes in cultures. Alternatively, in the terminology of biological reproduction, it is a K-mode reproductive strategy, but it transgresses multiple generations nurturing unseen progeny at unknown future time depths.

Events of capture are probably indicated archaeologically and historically by abrupt changes in conditions and material culture, but the packaging of this information may not be particularly visible. The package must consist of a holistic folkloric model that can be maintained by storytelling and ritual. This capture-and-retain process of folklore equips cultures, and the concept of culture, with a dynamic information-growth capacity that extends in time beyond immediate environmental circumstances. It is the cultural equivalent of linguistic displacement. It makes duration an important variable in understanding cultural development and complexity.

The term *capturing* comes to mind because it implies an event, limited in time and containing a discrete packet of information, which produces a reward with some duration of utility. An important aspect of capturing is that information may be carried forward in folklore even though it is not of immediate use. It can also be carried forward more subtly and unconsciously in motor habits.

In keeping with a multicausal definition, the concept of capturing should be expanded to include the ability of cultures to develop and retain solutions to a variety of conditions that may be precipitated by innovation, diffusion, or environmental change. In the case of environment, captured adaptations would consist of combinations of drought, moisture, flood, cold, heat, changing seasonality, and so on. If local circumstances are driven in part by a global temperature trajectory, as discussed above, cultures would capture solutions to a widening range of climatic states until all possible climates have been incorporated into its repertoire. Any given package would continue to exist until the culture succumbs, or the information decays below a threshold of utility. Cultures will accumulate solutions to various global temperature states and the regional conditions they dictate. The cultural changes will be channelized by historical experience in part, but they will be unpredictable, contingent on available resources and individual and group initiatives.[2]

An incident of environmental capturing is probably stored cognitively as a landscape or mental map with attendant adaptive behavior. This package is passed from generation to generation. It will be retained in folklore, and its practice and utility will be resumed in the event the circumstances that provoked its formulation arise again. In effect, it is a simulation of adaptation that can be run in the presence or absence of pertinent environmental circumstances. Folk tales are, in effect, running the simulation in the absence of environmental prerequisites to keep in practice. Calendrical rituals are runs of the simulation in anticipation of seasonal activities. Noncalendrical simulations appear to be evoked by a phrase(s). The phrase may be retained in the context of the mental map of the landscape. Thus, landscape locations also become a map of folkloric space. An interesting example is the songlines of the Australian aborigines in which history is mapped on trails crossing the continent (Chatwin 1987).[3]

The Duration of Collective Knowledge

The duration of the utility of captured information needs to be given open-minded consideration. Members of the Western technological and written tradition should give particular heed to their cultural biases on this matter. Western preconceptions tend to minimize the long-term (centuries and millennia) information capabilities of non-Western cultures, especially in the absence of writing. Chang (1986), on the other hand, argues that Chinese culture has been primarily an information culture from its beginning and that only in Western culture does the need to become cognizant of an "information age" exist. Supporting Chang's assertion is a tradition of knowledge unbroken for at least three thousand years, and perhaps for thousands of years more.

Perhaps most important in terms of sheer numbers of cultures and human beings is the retentive capacity of traditional urbanized non-Western cultures since they have dominated the culture change arena in the past ten thousand years. The capacity to retain adaptive information can be documented from the study of religion. The structure of pantheons of gods in China and India (Roberts, Chiao, and Pandey 1975) indicates that gods were sequentially admitted to pantheons as cultural heroes over many centuries. Each god first appears as a powerful figure with attributes implying that it supplied potent solutions to cultural crises. Following admission to a pantheon, a god evolves from a potent hero to a benevolent patron. This process takes about two thousand years. Pantheons universally consist of about twelve deities. It seems that with the introduction of a thirteenth deity after about two thousand years, the longest standing, albeit very benevolent, god is gradually forgotten.

The beliefs associated with heroes appear to reflect holistic and effective solutions to social and environmental crises. Once developed, they are retained in the collective memory as stories of the gods' lives, associated rituals, and so on. This situation is further illustrated by the New England case study presented below.

The Loss of Collective Knowledge

The rate at which information disappears from the collective memory depends on a number of circumstances. First, the decay function in the retention of cultural experience will be specific to individual cultures. Eskimo culture, for example, does not permit hyperbole and thus faithfully carries information forward, as with ice flow survival technology (Nelson 1969:98–132). One of the key elements of ice flow survival, the seal oil lamp, is no longer used in daily life; however, all ice hunters know about them, and designs are practiced and elaborated using aluminum foil and other nontraditional materials.

The faithfulness of Eskimo oral tradition is further supported by Eskimo accounts of exploration expeditions, which can be recognized 300 years later in ships' records. Traditional Indo-European cultures appear to have similar retentive facilities. A Scottish folk ballad was found, after hundreds of years, to report the events of an important battle more accurately than history textbooks on the subject (Buchan 1976). It might be supposed that since urban cultures tolerate hyperbole, or even deceit, they are less able to carry information forward reliably, at least in folklore. Also, a more sapiens-centric perspective veils much understanding of the functions of the environment. Will (1980) describes examples of literate capturing in disaster manuals in China. It may be that humor, at least so far as it is expressed in hyperbole, is allowable in literate cultures because written records have assumed the recordkeeping functions of verbal tradition.

Cultures of short duration are more susceptible to surprise climatic dislocations because of their limited repertoire. Droughts in the late 1800s did not prepare the culture on the American High Plains for the severe drought of the 1930s. Many individuals were forced to emigrate. A drought of similar scale in the 1950s did not result in mass exodus, in part because the culture was informationally and technically better able to cope with the circumstances (e.g., by chiseling dry fields, planting hedgerows, and receiving federal crop supports).

Practical Limits of Capturing

Perhaps the most ambiguous regions of continuity are in the New World. The New World has been subjected to substantial, though not total, disruptions of continuity by European, African, and Asian migration in the past five centuries. The question of Native American continuity with current populations is being actively investigated (Zubrow 1990) and may not accord with the standard historical perceptions of Native American extinction owing to diseases introduced from the Old World. In other words, it is still an open question as to how much regional information is retained from previous cultures.

In the United States the captured range of cultural experience depends on the amount and types of information passed through to the modern population by Native Americans. Important climatic fluctuations have occurred in the two hundred years since European emigration overwhelmed native cultures. The early 1700s was a warm and dry period in south Texas, which nurtured a hybrid Mediterranean-Mesoamerican agriculture (Gunn and Brown 1982). Its practitioners have since gathered a range of information on significantly variant climates. However, in the millennium preceding European emigration there was a greater range of global temperature variation, particularly toward the cooler end of the spectrum during the Little Ice Age (AD 1250–1900) but also toward warmer climate during the Medieval Climatic Optimum (AD 900–1250) than has been experienced since then. Thus, Native American cultures should have a broader repertoire of answers to potential climates, notably global warming, than Euro-American cultures. We know that the Native American adaptation to the globally warmer Medieval Climatic Optimum utilized species of corn developed in the monsoonal Southwest. Native American cultures sustained greater and more widely distributed populations during that time than any period before or after. It behooves us to learn more about the strategies and tactics they followed.

A review of some of the regional cultures in the modern United States will help define their relevance to studies of global climatic change. The Iroquoian societies along the Appalachian summit and in western New York have a millennium of time depth (Trigger 1969). They therefore should have passed on adaptive information on the Medieval Climatic Optimum. Some regions of the Southwest are populated by Native Americans with relatively long-lasting traditions representing a majority of the regional populations. The Hopi appear to have been in place for a half millennium and are probably descendants of the Anasazi culture dating to the Medieval Climatic Optimum (Cordell 1984; Dean et al. 1985). They should have captured a wide range of information on Southwestern climatic states, including globally warmer conditions than those at present.

The Mescalero Apaches in the Sacramento Mountains of New Mexico provide an example of a contrasting case: cultures with potentially incorrect information on regional climate owing to their short duration in a region. They arrived in the Southwest about 600 years ago (AD 1350; Cordell 1984), after the Medieval Climatic Optimum, and therefore should have a less accurate folkloric backlog of experience in the Southwest than the Hopi and other Pueblo groups. They should also have elements of Canadian climatic folklore dating to before their arrival, perhaps customs applicable to the Medieval Climatic Optimum in western Canada. Europeans in the United States have similar climatic baggage, that is, folkloric information that applies to Europe but not the United States. The groundhog legend is one such idea.

Case Studies

Eastern United States, 1816–40. Experience is captured in the form of folkloric knowledge which is evoked by phrases. Following the eruption of Mt. Tambora (Lesser Sunda Island, April 1815), 1816 was known the world over as "The Year Without Summer" (Stommel and Stommel 1979, 1983). One of the hardest hit regions in the world was New England, which experienced snow in June and killing freezes in July and August. It was an ice age summer: compare the climate of the same area when it was covered by ice at full glacial. The year of 1816 is still commemorated in New England by the phrase "1800 and froze to death." Expressing the phase evokes a range of thoughts about early and late freezes, unusual cold, hunger, and the like, even though the exact origin of the phrase is unclear to many who use it (Albert Leighton, personal communication). Social impacts following the event include famine, religious awakening, and use of new farming methods. Determining exactly what the phrase evokes in terms of knowledge and what the decay factor has been would be a useful ethnographic study. County histories, which are popular in the New England region, might document the development of such ideas (Glenn Hinson, personal communication).

Maya Lowlands. During a period of global cooling and global climatic instability (Vandic, AD 400–900), civilization flourished in the Maya lowlands. In the subsequent Medieval Climatic Optimum (AD 900–1250), when the world warmed beyond present average temperatures, the Maya civilization collapsed in one of the most spectacular disintegrations of civilization of which we have knowledge. Cities of 50,000 people in the central Yucatan were abandoned (Folan 1985).

Today water must be trucked to inhabitants living anywhere within

50 miles of Calakmul, such as Conhuas, a modern town located in an internal basin in the center of the Yucatan. This area receives moisture from upper-level disturbances generated by the annual movement of the intertropical convergence zone (ITCZ), and from a double sea breeze effect (Folan et al. 1983) during the rainy season from May to September. If the upper-level disturbances do not occur, and precipitation only comes from orographic uplift of moist air from the sea, only the seaward sides of hills are moist. Following the Maya collapse, the focus of Maya civilization moved to the coastal zones outside the interior basin (Adams 1977).

Although it is clear that climate was not the only cause of the Mayan population decline, soil degradation and deforestation being notable contributory candidates (Deevey et al. 1979), it is highly likely that if global warming caused a late rainy season, it would also result in negative impacts (Gunn, Folan, and Robichaux 1990). Drier conditions would have contributed significantly not only to availability of water but also to attendant hygienic conditions as rains failed to flush a heavily populated landscape with plentiful annual precipitation. Inhabitants of the area today know to move their *milpas* (cornfields) to the seaward side of hills when the rainy season is late. It is likely that the shift in settlement pattern following the Maya collapse reflects the same wisdom. Present-day Mayas may be acting on folkloric information captured during, or more likely previous to, the period of Maya civilization in the interior.

Western Europe. Civilization in western Europe has changed greatly in the past three millennia. It is well documented (Bryson and Murray 1977) that fluctuations in the fortunes of European civilizations were attended by climatic variations. The so-called Dark Age (AD 400–900), following the Roman Empire and preceding the High Middle Ages (AD 900–1300), was, on closer examination, a period of several alternating episodes of empire and regionalization, though none of the imperial episodes approached the cohesion and extent of the Roman Empire. The brevity of the attendant climatic episodes explains the attenuated development relative to that of Roman Empire.

The Medieval Climatic Optimum (AD 900–1250) and the attendant High Middle Ages are clearly distinct from the preceding centuries. Populations burgeoned and agricultural practices shifted markedly toward Mediterranean customs. Massive monumental architecture (cathedrals) was constructed. With the return of cool and moist summers in the late Middle Ages (AD 1250–1450), populations plummeted. Many of the skills required to survive in cool and moist climate, known by Celtic farmers previous to the High Middle Ages, had to be reinvented, such as manuring fields (Pfister 1988). Cheese was invented and moisture-tolerant crops were re-emphasized. After two or three centuries Europeans recaptured the tools necessary to survive in a moist and cool Europe, which included extensive external trade (Hugill 1988). Nevertheless, interior Europe was not free of famine until the railroads were completed in the 1890s (Pfister 1988).

Previous discussion by Gunn and Crumley (1989; also see above and chapter 8, this volume) of the global to regional relationships has shown that the trends of the High Middle Ages were not isolated events. The population movements and shifts of emphasis observed in the High Middle Ages recurred several times in the past three millennia and in fact reflect a continental-scale set of adaptive alternatives that were recalled or reinvented several times. Documented examples include the Gallo-Roman (Crumley 1987a; Gunn and Crumley 1989) and Bronze Age (Jäger and Ložek 1982) cultures. Similar migratory events may have occurred as early as 35,000 years ago with the first influx of *Homo sapiens* during a globally warmer period.

Comparisons. It is interesting to note that the appearance and disintegration of empires in Europe and the central Maya lowlands are exactly out of phase. When the Maya flourish, Europe is in dire straits. When Europe is blossoming, the Mayas retire into subsistence agriculture. The explanation for these phase differences can be seen through the global-regional climatic analyses and regional crop preferences. Warming global average temperatures dry the mid-summer in Europe, providing ideal conditions for maturation and harvesting of grain and grape crops. At the same time they delay the rainy season in the Yucatan ever later, depriving the central Yucatan of agricultural potential through milpa cultivation. Global cooling, on the other hand, rushes the rainy season in the Yucatan, providing thriving milpas, but locks Europe into dismal warm and moist summers. These conditions attenuate grain harvest, mildew the crops, and prevent proper drying and adequate storage. The net effects that support increased population and "civilization" in both regions are a subtle dance of global temperature, regional hydrology, traditional crop types, and cultural cropping strategies. Of course, the perception that the intervening periods are "collapses" or "dark" is the ethnocentric perspective of hierarchical "civilized" societies who write the histories (Crumley, this volume). The periods of lower population were intervals of gardeners and milperos who have their roots in the times antecedent to civilization, and as individuals may have viewed the disappearance of civilization as tax relief rather than the loss of the glory that was Rome or Calakmul.

Parallel Events

The European and Mayan case studies provide an illuminating example of parallel events propelled by a common external force, global climate. It is all the more fascinating that they are parallel in reverse, or negatively correlated, and that the reversed effects of global warming on the two areas define precisely the conditions that would be expected to foster the observed cultural phenomena. The argument for climate playing a role in the parallel events is strengthened by the separation of the two cultures by thousands of miles of ocean, precluding influences of one culture on the other (Galton's effect). Although these two examples, juxtaposed in time but separate in space, do not in themselves make a completely supportable argument, there are other similar parallel events, not only in cultures, such as the Greenland Norse (McGovern, this volume), the Saharan Kingdom of Ghana, the Buhaya region west of Lake Victoria (Schmidt, this volume), and the Mississippian cultures of the American Midwest (Fowler 1974), but also in biological systems (Wendland and Bryson 1974). The presence of parallel events in geographically separated regions of the world argues that their cause was climatic rather than historical, cultural, or individual. That is not to deny the presence of culturally specific solutions to regional effects of global changes.

CONCLUSION

This chapter suggests the basis of a dynamic, global-scale extension of cultural ecology that is designed to apportion the impetus of cultural change between various widely recognized causes, including global climatic change. This knowledge is valuable in the same sense as species diversity—they are resources that can and should be tapped to inform regional policy decisions. The cases cited above indicate that episodes of cultural change were, in part, the product of climatic change: they occurred as parallel events in time with little or no potential for influence by diffusion.

The import of this study for policymakers who are involved with disaster relief, or its anticipation, is that most regions have local solutions to a wide range of climatic problems. In some cultures this information may date to previous incidents of global warming. To provide regions subject to climatic stress with maximum relief, it is imperative that policymakers first determine the local cultural resources for meeting the crisis. To disrupt in-place cultural solutions to climatic changes only extends and deepens the crisis and is likely to destroy the local train of capture. Policies should be designed to preserve cultural diversity and the many solutions to global climatic change it offers. These polices should not preclude indirectly received knowledge, such as that passed to modern American farmers from Native American cultures who experienced events of global warming at considerable time depths. Policies should be designed to augment rather than replace local custom: failing that, the local population will end up on the global welfare line.

A study of past civilizations (Flannery 1972) has found that through time higher-level policymakers will tend to accumulate responsibility for local activities, even though the principals involved probably understand that it is better for local groups to make local decisions. This happens because small local governmental entities are more likely to fail under stress than high-level entities that depend on several lower-level entities. One lesson that has emerged from recent global benevolent relief for the Sahelian famine is that external relief must not undermine local social structure and custom. In summary, nurturing local traditions is more an issue of good knowledge than good intentions.

——— *Notes* ———

This paper is dedicated to John M. Roberts (1917–90), friend and instructor.

1. In this chapter I use the northern middle latitudes as examples. Similar examples could be constructed for the Southern Hemisphere and other latitudes by using appropriate atmospheric circulation principles.

2. In information terms this is white (random) and red (patterned) noise. Global temperature effects are white when culture is new or, if not present, off. Global temperature effects are reddened when culture is present, old, or on. Cultures redden global effects with time. It is a cultural red shift.

3. Motor habits need not be evoked. For example, walking in a way to enable movement on ice would continue through a warm episode.

Chapter 5

Historical Ecology and Landscape Transformation in Eastern Equatorial Africa

PETER R. SCHMIDT

A rchaeologists have an important role to play in land use and management policy in the tropics, especially in regard to perceptions that guide policy on tropical forest exploitation (Schmidt 1989). Given the rapidity with which tropical forests of all types are being eliminated, it is extremely important that we draw on our knowledge of prehistoric practices, both exploitative and managerial, used by prehistoric populations that utilized the tropical forests around them. Archaeological knowledge can provide important insights into both successful management and costly mismanagement of forests at extensive time scales. Moreover, anthropologists sensitive to the study of historical and contemporary thinking about tropical ecosystems have an important contribution to make toward informed policy that incorporates cultural beliefs about the potential and limitations of forested environments. If we merely indulge ourselves in polemical positions that assert that deforestation is a capitalist depredation, we shall miss an important opportunity to develop a more dynamic historical view. In this chapter I have tried to avoid this snare and instead adopt a historically informed, proactive posture that seeks to change the exploitative trajectory of modern human occupation of tropical forests.

A global systems view informed by macroeconomic analysis quickly reveals that the structural adjustment policies of Western governments and institutions, such as the International Monetary Fund and the World Bank, are responsible for most of what drives deforestation in the tropics today (Capistrano and Kiker 1990). This is sobering evidence. Nevertheless, recent policy formulations at these institutions have shown that it is possible to change policy at the ideological level—witness the use of the human rights sanctions program—if "scientific" evidence can be adduced to support such a shift. In other words, if we can demonstrate that the operation of various cultural perceptions, such as multiple use or increased export earnings, leads to deleterious effects on tropical forests, we will have a much better opportunity to develop sanctions, that is, exceptions to structural adjustment policy. But this is only the first step in any long-term change in policy. It must be followed with strong evidence of the long-term impact of different management systems on tropical forests. The history of complex forest ecosystems that have encompassed cultural systems offers invaluable lessons that can be applied to the present and the future.

One of our strongest assets as archaeologists is the longitudinal quality of our studies. We strive to demonstrate the consequences *through time* of human cultural perceptions on landscapes. No synchronic science can hope to meet the need to identify and explain long-term trends and consequences. If we are to influence policy making, our presentations must, by necessity, incorporate an empirical component, precisely because we must illustrate long-term trends to be credible. My remarks here thus initially assume a strong empirical orientation.

To my knowledge no long-term historical ecology of a tropical African ecosystem has yet been written. This chapter represents a first effort at focusing on the processes of landscape transformation in an area once under gallery and woodland forest. It is an enormously complex history, the rough outlines of which are disclosed mostly through vegetational history, industrial history, and strong continuities in belief systems embedded in industrial and agricultural economies. My object is to show the role of cultural perceptions in landscape management, through time, in one area of equatorial Africa.

The historical ecology of "westlake," the coastal zone west of Lake Victoria in northwestern Tanzania,[1] is one of transformations induced by human cultural systems over the past two to three millennia. Many of the changes that we read in the environmental record of the region are entwined with cultural belief systems, both as instruments of change and as refractions of ways of coping with stresses resulting from environmental change. "Unraveling" or "decoding" the historical ecology of this region within the Great Lakes region of east-central Africa introduces several issues: how cultural systems adapted to severe degradation of a once rich and varied forested environment; how a cultural preference for certain economic activities led to significant declines in population; how centralized control over a governing ideology led to improved management of natural resources; how shortages of critical resources led to significant changes in population dynamics; and finally, how beliefs about human reproduction may have sustained traditional behaviors that threaten the very existence of the culture extant in the region today. This paper can have only one logical ending: to ask if there is any link between the historical ecology of the past two and a half millennia and the terrifying incidence of AIDS in this region within the past decade, where the long-standing Haya culture now faces virtual extinction. Dreadful as the current health crisis is, this is not the first time that this region has confronted stresses caused by reduced environmental capacity and attendant disease. The westlake's historical ecology offers valuable insights into the genesis and rapid spread of AIDS among its people.

TECHNOLOGY AND THE ENVIRONMENT

The eastern part of the westlake region is occupied by the Haya people, a once prosperous folk who practiced a mixed economy expressed in an iron industry, fishing, hunting, and an agricultural system based on bananas interplanted with beans, as well as cash cropping and some cattle keeping. Over the past several decades culture change in the westlake region has led to the extinction or near extinction of traditional economies. The strongest sector of the productive economy, other than agriculture, was formerly steel production and its attendant industries, such as forging and wire drawing. Hence much of our environmental research has been directed toward this industrial sector and its distinctive needs.[2]

Our first research goals were to document when the most recognizable sectors of exploitative economy developed and were applied to the westlake landscape, and to analyze the cultural changes, particularly in technology and economy, that have occurred over the past two to three thousand years. This first step was more complicated than usual because no previous archaeological research had been done in the region. Moreover, very dense populations now live in the zone of greatest historical interest, the 25-kilometer-wide strip to the west of Lake Victoria. Most of the Early Iron Age settlements and industrial locales (200 BC–AD 600) are overlain by contemporary villages, which both hinders archaeological access to the ancient past and leads to significant transformations of ancient remains. Nonetheless our available evidence reveals patterns of development in the spread of industrial activity across the landscape several millennia ago. The combined impact of extensive, permanent agricultural communities and an active iron industry on the natural environment would have been both episodic and profound.

One of the reasons for the development of a technologically complex iron industry in westlake was the local availability of highly refractory, that is, heat-resistant, kaolinite clays. The region's traditional smelting procedure includes a preheating process that employs clay pipes placed mostly inside the furnace. These pipes must be of the highest possible quality (Schmidt and Avery 1978). Not just any clay will do: it must be capable of withstanding temperatures of 1500 to 1700°C, which occur in the furnace blast zone. Productivity and efficiency were closely linked to the quality of this ancillary raw material and to the skill of the technicians who procured and wrought it. Differential access to this critical resource thus ultimately meant a lot in terms of wealth and power as well.

Ironworkers in the region today have conveyed to us much important information about the resources they use, as well as their best scientific judgments about which materials are suitable for high-temperature iron smelting. Local craftsmen still know what kinds of restrictions—ritual, economic, political, and environmental—were traditionally applied to certain raw materials. Their knowledge has figured substantially in our assessments of iron ores, clays, tree species burnt for charcoal, and other materials used in the technological system. Folk classification of what constitutes acceptable, ideal, or even undesirable raw material has been central to our goal of eliciting spontaneous, emic mental and emic behavioral definitions of essential ingredients. If the advantageous mineral and chemical constituents of these substances can be isolated in the laboratory, we can begin to understand what raw materials were preferred over others, why specific resource zones were more intensively exploited, and why some resources led to greater technological efficiency. These environmental assessments, based on informant commentary and on material analysis, provide the standards by which we can judge why and how past cultural systems in the region used the natural environment.

Another important part of our environmental research strategy for westlake has been documentation of the region's vegetational history, with particular focus on the environmental changes initiated and effected by human populations. The physiography of the region—inhabited ridges alternating with swamps—provides an exceptional opportunity for studying settlement history in relation to the vegetational history available in the pollen record of contiguous wetlands. We hypothesized that intermediate swamps that lay close to settled hillsides would receive their primary pollen deposition from both the hillsides and the vegetation within the swamps; thus the pollen record from these areas might provide a good index to vegetational disturbance resulting from a variety of cultural activities, such as clearance of land for settlements and agriculture, use of forest products for industrial purposes, and the grazing of cattle.

The vegetational markers for some of these cultural activities are unclear, and there is a notable dearth of comparative pollen evidence in Africa. Though some rough indices exist (Hamilton, Taylor, and Vogel 1986), no precise comparative studies on agricultural clearance and cattle grazing have yet appeared that would enable definitive assessment of vegetational changes induced by humans during prehistoric times.

Our ultimate focus was on a dual goal: to trace the changes in the moist-forested landscape of westlake from ca. 2500 years ago to the present, and to discover how the exploitative economy and the cultural system have changed and adapted to a transformed landscape, by introducing systems of resource management and regulations that allowed continued utilization of key materials, at different spatial and temporal scales.

The significant contrasts we found between the bountiful forested environment of the earliest Iron Age (200 BC–AD 600) and the beleaguered environment of the very late Iron Age (AD 1700–1900) left us wary of models that would interpret prehistoric patterns of behavior in terms of patterns of the recent past. Yet the two eras share common features that must not be ignored simply because we see some problems in the application of "middle range" approaches. There are parallels in process, for instance, between the kinds of problems that Early Iron Age folk encountered when they had exhausted the forest along the lakeshore zone, and problems that ironworkers experienced with diminished forests during the nineteenth and early twentieth centuries. In fact, in certain contexts the recent past offered an appropriate model for environmental stress, patterns of which were discernible in earlier periods of the westlake economy.

Our most direct evidence for the ways in which early technologists in westlake exploited their environment has been recovered from archaeological excavations. The remains of smelting furnaces contain a critical material: the charcoal used to roast (presmelt) and smelt iron ore. Identifying the genus (and species if we are lucky) of this charcoal can tell us what kinds of trees were being used in smelting. This in turn can provide an index of the kinds of forests prevalent in the vicinity of the smelting sites and how that environment changed through time. Prehistoric charcoal can also suggest whether or not ironworkers preferred particular species, perhaps in different areas and eras. Such evidence is invaluable to our assessment of continuity and change in technological behavior as well as in forest resources. Preferences for certain forest species may be related to widely varying considerations, ranging from their chemical composition to human political and ritual concerns.

SETTLEMENT HISTORY AND THE ENVIRONMENT

The context for environmental and technological interrelationships in westlake is clearly situated in the behavior of ironworkers who work the swamps and hill flanks outside villages to obtain the resources they need for iron production. The recent historical environment represents a series of significant transformations over the past 2500 years. The quality and availability of resources during the past century differed substantially from conditions in the earlier periods of the Iron Age, in the transitional and relatively obscure period from AD 700 to 1200, when technological activity was much reduced or even absent in the region, and in the earlier part (AD 1500–1700) of the Late Iron Age.

Comparison of smelting furnaces from the Early Iron Age and the historical era reveals differences in the material used to fill the furnace pit. Early Iron Age wood charcoal from forest trees was small enough that its high carbon exposure was probably sufficient to create a carbon boil in the blast zone. This early technology was clearly more demanding of forest resources at a time when forests were bountiful. The change to *Miscanthidium* grass during the Late Iron Age marked an important innovative advance that had significant environmental consequences. First, it would have reduced economic demand for forest trees. It also substituted an annually renewable resource for forest trees. This development was, in our view, an important adaptation that was related to the depletion of forest resources. It was also a major technological innovation since the greater amount of carbon contact area in charred grass created a more efficient furnace environment.

Archaeological evidence thus far is not sufficient to indicate precisely when this change occurred. We have not yet excavated a complete furnace from the Middle Iron Age (ca. AD 1200–1400), but our observations of slag in a dated furnace at the Kasiramfuko site suggest that forest charcoal was still in use in the thirteenth century, when iron technology appears to have been reestablished on the landscape after a long absence between approximately AD 600 and 1200. This long hiatus in industrial activity and the concomitant contraction of settlement to the Lake Victoria littoral suggest that both may have been partly caused by the diminution of forests in the latter part of the Early Iron Age.

The likeliest interpretation thus far is that Early Iron Age peoples found the coastal zone of westlake in gallery forest. Over the course of extensive and long-term Early Iron Age settlement on poor forest soils, accompanied by intensive iron production, the zone gradually experienced deforestation, soil erosion and depletion, and resource scarcity in the industrial sector. Thereafter the settlement pattern shifted toward a predominantly lakeside adaptation with little or no practice of iron technology (none is yet documented); the once-forested environment to the west began its regeneration. Not until the thirteenth century do we find the return of iron smelting in the interior and the growth of settlements on the hills east of Lake Ikimba. The arrival of large numbers of cattle, brought by peoples of northern origin during the middle of the second millennium, inaugurated an era of greater agricultural prosperity and population increase, with the subsequent growth of centralized states and an increasingly intensified industrial economy. By the twentieth century, in many areas the productive economy had apparently stripped the environment of efficiently (that is, sustainably) exploited forests.

Two to three thousand years ago forests would have been readily accessible along the coastal ridges and their small valleys as well as in the permanently flooded swamps and in many of the seasonally flooded swamps.[3] The remote remnant swamp forests of the twentieth century-the last and only mature forests in the region-are an artifact of centuries of forest exploitation. Our observations of iron smelters today indicate that long treks through *Miscanthidium* and *Syzygium* swamp are necessary to reach the preferred tree species for smelting, *Syzygium guineense*. This may be one of the few remaining trees whose characteristics are adequate to meet the requirements of current Haya iron technology. Its exploitation is labor-intensive; high labor costs for charcoal production are one of the environmental factors that have militated against iron smelting. These recent historical exploitative practices may offer insights into Late Iron Age behavior, but they do not furnish an appropriate model for Early Iron Age forest use.

By the beginning of the present century, in most areas fuel was thus a much more highly restricted commodity than was iron ore. Iron smelters in the northern part of the region, particularly in Kiziba, were forced to relocate to the south near Lake Ikimba because of the depletion of forests in their home area. Direct historical testimony from these ironworkers indicates that they favored several species of trees and moved their smelting locations periodically to save labor costs in fuel transportation. In other words, they followed the availability of certain forest resources in an environment completely remade by humans. Exploitation of forests for iron smelting had become a cyclical process, in which ironworkers harvested both from immature groundwater forests in the valleys and from seasonal swamp forests. Archaeological survey confirms that smelters of the late nineteenth and early twentieth centuries were locating their industrial activities along the margins of seasonal swamps contiguous to fuel resources (Schmidt 1980).

The severely restricted forest resources of the past century offer one of several explanations for the demise of iron technology in westlake. That the region was no longer self-sufficient in iron production by the late nineteenth century is confirmed by early European observers, who noted that iron imports, perhaps substantial, were obtained from Biharamulo (to the south), Ankole (northwest), and Karagwe (west) (Richter 1900).

ENVIRONMENTAL PERSPECTIVES ON LANDSCAPE CHANGE

The size and distribution of Early Iron Age settlements and their industrial locales suggest that those populations and their land clearance for agricultural and industrial purposes would have had a major impact on the natural environment. The density and complexity of Early Iron Age industrial sites offer unquestionable evidence that the ridges next to Lake Victoria had been cleared of most forest vegetation by AD 500 and that the first cycle of clearance may have occurred as early as AD 200. The era extended until ca. 600–700, when settlement began a retreat to the lakeshore zone, where communities are dated to the turn of the millennium.

Prehistoric Industrial Charcoal

Charcoal from prehistoric smelting furnaces in westlake provides an exceptional opportunity to study the type and location of forests used for iron-working purposes. We have often excavated charcoal in significant quantities at such sites, and extensive samples have been recovered from all sectors of furnace pits. We submitted some of our charcoal samples to the Musée Royale de Belgique for paleobotanical analysis. Because charcoal had been excavated from tightly dated furnaces, these analyses provided a way to trace changes in forest ecology as well as variations in the range of forest species used in the iron industry over the entire span of the Early Iron Age.

Forest clearance to supply charcoal for smelting and forging iron can be linked to specific features of the cultural landscape. Variations in the species used can also indicate changing preferences for materials as well as differential access to critical materials, for any number of reasons ranging from ecological to political and ritual. We have amassed substantial amounts of data about the kinds of forest products used by Early Iron Age residents, particularly on the hills above Kemondo Bay, from which we may pose some important questions and offer some tentative interpretations.

First, one of the earliest iron-smelting furnaces at one of the Kemondo Bay sites (KM3) shows the use of at least twelve genera of forest trees. This remarkable range of types, derived from various microenvironments, gives the initial impression that by the early first century BC iron technologists were exploiting predominantly first-growth, mature, wet-forest trees. Some, such as *Celtis durandi,* are huge; others, such as *Entandrophragma cylincrium* (mahogany) and *Chatacme microcarpa* (which grows on shallow, ridge-top soils) are very hard, very large forest trees. Yet at the same time, middle-story trees and larger swamp trees (such as *Uapaca,* which makes excellent charcoal) were also in use. At another site (KM2) a furnace of similar date yielded charcoal made from sixteen different genera. The great diversity of genera and species in this case likewise points to a predominance of mature, moist-forest trees, including mahogany and ironwood (an extremely difficult tree to cut down), supplemented with middle-story trees and trees common to swampy and riparian environments. Here, however, several large forest trees with light, soft woods (such as *Canarium schweinfurthii*) are also represented.

The overall impression is that Early Iron Age furnaces in this earlier era were rather like a forest stew: bits and pieces of any tree that was available were tossed into the furnace, even though some species would in fact have had little caloric value. The most parsimonious explanation for the time being is that the first iron technologists along the lakeshore were working in an environment where forest clearance for agriculture, perhaps under swidden conditions, was being practiced. If mature, moist forest was being cleared, as seems to have been the case, great quantities of readily available wood (much of it of high quality) would have been left lying about near the new farm plots, sometimes for long periods. The presence of charcoal from light and soft woods, as well as from wetland trees, supports this picture of "omnivorous" use of wood, especially surplus wood from other activities.

As we shift our focus three to five centuries later a different picture emerges. Fourth-century evidence from the KM3 site shows a much more restricted list of fuel: only two moist-forest species were used at this site, immediately beneath the crest of an otherwise inhospitable rocky hill. The KM2 site, along the shore of Lake Victoria, shows only slightly less confined utilization of fuel woods during the fifth century. In one furnace pit only three species are represented: an older, wet-forest type; a secondary tree that colonizes the fringe of the forest; and a tree with soft, light wood that today is commonly used to make beer boats (large vessels resembling dugout boats that are used to brew beer). In a nearby furnace from the same era we found a similarly limited mix of mahogany, two other forest species now uncommon in East Africa, and two very common swamp species. Clearly the variety of forest species formerly common to the environment was no longer available. Large remnant trees were used, but the iron smelters were now consistently venturing into the swamps to obtain supplementary fuel.

We may conclude that over the several centuries after the first practice of iron smelting along the coastal hills, the environmental plenty of moist forests diminished to the point that iron smelters were obliged to use only a few remnant moist-forest species and some secondary regrowth and were ranging farther afield to exploit the swamps for supplementary fuels. The human industrial record thus gives a clear picture of the spatial form that forest clearance took and its precise expression in the range of species eliminated from the landscape. From it we can also estimate the scale of early forest exploitation for both land clearance and industry, until forests were eliminated from the coastal valleys and ridge tops and ironworkers increasingly sought out other suitable fuels.

Palynology

To obtain an alternative view of the vegetational history of the central west-lake coastal zone we developed pollen histories by analyzing core samples taken along several east-west transects from the drier central depression to the moist ridges next to Lake Victoria: we thus gleaned evidence from the lakes as well as the swamps between the north-south ridge systems. Because Lake Ikimba lies in the rain shadow of the coastal ridges, vegetation today tends toward grasslands, patches of woodland, and woodland savanna. The production of storms over Lake Victoria and their very particular vectors over westlake would suggest that the precipitation pattern in the eastern part of the region has not altered significantly over the past 2500 years.

One sample taken from the eastern part of Lake Ikimba (basal core deposits radiocarbon-dated to 1685 BP, ca. AD 265) shows an erosional horizon that began as a catastrophic environmental event (Laseski 1983). The deposition in the lakebed of limonite nodules from the hillsides above and east of the lake suggests that land there had been severely degraded, perhaps even stripped of protective shrub and grass cover, which meant that high-velocity erosion carried nodules into the lake. This episode occurred at approximately AD 450–500 and provides a definitive environmental marker. Lower deposits (prior to this erosional event) show, first, a decrease in arboreal pollen, apparently related to deforestation, and then a decrease in nonarboreal pollen. This marked and rapid pattern of environmental degradation is particularly indicated by the fall in nonarboreal pollen, which indicates widespread alteration of low-lying vegetation and shrubs, presumably owing to agriculture.

I believe that these changes, along with the severe erosion, resulted from Early Iron Age cultivation and settlement in this zone to the east of Lake Ikimba. Thus far we have no evidence that iron production was widely practiced there. Archaeological survey around Lake Ikimba shows a shorter settlement history during the Early Iron Age than along the coastal swamps. From dating evidence for the area between Lake Ikimba and the coastal zone, one can reasonably project initial Iron Age settlement in the Ikimba Basin at ca. AD 300–400. The spread of Early Iron Age agriculture and technology to the woodlands of the central basin would have posed a different array of adaptive problems compared to the moist-forested coastal ridges and the well-watered central plateau. Land clearance would have occurred at a much more rapid rate in the woodlands, a phenomenon that may be reflected in the severe erosional episode of AD 450 to 500.

Further understanding of human-land relations can be gained from the history of evergreen forest genera, especially *Podocarpus*. According to conventional wisdom, *Podocarpus* usually occurs in drier montane forest conditions. Yet the predominant forest type in the northern part of westlake today is the *Baikai-Podocarpus* forest, found on the alluvium flats of the Kagera and Ngono rivers and filling large tracts of seasonally flooded swamps that extend south from the Uganda border. These forests contain *Podocarpus milanjiamus, Podocarpus usambarensis,* and *Ilex mitis*—species usually restricted to montane forest. In seasonally swampy locales these trees are mixed with a matrix of typical medium-altitude species (Langdale-Brown, Osmaston, and Wilson 1964:75). In these special environmental circumstances *Podocarpus* pollens mark climax swamp forest in the northern part of the region, a condition that has remained constant since prehistoric times. In our core sample from Lake Ikimba, *Podocarpus* pollen declined slightly before AD 400, then recovered, then nearly disappeared about 700, the end of the Early Iron Age in this area. Collateral evidence for change in ridge-associated species over the same period (ca. AD 300–700+) shows a process of forest clearance parallel to that observed in southwestern Uganda: first the valley bottoms, then the slopes, and finally the ridge tops (Hamilton, Taylor, and Vogel 1986).

The other most notable period of environmental change around Lake Ikimba came in the early to middle second millennium. Archaeological survey has recovered evidence of reestablished settlement on the hills along the eastern edge of the swamp south of Ikimba ca. 1200 to 1400, about the same time that shrubby species took hold in the swamps, apparently after the swampy forests were cleared. An increase in grasses and nonarboreal pollen and a corresponding decline in arboreal pollen during the mid-second millennium also suggest increased clearing of the land around the lake, if not in the swamps. This period would have been approximately the time (documented in local oral traditions) when peoples with large numbers of cattle arrived from Ankole in the north and from Karagwe to the west.

Another record of vegetational history comes from Kiizi, three kilometers north of Kemondo Bay between the two largest ridges along Lake Victoria, the first area to be settled during the Early Iron Age (Laseski 1983). The Rugomora Katuruka site—first used for iron production ca. 500 BC and occupied as a Bahinda capital in the mid-seventeenth century—overlooks this core-sampling locale from a hilltop to the east. Numerous Early Iron Age industrial sites (including KM2 and KM3, mentioned above) appear five to ten kilometers south within the same basin; several have yielded dates around 200 BC. For a six-hundred-year phase of diminished human activity beginning ca. AD 600 we have found no archaeological evidence for iron production along the coastal ridges, but populations with characteristic Early Iron Age pottery continued to inhabit the margins of Lake Victoria until at least the eleventh century.

The Kiizi core gives a more sensitive reading of cultural developments over its upper (later) half, where we can see the opening of land to more intensive exploitation. Moisture-loving forest trees declined rapidly. Grasses increased significantly, and shrubby trees in the swamp gave way to *Miscanthidium* grass near the coring site. This suite of changes indicates a direct encroachment into the swamps by Iron Age peoples, probably between AD 1200 and 1500.

The parallels between the upper cores from Kiizi and Lake Ikimba suggest that similar processes of change were simultaneously at work in both areas. These were undoubtedly linked to cultivation, iron smelting, and the coming of larger cattle herds to the region. I feel confident that we can attribute the mid-second-millennium forest clearance, particularly in the swamps, to iron smelting during the Late Iron Age, when the swamps provided one of the few sources of fuel in those densely settled landscapes.

Synthesis and Interpretation

This first attempt at a vegetational history of the coastal zone of westlake yields some important insights into how early populations remade the landscape. We have been able to assess the first impact of Iron Age peoples in the Lake Ikimba area quite successfully. During the Early Iron Age the southern margins of the unique "montane" swamp forests were gradually cleared until woody shrubs and grasses prevailed, but the most profound changes occurred around Lake Ikimba. In that area initial agriculture apparently had a severely degrading effect. The consequences can be read in a major erosional event and in the subsequent abandonment of the area. The causes of human depopulation in this area cannot be definitively attributed, but analogies drawn from similarly stressed environments in East Africa today indicate that severe malnutrition leads to high susceptibility to a broad spectrum of diseases. We have no specific archaeological evidence that disease was the direct cause of population decline in westlake, but the region's history over the most recent century strongly suggests that human disease is a common response to conditions of ecological stress.

Following the Early Iron Age at Ikimba there was an apparent regeneration of both swamp and other forests. The increasing populations of the Middle Iron Age and earlier Late Iron Age began an exploitative process that eventually led to profound vegetational changes. These changes were met by management practices hinged to ritual protection of certain tree species, as well as the ritual mystification of certain sectors of the landscape, so exploitation could occur only under special ritual-political sanction. I consider these cultural factors below. Under the present heading we may only point to a set of general processes—increased use of forests for iron production, clearance of forests for agriculture and settlement, and the coming of large numbers of cattle to the region—as the major causes of this second significant transformation of the landscape, which was under way by AD 1400 to 1500. Deforestation during this later era became so widespread that the conditions for the development of adaptations to depleted forests were certainly present.

The clearest indication of technological adaptation to the radically transformed landscape is the change in the fuel used in the bottom of the smelting furnace. The shift from tree charcoal to charred *Miscanthidium* grass is linked to increasingly scarce forest resources. *Miscanthidium* grass replaced a succession of forest trees and then woody shrubs in the swamps. In our analyses it appears first on the periphery of swamps in areas most accessible to iron smelters working there. The physical hallmarks of this change are the imprints of swamp reeds in the frozen prehistoric slags. As noted earlier, *Miscanthidium* grass offered two distinct advantages: it was an annually renewable resource, and it provided an ideal charred, ashy matrix with a high carbon contact area particularly suited to the reduction technique used in the region's iron smelting technology at that time (Schmidt and Avery 1978).

IDEOLOGY AND LANDSCAPE TRANSFORMATION

The most difficult challenge in constructing the historical ecology of any prehistoric region is to integrate the interplay of cultural systems with the physical environment. It is clearly easier to construct relationships that prevailed between the productive economy and the landscape, the transformations that these relations induced, and subsequent adjustments and adaptations. The task quickly becomes more difficult, and "middle range" approaches more complex, when we arrive at structural questions such as organization of production and look to the superstructure for understanding of the ideologies that regulated production. One distinct advantage in the equatorial Bantu-speaking areas that practice iron smelting is that the existing cross-cultural systems of organization and ideology enable us to construct a more reliable context for prehistoric landscape transformation and management (or mismanagement).

Political Economy and Symbolic Mystifications

Our endeavor to explore the social relations of production and to probe the ideology that regulated exploitative practices naturally began by decoding belief systems that have governed the use of natural resources and affected perceptions of the landscape. In westlake the obvious starting point is the Kaiija tree shrine (situated within Katuruka village), the region's most important symbolic space associated with political legitimacy and with iron production. In Bantu-speaking Africa these two domains form an identity.

Both are invariably linked such that chiefs and kings, invested under eso-teric rituals conducted by ironworkers, are given iron emblems of power that symbolically tie authority to reproduction, both sexual and agricul-tural—an interdependent domain.

A key observation to unlocking this code lies in the meaning of the name of the shrine tree, Kaiija: derived from *luiija,* "anvil" or "forge," it means "Place of the Forge." It is no coincidence that the shrine tree stands next to an Early Iron Age forge (now excavated and dated to 500 BC). The forge and the tree derive mutual meaning from their contiguity. The most important conferral of meaning, however, comes from a myth attached to the same place, that King Rugomora Mahe of the early Bahinda dynasty once built an iron tower there, which eventually collapsed, killing many of its fabricators. The iron tower, the forge, and the tree share a bundle of interrelated symbolic meanings rooted in the material past.

Kaiija is a commemorative shrine that connotes the origins and im-portance of iron working in the region's culture. The ancient, pre-Bahinda myth and the forge share a great antiquity, which may explain why the site fits so neatly into Bahinda ideological representations that link the dynasty to the ancients. A double metonymy comes into play: Bahinda occupa-tion of the site in the seventeenth century incorporated the shrine and its related myth within the Bahinda palace boundaries, at the same time that Bahinda history became contained within a much broader and more powerful domain of iron-working symbolism. A legitimizing mystification occurred whereby reference to any part of Rugomora Mahe's history on the site evoked common images of the larger ancient, symbolic whole and made Bahinda association with and control of iron working seem natural.

Bahinda political manipulation of the symbol systems that originated in iron production occurred in a period of radical change in the social and political orders that marked the ascendancy of cattle-keeping people from the north over indigenous folk who produced iron and traditionally held political authority. These events, in the seventeenth century, unfolded approximately two hundred years after the cattle keepers had arrived in westlake. This was also a period of ecological stress. Deforestation of the region was well underway, exacerbated by the presence of cattle, which prevent secondary regrowth.[4] Iron production, traditionally controlled by indigenous clans who also believed in the ancient Bacwezi gods, was ap-parently already subjected to regulation and taxation by a central authority under the aegis of an alliance of indigenous groups identified with rain-making. Other similar changes gripped the related kingdom of Kiziba just south of the Uganda border, where Bacwezi priests were challenged by a new cult of affliction sponsored by the new royal house (Schmidt 1978). In this instance the new dynasty colonized areas of wealth (and iron production) by establishing rival cult centers based in confiscated estates.

In both these kingdoms the new royals and their cattle-keeping allies controlled a precious commodity, manure, that was essential for maintaining human activity in a degraded environment. Cattle manure, with mulch and green manuring, could sustain continued agricultural production and settlement. What developed was the transfer of rights over land in exchange for cattle and their manure, as well as a "legitimate" centralized control over industrial production. Bahinda seizure of the Kaiija shrine was a keystone in that dynasty's control over indigenous industry. The symbolic harnessing of the industrial economy meant royal hegemony over the productive economy.

The Symbolic Transformation of the Productive Landscape

The transformations described thus far lead us naturally to an exegesis of the iron-working symbolism attached to the general landscape. One important aspect was first opened to us through conversation with the young men who worked as our assistants. As we daily drove through the village on the next ridge west of our Katuruka site, they would guffaw, "We've arrived at Katerero!" Katerero is the place on which King Rugomora Mahe's mythical iron tower is supposed to have fallen. I eventually learned that *katerero* (from *okutera*, "to hit") means "beating, beating," a sexual practice in which the man taps or beats his penis on the woman's clitoris to draw forth significant amounts of vaginal secretion, called *kiizi*. This is the first phase of intercourse, preparatory to *kanyinya*, "pushing, pushing" (from *akinyinwa*, "filling up").

A much deeper understanding of local place names attached to the landscape around the mythical tower began to emerge with these revelations. When the iron tower, a cosmic phallus, collapsed on Katerero, it replicated the same motion as human *katerero*. This relationship affirms the iron tower as a symbol of human procreation. As an *axis mundi* it also unites a mythic, heavenly image with earthly, human reproduction. Iron is central both to this symbolism and that of agricultural productivity (see below).

Other place names in the surrounding landscape further amplify the symbolic meaning of the Kaiija shrine and its iron tower. The mythical iron tower is said to have been constructed at the western end of Katuruka, overlooking the contiguous village of Kiizi, which takes its name from a stream that originates not far from the supposed base of the tower and then passes through the village center. Thus the Kiizi that flows from beneath the beating iron-tower/phallus is, through metonymy, symbolically the *kiizi* (vaginal fluid) generated by *katerero*. Katerero itself is located across the swamp from Katuruka on a high hill to the north of a low saddle, a unique geographical feature on the shoreline that stands between Lake Victoria and an enormous interior swamp. The saddle is named Kanyinya (*kanyinya*, "pushing, pushing," "filling up"). As one moves down from Katerero, one moves into the saddle at Kanyinya. The topographical structures and movement between places replicate the stages of the sex act and the movement of the phallus through them.

A Symbolic Armature in the Productive Economy

The iron tower, with all the attributes of a phallus, is a symbol of both human procreation and the production of iron. It unites both domains and also symbolizes their interdependence. Iron is also central to the production of food: prosperity in industrial production is directly translated to agricultural well-being, which in turns leads to the capacity of society to reproduce itself and provide labor for the industrial and agricultural sectors. Exaction of tribute and monopoly over the wealth that results from such a technology are obviously important, in very pragmatic terms, to the development of centralized political authority. With an eye toward such realities, the groups that traditionally held direct control of iron production at least in part maintained that control through an esoteric technological and ritual repertoire. The ritual that surrounded iron production was exceedingly complex. It mystified the technological process to such a degree that its adepts appeared to enjoy mastery not merely over specialized technological knowledge but also over human fecundity. This mystification protected the special interests of the iron-working clans that controlled the economy.

Aside from its significance as a symbol of human and economic fecundity, the iron tower also relates to the cultural phenomenon of iron working in other crucial ways. It provides an etiological explanation for the origins of iron working (see Schmidt 1983). At the Kaiija shrine it is directly connected with archaeological evidence for ancient iron working. And it belongs to a broader and fabulously rich symbolism that arises from the process of iron smelting, a profoundly transformational phenomenon that alters a natural substance, earth, through fire into life-giving cultural matter, iron.

While engaged with the iron-smelting furnace, each smelter is in a highly virile state. He has reserved his sexual energy, via taboos that prevent sexual intercourse, for exclusive devotion to the furnace in order to produce as much iron as possible. His first sexual responsibility is to the furnace; for example, he must not sleep with his wife during the smelting season.

The taboo of greatest consequence, however, is that menstruating women must be prevented from contact with any part of the smelting furnace, ore, or apparatus. Contact with a menstruating woman would pollute the smelting process and result in its failure (that is, the smelt will not be productive). Menstruation, a state opposite to fertility, is the height of sterility, for menstrual blood suspends fecundity. The contiguity to the furnace or its ingredients of anyone in a sterile condition transfers that attribute to the furnace. The ritual taboos thus insure that a state of fecundity will prevail in the domain of the furnace. They are primary contextual indications that the furnace is perceived as both female and ideally fecund.

These ritual taboos mask deeper material relationships. In westlake, as in other neighboring Bantu-speaking cultures, knowledge of iron working, as well as the considerable economic wealth and political power that it produced, was traditionally confined to patrilineages. Passed on under conditions of great ritual secrecy from father to son within specific clans, this knowledge was endangered by the presence of women who had married into the line from non-iron-working groups. Principles of production—along with the wealth and power thus conferred—could be lost to other groups if these women witnessed smelting or otherwise learned its secrets (either of natural resources or of master technology) and then talked with their kinsmen. Hence the taboo that the smelter must not sleep with his wife during the smelting season had material as well as symbolic implications, for a man in the arms of a loving wife is more inclined to let trade secrets slip than one who keeps his own company. And in this sense the various taboos against female contact with the smelting process likewise protected critical economic trade secrets.

We know that a wide variety of African cultures practice rituals in which special blood sacrifices are conducted prior to the smelt or small pits are dug in the bottom of the furnace pit to receive special offerings that insure a successful smelt or protect the smelt from those who would do it harm. In westlake such practices include special rituals for inserting into a hole at the bottom of the furnace pit a white, semenlike liquid called *empuri*, a remedy usually given to sterile women to make them capable of bearing children. Extensive archaeological evidence points to the application of similar rituals over the past two millennia, which indicates great continuity in the belief systems embedded in iron production.

Other ritual practices were linked directly to resource acquisition. In Kiziba kingdom iron smelters carefully performed blood sacrifices to Irungu, the Bacwezi god who oversees the resources of the hinterland (such as clay, iron ore, and charcoal). Consultations with Bacwezi diviners who supervised these affairs led to a flow of payments from iron smelters to the religious overseer. After smelting, a portion of the product was also paid to the king. Thus a regulatory system, a kind of checks-and-balances, arose between the local ritual authorities—indigenous Bacwezi diviners and priests—and the taxing central authority.

Any attempt to devise a historical ecology of westlake must come to terms with these social relations of production as well as the effects of ideological systems and their role in constructing successive landscapes. Over time, particularly during the most recent three centuries, for which more diverse historical documentation is available, we can observe processes of landscape transformation mediated by complex belief systems, sometimes in competition, but sharing the fundamental perceptual posture that the natural environment is in the service of the reproduction of culture. This fundamental symbolic armature, I believe, may be linked with some of the more profound ecological changes in the area.

For example, the introduction of central taxation in the seventeenth century, along with local ritual regulation of forest resources, meant a decrease in the profit margin in iron smelting, especially as critical resources such as wood became scarce during the nineteenth and twentieth centuries. By the early twentieth century many Kiziba smelters found forest resources insufficient and relocated to Kianja to the south. There they found a different landscape north of Lake Ikimba, a place without an ancient history of iron smelting, without large stands of swamp forests, and without an indigenous ritual system that regulated hinterland forest exploitation. The forests were small, secondary riverine growths not far from villages and were under the management of local heads of clans, who ultimately had to account to the king in matters involving outside exploitation.

Insights can be similarly gained from the social contexts of smelting. Smelters operate in the domain of Irungu, the Bacwezi god of the hinterland who controls such resources as iron ore and forests. The most important ritual performed by the Kiziba smelters was the construction of a spirit house for Irungu and a blood sacrifice to propitiate his spirit. They also assumed the role of *muharambwa* for their furnaces.

The primary ritual figure in matters concerning Irungu in a traditional

Haya village, the *muharambwa* was a respected elder who controlled allocation of resources within Irungu's domain. He was distinguished by his ap-
parel: he wore a woman's raffia skirt (*kishenshe*). Besides interceding with
Irungu, he ritually blessed the women's hoes to ensure their productivity.[5]
But most important was his power to bless women so that they might
bear children. He was the most powerful public ritual official concerned
with matters of female fertility. Thus the smelters not only operated in the
domain of Irungu, but each dressed as (in a way, became) a *muharambwa,*
ritually acting out a liminal role as both husband and midwife to the furnace. Though Bacwezi diviners may have partly controlled resource extrac-
tion by iron smelters, their influence appears to have been partly neutral-
ized, at some junctures, by the independent ritual role playing of smelters
who assumed the guise of Irungu's representative during the actual work.

The social dominance of the smelters and their exploitative posture
can be further understood from other contexts, particularly their songs.
Some songs have considerable symbolic content and clearly indicate that
the furnace is a womb—a widespread motif among Bantu-speaking iron
smelters. One example is "Emondo," replete with esoteric metaphors,
which is commonly sung during the regular smelt.

Call	Response
The 'Mondo	Has flowed (with the current)
The 'Mondo	Has flowed (with the current)
The 'Mondo	Has flowed (with the current)
Beware! The Spotted one may eat you!	
The 'Mondo	The Spotted One may eat you!
The 'Mondo	The Spotted One may eat you!
The 'Mondo	The Spotted One may eat you!
Oh, you women scooping up the water	
Do stop my emondo for me.	
Oh, you women scooping up the water	
Do stop my emondo for me.	
The 'Mondo	It has flowed (with the current).
The 'Mondo	It has flowed (with the current).

The song is filled with sexual metaphors that refer to human reproduction.
The *emondo,* a small aquatic mammal similar to an otter, is an image widely
used in sexual symbolism—in this instance as a metaphor for flowing
semen during sexual intercourse. (This too has its place in the sexual landscape near the iron tower and Katerero: Kemondo Bay, the major body of

water that lies between Katerero and Kanyinya, is the "place of the flowing semen"). The Spotted One is *kagondo,* a generic term for spotted animals such as the leopard, serval cat, or indeed the *emondo* itself. In this context the word is a metaphor for the penis. The phrase *Yakulya kagondo* literally means that the animal might eat you, but its implications are enriched by the metaphorical use of "eat," which can also mean to make love to a woman. The call to the women downstream, who are scooping up water, metaphorically means that the semen is headed their way—and they are enjoined to stop it, to catch the *emondo.*

The reproductive metaphor that links iron production to agricultural production and to reproduction of labor sets a perceptual context that governs the most fundamental exploitative activities. The belief that reproduction of culture hinges on iron production is the engine that also drives the exploitation of forest resources, powered by the same symbolic elements. During the production of charcoal, for example, as the fire burns down and dousing begins, the smelters set a spell on their effort:

> Say the following:
> "I am digging a well
> For killing the charcoal
> So that it may not burn away
> So that all may be happy
> And not complain that things are not well
> That is as it should be
> So that we may make those who bear breasts reproduce
> Even the mudfish may come from it
> Even the fishtraps may come into it."

The dousing, the final phase of charcoal making, entails throwing water up from a ditch or "well" that has been dug around the burning platform in the swamp. The charcoal is destined for the inside of the furnace, "So that we may make those who bear breasts reproduce"—the allusion here is to the smelting furnace, not to women. Another key metaphor is the reference to the mudfish, that is, the lungfish, which because of its "breasts" represents women in Haya culture. As the smelters squelch about in the mud, they are in the "reproductive domain" of the breasted ones (lungfish), a symbolic meaning that continues with the placement of the resulting charcoal inside the female furnace.

Beneath the particulars of this exegesis lies my main point: that fundamental exploitative activities such as iron smelting, which consumed an enormous proportion of forest resources in westlake, were conducted as elaborate, sacred rituals that reaffirmed the very essence of the human experience—the reproduction of labor, the regeneration of life. The integration of this belief system with industrial activity established an abiding perception of the landscape as an abundant, sustaining, and responsive mother.

TOWARD A SYNTHETIC HISTORICAL ECOLOGY

Did the universal ideology of renewable fertility and its integration into industrial production, as an integral part of the division of labor, contribute to the inexorable degradation that we witness in the environmental record? The other component of this ideological equation would be the regulatory systems that conserved resources through the checks and balances provided by sacrifices and payments to Irungu's priests, as well as the ritual protection of many forest species located in villages and managed as shrines. The application of religious-political sanctions against those who disturbed trees that functioned as ritual locales effectively preserved and assured the management of countless groves of mature forest species both within and outside villages.

The seizure of the Kaiija shrine by the Bahinda royals marked an important new period of centralized management of sacred shrines and other forest resources. The patronage of the central state was essential in maintaining a cadre of ritual officials who oversaw and managed forest products. Also, via a land tenure system of estates awarded to loyal subjects, either Bahinda or indigenous, the state controlled agricultural surplus and labor, both essential to the expensive upkeep of numerous ritual officials and their retainers scattered across the landscape.

The introduction and subsequent widespread acceptance of Christianity during the first half of the present century brought a major change in the delicate balance of ritual management. Most of the traditional priests invested with protection of the shrines and the forests either converted and abandoned their roles or died without passing on their traditional authority. The kings, now Christian too, no longer maintain caretakers at the royal ancestral shrines, many of which have been converted to agricultural land. Similarly, the sacred significance once attached to groves dedicated to the Bacwezi gods has gradually eroded, sometimes to the point where shrine trees have been cut to make way for much-needed crop expansion.

As recently as forty years ago this behavior would have been met with outrage and severe punishment.

Syzygium guineense, the wood preferred during the first quarter of this century for iron-smelting charcoal, is locally known as *muchwezi*—the singular form of the name for the ancient religious-political groups that once controlled iron working in the region. (In recent times Kiziba smelters likewise preferred it.) [6] Ordinarily one expects to find *Syzygium guineense* in riparian forests, but in westlake it now occurs only in remote stands of swamp forests. Deforestation over the past four centuries has increasingly restricted options and may have focused preference on a dominant species with the requisite chemical properties. Or perhaps centralized regulations may at some point have required smelters to exploit a species outside of day-to-day demand. In any case the long-term shift from omnivorous use of multiple species in the Early Iron Age to use of a very limited range of species during periods of diminished forests and then to use of only one species in recent times represents a significant, large-scale change in the landscape.

In sum, the values and religious-political sanctions that once checked unbridled exploitation have passed into distant memory. In their place has arisen a system of forest management based on village and regional authority, an uneven scheme with overlapping and ill-defined responsibilities that promotes corruption and widespread abuses. The few remaining secondary forests are fast disappearing, and the remnant groundwater forests of the large swamps are being exploited as never before. Within the villages some trees are specifically planted along farm boundaries and cropped for building poles and firewood. During the late colonial period and the first decade of independence (that is, the years following World War II until the 1960s) people were actively encouraged to start small plantations of eucalyptus on fallow land; these plots have indeed become alternative sources of fuel and building poles, but they are now being cut without replanting.

These events are occurring in a perceptual universe still guided by belief in reproductive abundance. Yet for many decades it has been clear that the limited distribution of good soils, a system of partitive inheritance, the decrease in the practice of fallow agriculture owing to competition with plantations for open lands, and dense cattle and human populations do not allow continued expansion of Haya villages along the coastal ridges (Reining 1967; Schmidt 1978). A once finely balanced agricultural system has come under stress as fallow lands have been converted to tea (and smaller tree) plantations, resulting in shortened fallow cycles and decreased production. Established farms cannot support further division, and for several decades young people have been forced to settle on marginal interior land or seek their fortunes in other districts or regions. Those who elect to stay and try to cultivate the poor soils on fallow land at the periphery of permanent villages risk low productivity and family malnutrition.

These and other interrelated causes have created an agroecological system that long ago reached its carrying capacity. Outmigration has been one solution; Haya men and women have been leaving westlake in significant numbers since World War I. This departure was the natural culmination of declining productivity in the region, linked to human disease and the rinderpest cattle epidemic of the early 1890s. The decimation of the herds, whose manure was essential to the agricultural system, would have had a lasting impact on soil fertility (Kjekshus 1977). This severe environmental stress was accompanied by famine and smallpox. With the almost complete elimination of herds from the landscape, bush encroached from the east, bringing with it the ravages of tsetse flies and trypanosomiasis, further suppressing the regeneration of herds and decreasing the carrying capacity of the once productive agricultural zone. The disease and outmigration seen in the twentieth century is an outgrowth of the collapse of an agroecological system deprived of essential inputs.

One notable feature of this decline was the departure of thousands of young Haya women to urban centers in East Africa in search of work, often as prostitutes. British colonial officials despaired of halting this constant traffic; sometime in the 1920s one baldly admitted (in a Bukoba District report) that he was powerless to prevent yet another lake steamer, loaded with young women, from leaving.[7] Many women eventually returned, some to invest in their own land. But often they brought with them the ravages of syphilis and other sexually transmitted diseases.

The pre–World War II syphilis epidemic in westlake was a terrible scourge and contributed to very low population increases during the 1930s (Kaijage 1989). Fertility rates in the postwar period were generally low for East Africa (Reining 1967) but are not linked to high rates of syphilis infection. Widespread administration of antibiotics ultimately saved the Haya from catastrophic disease rates and reversed the decline in population. But subsequent decades have seen a continuation of the pattern of outmigration for economic opportunity and better land, which still includes a flow of prostitutes away from and back to westlake.

The region's arable land is very limited and sells at exorbitant prices. The only option remaining to many is colonization of land with low fertility and marginal rainfall, usually in the drier central basin. The prospect for young women is grinding agricultural work and poverty. Alternative urban "opportunities" seem undeniably attractive in this context of over-population and impoverished lifestyles, a syndrome that began in earnest one hundred years ago but whose genesis goes back two thousand years or more.

Out of this milieu has arisen the latest danger to westlake populations, the AIDS epidemic. Like the earlier syphilis epidemic, AIDS has decimated the reproductive populations of many westlake villages, particularly those on the coastal ridges. By the late 1980s seropositive rates were running as high as 41 percent among some age groups (Lwihura 1988). Tens of thousands have died, and massive socioeconomic disruption prevails. The tragic paradox is manifest: in a culture whose central system of meaning is derived from human reproduction, the act of human procreation now threatens the very existence of the cultural system. Nowhere else in the world is the threat of cultural extinction from disease so real. We are com-pelled to ask how the historical ecology of the region might figure in this phenomenon.

As the Haya bury their dead, a palpable fatalism grips their commu-nities. Death has been an omnipresent part of life, but now it is immediate and appears inevitable before the natural life cycle is complete. Many in-dulge in promiscuity, reckoning that because they are fated to die soon they might as well have a good time now. This attitude accelerates the transmission of AIDS, and widespread suicide, often at the first sign of any common symptom, adds to the crushing despair. Scientists have searched for some—any—explanation of why it is precisely here, and just across the border in Uganda, that the epidemic has taken such a cruel toll. The war with Uganda in 1979 and the concomitant high concentration in the area of prostitutes from all around East Africa have been cited among the possible causes for both the localization and the high rates of transmission (Kaijage 1990).

That AIDS may be more readily transmitted by uncircumcised males must also be acknowledged as a contributing factor (Bongaarts et al. 1989). Clinical studies have shown that HIV thrives within the moist environ-ment of the uncircumcised prepuce and passes easily through if that mem-brane is torn; or it is stored and later transmitted to a partner (Simonsen, Cameron, and Gakinya 1988). Some Tanzanians have questioned, and I join them, whether the practice of *katerero,* the beating of the penis against the female genitals, might tear the prepuce as well as the female mem-branes, thus increasing the probability of viral transmission.

All these speculations, however important, cannot be isolated from other issues of sexual behavior and must not be allowed to obscure the

reality that westlake is in the midst of a health crisis of staggering proportions.

In the past, social relations of production led to the differential acquisition of power and wealth by those who controlled critical knowledge of
the westlake region's iron-working technology. That knowledge was protected by ritual mystification of the industrial process and sustained by
a central symbolic armature of belief in unlimited reproductive capacity.
The social relations of production promoted by this ideology ultimately
led to severe degradation of the region's ecological system. Adaptations—
in the form of both technological change and, eventually, institutional adjustments under centralized authority—nevertheless enabled a dynamic
cultural system to thrive on the changing landscape for some centuries. In
the latter case, the centralized state intervened in the relations of production through taxation and through new regulatory devices that employed
religious-political sanctions to balance and to counter a dominant exploitative ideology.

Any historical ecology of westlake must address the rapid culture
change that began at the opening of the twentieth century. The coming
of Christianity undermined the fragile ecosystem by dissolving systems of
restraint and management that had been vested in religious authorities in
the employ of the state. That historical ecology must also recognize the
historical effects of the ideologies that have driven exploitation and justified social control over the productive economy since prehistoric times, as
well as the unfolding of a religious-political revolution in the seventeenth
century that imposed a new order in the relationship between nature and
culture. This ethnohistoric approach to human-land relations introduces
cultural perspectives into environmental history and provides important
insights into the relative success—over long periods—of different exploitative and management systems, some of which may provide guidelines if
not blueprints for the future.

——— *Notes* ———

1. The area is also called Buhaya, after the Bahaya or Haya people who live there.

2. I have used the first-person plural throughout this paper to refer to the cooperative
team of scientists under my guidance who have contributed to the synthesis of ideas presented here. The interpretations are solely my own.

3. Recent research into the history of forest clearance and environmental degradation
in southwestern Uganda (Hamilton, Taylor, and Vogel 1986) shows intriguing patterns of
forest clearance, some as early as 4800 BP. Any interpretation of the pollen record that
claims that this forest loss was caused by early cultivation must be viewed with great cau-
tion. Such an interpretation is not confirmed by any archaeological evidence for agricultural settlements in the area. Hamilton and Taylor's pollen diagrams from the Ahakagyezi

swamp do show that clearance of the lower slopes and valleys was probably under way by 2800 BP and that the valley forests had been completely cleared by 2200 BP. We agree that this deforestation can very likely be attributed to cultivation, most probably by Bantu-speaking peoples. Whether they were iron producers remains an open question.

4. Note that this was the second serious phase of deforestation in the landscape within a thousand to twelve hundred years. As indicated in earlier discussion, the deforestation east of Lake Ikimba ca. AD 450–500 bears similarities (decline in arboreal pollen, then in nonarboreal pollen) to patterns we see in the area again by the mid-second millennium.

5. For further information on the liminal state of the *muharambwa* see Cory and Hartnoll (1945:266).

6. During experimental smelting in 1976, 1979, and 1984 the smelters of Kiziba required this species and identified it as the species used in the 1920s.

7. White (1990) documents the accumulation of wealth and the transfer of this wealth to westlake by Haya prostitutes beginning in the 1930s. However, it is apparent that out-migration for prostitution was well established at least a decade earlier.

Chapter 6

Management for Extinction in Norse Greenland

Thomas H. McGovern

Five hundred years before Columbus arrived in the Caribbean, Scandinavian communities sharing a common language and a common culture stretched from western Norway to eastern North America. Between ca. AD 800 and 1000, Nordic warriors, traders, and settlers colonized the Faroes, Shetlands, Orkneys, northern Scotland, the Isle of Man, parts of Ireland, England, and Frankland, as well as the western Atlantic in Iceland, Greenland, and Vinland (see Bigelow 1991; Jones 1985; McGovern 1990). By the early Middle Ages, thriving European communities existed in arctic Greenland and subarctic Iceland, and the great saga-men of the western North Atlantic were producing medieval Scandinavia's first histories and finest historical novels.

Because the medieval Scandinavian North Atlantic route to North America was ultimately fruitless, Columbus surely deserves credit for the effective connection of the Old World with the New. By the time Columbus sailed, the Norse North Atlantic had long been an economic and social backwater, and its island communities were undergoing contraction and a desperate struggle for survival. In 1492, it is just possible that the very last of the Norse colonists of Greenland were losing that struggle, slipping into social and biological extinction. This westernmost European colony of the Middle Ages probably fell vacant within a few decades of the first Iberian voyages to the Caribbean (ca. 1475–1500).

What caused the failure of the early, northern route to the New World? Why were the early centuries of Scandinavian exploration and relative prosperity followed by isolation, impoverishment, and extinction? Were the Scandinavian colonists of Greenland simply overwhelmed by the challenges of global climate change and contact with Thule Inuit? Did critical failures of human resource management doom the settlements? Does the grim case of Norse Greenland hold any lessons relevant to a modern world faced by climate change, universal culture contact, and the consequences of human management choices on a global scale?

In this paper I briefly explore the 500-year-long interaction of culture and nature in Norse Greenland, explicitly attempting to draw lessons of wider potential relevance. The data employed are archaeological, documentary, and paleoecological. (Recent archaeology is discussed in greater detail in Berglund 1991; Keller 1991; McGovern 1985a, 1985b, 1992; McGovern et al. 1988. For a more complete discussion of the documentary sources, see Arneborg 1991; Gad 1970; Jansen 1972; Keller in press.)

Documentary sources for Norse Greenland are few (and historically reliable documentary sources even fewer), and they do not provide much information about basic subsistence, settlement pattern, land-use changes, or culture contact (Gad 1970). They do, however, provide a great deal of information about medieval Norse world view and cultural evaluation of "correct" social and environmental relations. Sagas, law codes, myths, and popular stories all provide a rich data set only now undergoing systematic analysis from an anthropological perspective (Durrenburger 1991; Durrenburger and Palsson 1989; Hastrup 1985; Miller 1986).

Thanks to the work of Scandinavian and English-speaking scholars of Greenland over the past three hundred years we now have a rich archaeological data base for many of the aspects of life not deemed "saga worthy" by the Norse themselves. In Atlantic Scandinavia it is thus possible to combine the long, diachronic perspective of history and archaeology with the emic, "inside view" usually restricted to ethnographic cases. Historical archaeology is only beginning to exploit this sort of interface, but a rich potential surely exists for a combination of standard environmental analyses of resource exploitation and land-use patterns with cognitive approaches incorporating concepts of limited knowledge, management hierarchy and heterarchy, and a world view significantly different from our own.

SETTLEMENT PROCESS

As described in Landnamabok, The Book of the Greenlanders, and Eirik the Red's Saga (Jones 1985), the settlement of Greenland began with competition between chieftains in Iceland. The loser in this power struggle was Eirik the Red, who departed hastily to investigate reports of new land to the west. This voyage replicated earlier Norse voyages of exploration and settlement, since chiefly competition in the previously settled island colonies encouraged further emigration under the sponsorship of the defeated elites. Many such desperate or hopeful voyagers simply disappeared in the gray waters of the North Atlantic or were forced to accept subordinate positions in already settled colonies. But for a lucky few like Eirik, the special status of Landnamsmann (first settler) rewarded the exploration of a new settlement area.

A first settler was not necessarily the first to discover a new land; he was the one who pioneered a successful settlement, discovering firsthand both the potentials and the hazards of an unknown region. Not all would-be first settlers were successful. Iceland's legendary history describes two failed settlement attempts before the eventual success of Ingolfur Arnarsson around 870 (Jones 1985). The Vinland settlements did not survive the first few years when they were most vulnerable (McGovern 1980–81; Wallace 1991). The risks of pioneering were exceptional since the normal buffering effects of a larger Norse community were absent, the timing and length of the growing season (and its variability) could only be estimated, and the potential hostility of unpacified native humans, elemental in-dwelling land spirits, and nonhuman magical beings (trolls and elves) would be a real threat to a small and restricted settlement. Success could come only to a strong chieftain with both the economic resources (ships, animals, seed, and laborers) and the personal, semimagical "luck" that could overcome great natural and supernatural obstacles.

Successful first settlers were able to claim lasting privileges in return for their luck and their early economic investment. The primary first settlers (like Eirik) could lord it over later-arriving chieftains and could count on playing a leading role in the new colony for the rest of their lives. Many primary and secondary chiefly pioneers set up pagan temples and, later, Christian churches on their home farm, ritually reinforcing their early authority and forcing other settlers to come to them for religious observances (see discussion in Keller, in press). The first settlers often arranged the location of the local *thing* (assembly, attended annually by free farmers who meet minimum property requirements) and had a great deal to say about its operation.

The first settlers named broad tracts (often naming whole fjord systems after themselves) and local landscape features, giving meaning and form to a culturally blank wilderness. Names had lasting power, both magical and legal, and so did this initial division of landscape on the chieftains' terms. Eirik the Red named the longest fjord of the eastern settlement Eiriksfjord and then claimed the best land in Greenland at its head, naming his manor Brattahlid.

First settlers usually centered their main farms on the best agricultural land, then parceled out less-desirable tracts to followers (see Keller, in press). The Icelandic first settler Skalla-grim was well known for skill in integrating coastal, valley floor, and upland resources. He sent slaves and subordinates to harvest seasonally available seals, birds, and fish. He also assigned workers to *saeters* (shielings, summer pastures with shepherd's huts) in higher elevations, while overseeing the working of the main farm in the prime agricultural zone himself (Durrenburger 1991). Skalla-grim's manor thus was said to "stand on many feet": in modern terms, enjoying a wide niche breath as well as a large foraging territory.

This early "Skalla-grim effect" may have initially dispersed chiefly centers over the whole habitable landscape rather than encouraging villagelike clusters. Certainly in Greenland the archaeological data (backed by a small but growing series of radiocarbon dates) suggests that all of the pockets of potential pasture vegetation in the fjords of West Greenland were occupied by Norse settlers within a generation of first settlement (Berglund 1991; Keller, in press; McGovern 1981). The Norse in Greenland seem to have settled two major regions: the eastern settlement around the modern Qaqortoq and Narssaq districts in the southwest and the smaller western settlement in the more northern Nuuk district.

Initial settlement may have been broad but thin, but as immigration and reproduction continued, the landscape seems to have filled in with small, less-extensive holdings. Many small holdings may initially have been special-purpose seasonal stations later upgraded to year-round farms, or they may have been created by subdividing early chieftain farms among siblings. As the filling in process continued, the niche breadth of individual farms may have narrowed, and access to localized wild resources may have required the cooperation of a local community rather than the coordination of a single chieftain's household labor. As the Viking period ended and local populations increased, slavery was replaced by the use of tenant labor (Durrenburger and Palsson 1989; Hastrup 1985). By ca. 1100, the initial impact of first settlers and the Skalla-grim effect may have been history, but it was to prove a pervasively influential history for the rest of the settlement.

LATER SETTLEMENT AND ARCHITECTURE

West Greenland's plant communities are similar to those of Iceland and the eastern North Atlantic (Buckland 1988) but are restricted to the lower elevations of the warmer inner fjords of the south and southwest—precisely the location of the Norse eastern and western settlements. Virtually every meadow is marked by a Norse ruin, with close correlation between pasture productivity and settlement density in most regions (Christensen 1991; Keller 1991, in press). Summer pasture and hay for winter fodder were critical determinants of the number and productivity of domestic animals, and North Atlantic farmers were keen observers of pasture potential (see McGovern et al. 1988 for examples and discussion).

The distribution of these critical resources was certainly a key variable politically and economically, as well as environmentally. By the height of the settlement, productive pasture was far from evenly distributed. Figure 6.1 presents the pasture area available to a series of well-surveyed western settlement sites we have reason to believe were contemporary (McGovern 1985a) and illustrates the correlation of pasture area with the size of the farm. The site of W51 (Sandnes) was a chieftain's (probably first settler's) farm with one of the three churches in the western settlement (and the only church farm in this sample).

Table 6.1 summarizes available floor areas of halls (a proxy for human space), byres (cattle sheds), barns (hay storage), storage features, and churches for both settlement regions. The larger farms had a distinctive architectural pattern, with byres and storage buildings having far larger floor areas relative to human dwelling spaces than is found on smaller holdings (see McGovern 1992 for discussion). The site with the largest total floor area, and also the site showing the greatest surplus of storage capacity and cattle production, is the bishop's manor at Gardar (site E47; modern Igaliko).

The later Norse Greenlanders were indeed Christianized and eventually acquired a small monastery and nunnery as well as a bishop. The first bishop, Arnald, was provided by the king of Norway around AD 1127 in exchange for a live polar bear. According to Einar Sokkason's saga, the bishop became an active player in Greenlandic elite politics, eventually causing the deaths of most of the important men in the eastern settlement (Jones 1985).

The architectural and settlement data certainly indicate that Arnald and his successors were effective land managers as well as serious competitors with the other, nonclerical chieftains. By the later phases of occupation the episcopal manor at Gardar far outstripped the old first-settler's

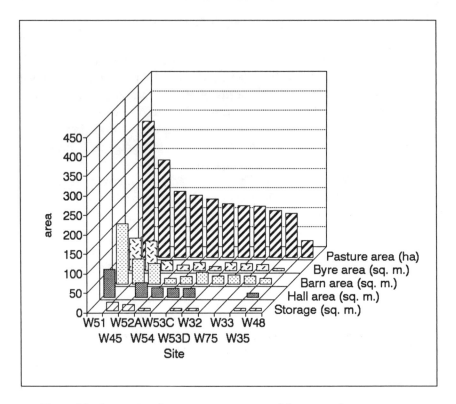

Figure 6.1. Comparison between pasture area and floor space for various uses at eleven sites in the western settlement.

farm at Brattahlid in all our architectural measures. Gardar's massive byres may have held more than 125 cattle (an average farm might have had between three and ten cattle), and an elaborate system of irrigation channels watered the bishop's pastures (Krogh 1982).

It also appears that Gardar was better able to suppress nearby settlement than Brattahlid had been. An excellent locational study by Keller (1991, in press) comparing ruin density and modern pasture productivity in the eastern settlement area reveals that the Gardar area maintained a surplus of pasture relative to site density, while the Brattahlid area did not. In other parts of medieval Europe, churches were often able to maintain and extend landholdings while the secular aristocracy was eventually forced to divide manors among siblings and retainers. A single (rather unreliable) document dating to the mid-fourteenth century and listing church property indicates that the church then owned outright or controlled access

TABLE 6.1.

Comparison of floor space at sites in the eastern and western settlements of Norse Greenland

Site	Site Rank (Name)	Floor Area (sq. m.)				
		Hall	Byre	Barn	Storage	Church
Eastern settlement						
E47	1 Gardar	131	389	353	361	154
E83	2 Hvalsey	82	53	107		68
E29N	2 Brattahlid	66	127	105	118	59
E111	2 Herjolfsnes	66	48	43	59	86
E105	3		20	20		53
E29R	3	35	77	56	51	
E20	3	32				
E66	3		44	36		
E64C	4	19	18	25	7	
E64A	4	14	10	18	8	
E78A	4				5	
Mean		56	87	85	87	84
Western settlement						
W51	2 Sandnes	72	84	155		40
W7	2 Anavik		50	54	38	58
W45	2		77	64	21	
W52A	3	38	25	52	15	
W54	3	24	15	15	6	
W53C	3	23	20	19		
W53D	3	23	11	30	6	
W8	3	21	12	14		
W16	4	14	14	11	12	
W35	4	11	6	14	6	
W32	4		20	20	6	
W33	4		16	20		
W75	4		18	23		
W44	4		14	13		
W48	4				6	
Mean		28	27	36	13	49

to most of the most productive resource spaces in the eastern settlement (Gad 1970; cf. Keller in press).

Whether sponsored by chiefly patrons or ambitious clerics (not mutually exclusive categories in the early Middle Ages), the churches of Greenland clearly played a role in the expression of both status and piety. As has long been noted (Bruun 1918), the stone churches of Greenland are very large by the standards of Atlantic Scandinavia. The episcopal cathedral at Gardar was nearly as large as its counterparts in Iceland (contemporary population estimated at ca. 60–80,000), and it was only one of several large stone churches built during the thirteenth century in Greenland (maximum population ca. 6000). These stone churches were modeled on the latest European fashions and included imported stained glass and English bells as well as costly timber and appropriate vestments. Even if we assume that most of the heavy work of dragging and raising stone was done in the winter, the amount of labor and resources allocated to such ceremonial structures remains impressive for a community whose domestic architecture consisted of a series of low sod huts.

SUBSISTENCE ECONOMY

Our evidence for subsistence economy in Norse Greenland is largely zooarchaeological and locational. Faunal data are available for a large number of Norse sites in Greenland (see McGovern 1985a for summary), as is a rich body of modern biogeographical information (Vibe 1967) and a growing number of paleoecological studies (Buckland 1988; Fredskild 1986; Sadler 1991).

From both documentary and climatic studies, we know that cereal agriculture was never possible on an economic scale in Norse Greenland. Herding and hunting supplied the surpluses that fueled clerical and chiefly building projects. Although the location of the Norse farms in the pasture-rich inner fjords suggests the importance of domesticated cattle, sheep, goats, horses, and pigs, the zooarchaeological evidence indicates a major reliance on wild species of the coast and mountains (see McGovern 1981, 1985b for discussion). Seal and caribou bone often make up the majority of the site archaeofauna, followed by caprines (both sheep and goats) and cattle (fig. 6.2).

The majority of the seals in the assemblage were migratory harp (*Pagophilus groenlandicus*) or hooded (*Cystophora cristata*) seals, while harbor or common seals (*Phoca vitulina*) were locally important in the eastern settlement. Ringed seals (*Phoca hispida*) are rare or absent. The migratory seals were probably caught in the outer fjord zone during their spring migration. Two small seasonal hunting stations have been documented in the outer fjord islands of the western settlement (Gulløv 1983), and it appears that nets and communal boat drives were used to catch groups of

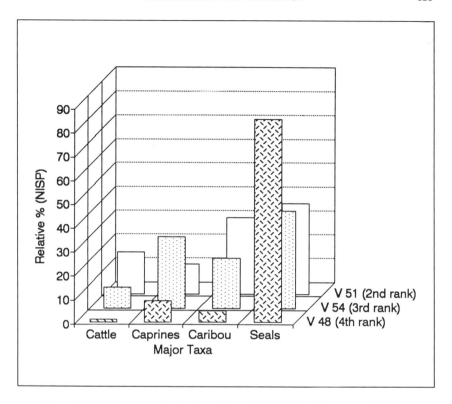

Figure 6.2. Major taxa in the faunal assemblages from three sites of different ranks.

seals at the same time (probably like modern Faroese pilot whale drives). Harpoons, absent from Norse artifact collections, are post-medieval introductions in most of the Scandinavian North Atlantic.

The seasonal round of the Norse Greenlanders (partly based on unpublished tooth sectioning studies carried out by Bryan Hood) may serve to underline the key role of seals (especially the spring harp seal migration) in the Norse subsistence round (fig. 6.3). By late winter, domestic stock would have long since ceased milk production, and stored food would have run short on many farms. Cattle and some sheep and goats were kept in the warm dark byres most of their lives, standing nearly immobile in a rising tide of their own dung. Many of the small Norse cattle had to be carried out to pasture in the spring because their muscles were too weak after a winter of severe inactivity, and it is clear that Greenland was always near the limit for even the most skillful Scandinavian stock-raising techniques.

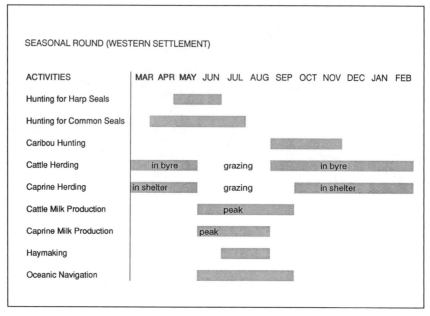

Figure 6.3. Hypothetical Norse seasonal round (western settlement).

These difficult conditions, combined with the very small size of most cattle herds (probably between three and eight animals), suggest the importance of the few large herds (and especially the 100+ herd at Gardar) in buffering the whole community against catastrophic losses and in maintaining the biological viability of the domestic animal population. If they were organized as in Iceland, local communities (*hreppur*) of 15 to 25 farms centered on a single church operated as minimal subsistence units, pooling labor for critical seasonal tasks (like hay harvests and seal hunts), sharing upland common grazing, and providing fodder, food, and replacement stock to members whose holdings were damaged by fire or other disaster. Several authors have independently employed a range of locational techniques centered on known church locations in an attempt to reconstruct Greenlandic regional divisions in both settlement areas; all of them have modeled basic units in the same size range of 15 to 25 farms (Berglund 1982; Keller 1991, in press; McGovern 1980).

The distribution of animal bones in Norse sites further suggests the communal nature of Norse hunting and resource redistribution. The sites with the highest percentage of harp seal bones are those at the highest elevations, often several hours' walk from the nearest salt water. Seabirds most commonly found in Norse middens (alcids, mainly murres and gullemots) are those best taken by groups of hunters exploiting seasonal concentrations, and these bones too are found many kilometers inland.

At the same time dead seals and sea birds were being moved uphill, dead caribou appear to have been moved downhill. Norse caribou hunters appear to have used crossbows (Roussell 1936) and drive systems (Christensen 1991; McGovern and Jordan 1982) to intercept migrating caribou in the higher elevations. Strangely, the highest percentages of caribou bones are found not on the small holdings nearest the drive systems, but on the larger manors closer to the sea (McGovern 1985b). Patterning so contradictory to the normal assumptions of site territory points to the social dimension of resource exploitation in Norse Greenland.

Social hierarchy is apparent in the bone collections as well as in pasture distribution and site architecture (zooarchaeology, architecture, and locational data show high levels of correlation; see McGovern 1985b). Figure 6.2 compares three archaeofauna typical of western settlement sites of second, third, and fourth rank. The role on the larger farm (W51) of domestic mammals, especially cattle, is clear, as is the inverse role of caribou and seal. While elite farms were able to emphasize cattle production and enjoy a diet of dairy produce and deer meat, lowest-ranking farmers must have been strongly dependent upon seal meat taken in the communal drives.

The Norse subsistence economy in Greenland was thus a balanced exploitation of the inner fjord pastures required by the imported domestic animals and of the outer fjords frequented by the migratory seals. Both communal organization and economic hierarchy seem well marked, with the larger holdings playing a critical role in buffering short-term resource crises. Norse Greenland's productive subsistence economy depended upon careful management of socially structured land and resources in a marginal environment relative to traditional forms of European agriculture. Coordination of labor with seasonally variable resources (especially the migratory seals) was critical for the survival and prosperity of the community as a whole. The skills of Norse community managers at different levels are visible today both in the impressive stone churches built so far from the centers of Christendom and in the piles of seal bones in inland middens so far from the sea. Both communal cooperation and social hierarchy shaped the Norse economy more than simple proximity to resources, either material or social.

TRANSATLANTIC TRADE AND
LONG-RANGE HUNTING

Communal cooperation, hierarchical control, and willingness to exploit distant resource spaces are all evident in the remarkable trips to the Nordrsetur, or northern hunting grounds. Documentary sources describe long and dangerous journeys far north of the settlement areas by groups of hunters seeking a range of arctic products but concentrating on walrus ivory and hide (which was used to produce exceptionally strong ships' cable). This hunting ground appears to lie in the modern Disko Bay–Holsteinsborg area, still home to one of the largest concentrations of walrus in the Eastern Arctic. The trips north were apparently an annual event, with a few men probably overwintering regularly (see McGovern 1985a for more complete references and discussion of the Nordrsetur hunt).

Despite the documentary and archaeological evidence for the northern hunt, walrus ivory itself is extremely rare on Norse sites in Greenland. Most of the "ivory" artifacts produced for home consumption are in fact fabricated from the peglike post-canines of the walrus. Rich in walrus, Norse Greenland was singularly poor in walrus ivory; most of this valuable arctic treasure was evidently reserved for overseas trade.

Unlike their contemporaries in Norse Shetland, the Orkneys, and Caithness (Batey 1987; Bigelow 1989; Morris 1985), the Norse Greenlanders did not enter into the expanding exchange of fish for grain that enabled survival and some prosperity to the eastern North Atlantic islands in the later Middle Ages. Instead, the Norse Greenlanders seem to have been locked into an early medieval–Viking period pattern of exchange of durable high-value goods suitable for elite consumption (Keller, in press). In exchange for walrus products and skins, we know that the Norse imported stained glass, church bells, elite clothing and church vestments, building timber, wine, and iron. A careful analysis of the documentary sources (Gad 1970) indicates that no great volume of material could have been imported at any time, and that most Greenlanders probably had only occasional access to imported goods. The rarity of imported artifacts in Greenlandic excavations, even in comparison with Iceland and Shetland, and the finds of bone or antler substitutes for items normally made of metal (including a spectacular whalebone battle axe) serve to confirm Gad's analysis.

While overseas trade may have brought only limited benefit to most Norse Greenlanders, the Nordrsetur hunt may have been costly to many. The northern hunt was described as dangerous, and the wild northern heaths were apparently dangerous places for the medieval Norse hunter.

Pierced amulets carved from walrus post-canines to represent walrus and polar bear have been found on several sites. Whole walrus and narwhal skulls (which normally would have been broken up at the kill site) were deliberately buried in the consecrated soil of the episcopal churchyard at Gardar (Norlund and Stenberger 1934).

Despite such sacred and magical protection, it seems likely that many hunters failed to return from the north. The vessels used were not the ocean-going ships of the Viking period, but small open "six-oared boats" vulnerable to the ice, rocks, and bad weather of the Greenland coast. Even these small boats must have been extremely valuable to a community lacking most shipbuilding timber, and the loss of such vital tools of production must have been felt almost as keenly as the loss of lives when one of the boats went down. These losses were not the only price of the northern hunt and the transatlantic trade it fueled, since the absent hunters could play little role in the labor-intensive summer activities back on the home farms. The northern hunt was expensive in lost lives and resources, but also in deferred or blocked alternate uses for scarce labor and summer days.

CULTURE CONTACT

When the Norse arrived in West Greenland, they found only archaeological traces of the earlier Paleoeskimo inhabitants (Jones 1985). Their first contact with the ancestors of the modern Inuit came ca. 1100–1150, as the Thule folk pushed across from Ellesmere Island and moved down the coast of West Greenland (Schledermann 1990). The *Historia Norvegiae* of ca. 1170 noted that Norse hunters in the Nordrsetur had encountered strange skin-clad *skraelings* (the same term was applied to Native Americans in Vinland one hundred years earlier; see McGhee 1984, Fitzhugh 1985), who did not know metal and used stone and ivory tools. The most remarkable feature of these skraelings was that when merely wounded, they did not bleed, but when finally killed, their blood rushed out dramatically (Gad 1970).

This strange and bloody encounter did not prevent further Inuit migration southwards, and by ca. 1300 large Inuit settlements had been established in the Disko Bay region, and some winter houses had been constructed in the outer fjord zone of the western Norse settlement (Gulløv 1983). The two cultures must have been in increasing contact from ca. 1100–1500, or approximately as long as Native Americans and Europeans have been in contact in the eastern United States following the Jamestown settlement in 1607. Despite ongoing research, we still know frustratingly little about the details of this earlier contact situation (McGhee 1984; McGovern 1979, 1985a). Inuit legends, and scattered references to the skraelings in Scandinavian documents, indicate both peaceful and hostile relationships.

The archaeological evidence for Norse-Inuit contact is strangely one-sided. A growing number of Norse artifacts have been identified in Inuit contexts, including metal objects and woolen cloth, as well as souvenirlike trinkets such as Norse draughtsmen converted into Inuit-style spinning tops. Although no major realignment of Inuit settlement, subsistence, or material culture seems to have occurred, there is abundant evidence on the Inuit side for contact with the Norse settlers.

On the other side, Inuit objects in secure Norse contexts are very rare. A handful of finds, mainly of the nonfunctional souvenir category, are known from the many late phase Norse structures that have been investigated. Notably absent are harpoons or any of the host of refined sea and ice hunting gadgetry so characteristic of Inuit sites. Also absent from Norse collections are the bones of the species of seal most commonly taken with this Inuit technology—the ringed seal (*Phoca hispida*). In the tens of thousands of seal bones from Norse middens examined by three generations of zooarchaeologists, fewer than a dozen have been identified as ringed seal. Although a mainstay of Thule through modern Inuit subsistence (especially in winter), this common animal was not regularly taken by Norse sealers.

Climate Change

As many scholars have observed, the weather turned rotten on the Norse expansion (Lamb 1977[2]). Between ca. 900 and 1200, a period known as the Medieval Climatic Optimum (MCO) produced mean temperatures around 1 to 2°C above the 1930–60 modern baseline. Beginning around 1250, temperatures cooled to around 2 to 3°C below this baseline (Lamb 1977[2]; Ogilvie 1985), producing what many have called the Little Ice Age (LIA). Increasing variation between years and between decades (extreme in the fourteenth century; Dansgaard in Lamb 1977[2]) may have further complicated human economic response. These global climate shifts were of a magnitude to cause significant impact all across the Scandinavian North Atlantic, but they were probably felt first and most strongly in Greenland.

The growing season for pasturage would decrease, probably irregularly, reducing fodder yields and complicating harvest labor scheduling. Longer winters would increase winter fodder demand, just as the capacity to produce fodder would be reduced. Increased drift ice made navigation more dangerous, requiring a new sailing route from Iceland and probably discouraging transatlantic contacts. All these effects would certainly have presented challenges to the Norse Greenlandic economy as we now understand it, and many writers have cited the case of Norse Greenland as a prime remaining example of simple climatic determinism in human affairs. Many climate impact theories have been proposed (see McGovern 1986 for discussion), but most may be reduced to the simple statement "it got cold and they died." The Norse are seen purely as passive victims, overcome by an unanticipated and unstoppable force of nature.

This view is attractively simple, but it ignores several relevant points:

1. The Inuit of West Greenland did not die out, but instead spread and prospered during the same period that saw the extinction of the Norse Greenlanders. Greenland clearly did not become uninhabitable for humans, even during the depths of the LIA, ca. 1650–1700.

2. The Norse Greenlanders also did not die out the moment the climate changed. Much of the impressive church construction occurred after the onset of LIA conditions, and the colony probably endured in some form until ca. 1475–1500. Medieval Scandinavians had developed a multilevel subsistence system, with extensive social buffering, that had survived many short-term climate shifts. Norse Greenland did not succumb to the first, or the hundredth, bad winter. If climate change did play a major role in Norse Greenland's extinction, it cannot have acted alone.

3. When Norse society in Greenland did perish, it did not die in a resource-depleted environment after using up all possible means of survival. In fact, the Norse Greenlanders had failed to make full use of resources locally available, while continuing to deform the subsistence economy to produce inedible prestige goods for export.

These points, particularly the last, require further discussion, for the Norse Greenlanders did indeed die out, and a resource crisis of some sort remains the most likely proximate cause. If simple climatic determinism fails to explain the collapse adequately, then why did they die when it got cold?

Combining modern pasture productivity data for southwest Greenland and Iceland with archaeological and biological survey data and zooarchaeological evidence in a simple spreadsheet model, we can get an idea of the relative productivity of pasture communities within the holdings of

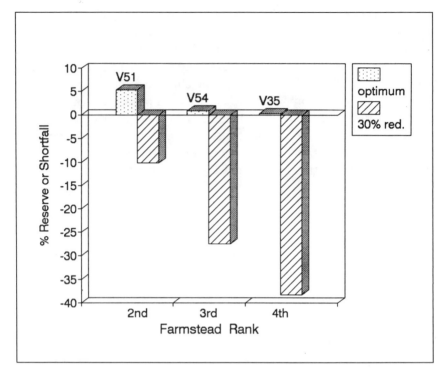

Figure 6.4. Effect of variation in fodder supply on farms of different ranks, modeled under situations of optimum productivity and 30 percent reduction therein.

farms of different rank, and the adequacy of this pasture productivity to supply the fodder needs of the farm's domestic animal stock (see McGovern et al. 1988). Figure 6.4 illustrates the model output for optimum levels of pasture productivity and for a 30 percent reduction in this level (a realistic worst-case scenario given the results of temperature decline impact models and 1920s–80s weather data).

Note that colder periods will not affect all farms equally. The second-rank farm (Gardar is the only example of the first rank) typifies an old first-settler's farm near sea level with relatively abundant pasture and a major investment in cattle. The modeled effects on third- and fourth-rank farms are based on data from less well sited farms with poorer pasturage, smaller numbers of domestic animals, and a greater emphasis on sheep and goat herding. Although all three types experience fodder shortfalls that would require stock reduction, note the disproportion between good year/

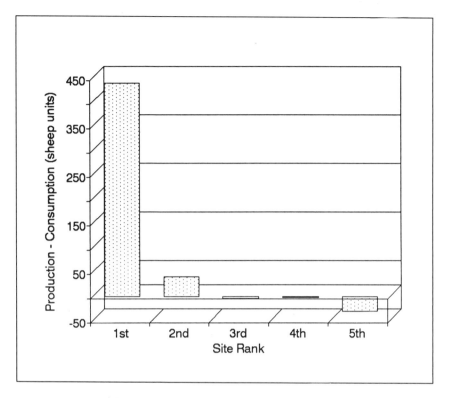

Figure 6.5. Ability of farms of different ranks to be self-sufficient (based on floor space as an indicator of population).

bad year outcomes for the three types. In the western settlement, between 60 and 70 percent of sites fall into the fourth rank. Any adverse climate impact would affect these smallholders first and worst. The pattern of extensive use of wild species (particularly seals) by smallholders observed in the zooarchaeological data makes sense in light of this model prediction.

Using floor space as a proxy indicator, we can also model the balance between probable human population and domestic animal production (meat and milk) on a given site. Again using excavated sites as examples of a given site class, figure 6.5 compares the production-consumption balance for all four site ranks. The unique position of the episcopal farm at Gardar is evident. Even if model assumptions are only broadly correct, it. is clear that Gardar could potentially produce a surplus above its own consumption needs far in excess of any other holding in Greenland.

These models and our locational and zooarchaeological data indicate that by the later phases of occupation, elite farms had a set of characteristics in common:

1. They were least and last affected by adverse climatic impacts on pasture productivity. Bad seasons will first impoverish lower- and middle-ranking farmers, while having comparatively minor effects on upper-ranking farmers. The immediate impact of LIA conditions would have been to steepen the economic and political gradient in the favor of the heirs of the first settlers.

2. They were most involved in domestic mammal (especially cattle) production. Although wild resources were clearly important to elite farms, they probably did not serve the same critical staple role as they did on smaller farms. The commitment of the elite farmers to cattle and to the best pastures would tend to increase as they became increasingly scarce and valued commodities.

3. They played a buffering role as sources of replacement stock and dairy produce for middle- and lower-ranking farms suffering periodic shortages. The more frequently the buffering role was played, the greater probability of loss of real or effective independence on the part of the recipients. The economic functioning of the local community would increasingly depend upon a few major households, even if the majority of farmers did not become actual tenants as they did in contemporary Iceland (McGovern et al. 1988).

The episcopal manor at Gardar played a critical buffering role for the settlement as a whole during large-scale resource crises. Whether managed by Greenlandic elites or foreign-born bishops, Gardar must have exerted unrivaled economic and political influence by later phases.

Social Stratification and Economic Management

Our current data and the results of our various land-use models suggest that later Norse Greenland was neither a haven for independent-minded individualists nor a home for any form of primitive democracy. Although Norse Greenland lacked all the trappings of high medieval feudal society (Keller 1991), it was clearly no longer the flexible, pioneering society of the first settlement era. Getting through the average year required community cooperation, and that community was increasingly likely to be dominated by a few great landowners. Bad years activated a nested series of community buffering strategies, none of which were cost-free to the recipient.

Studies by Arneborg (1991) and Keller (1991) have raised the possibility of significant doctrinal conflict between Greenlanders and the papacy, as well as probable internal elite competition, rather than unquestioned compliance with royal and papal demands (contra McGovern 1981). As in Iceland, the partly ecclesiastical elite may have had more than changing weather to worry about, and they may have been as concerned over the latest papal edicts as over this year's seal harvest. The disproportionately large and elegant churches of Norse Greenland may reflect growing internal competition and local display as well as orders from the continental core. Certainly the remarkable northern hunt could not have been carried out without the active sponsorship and direction of the local elite, who must have played a leading role in ensuring the remarkably efficient collection of processed walrus tusk for export.

In any case, the Greenlandic elite did not hesitate to employ a full range of positive and negative sanctions to enforce their leading role in this tightly managed society. Our last written record of Norse Greenland (from 1408; see Gad 1970) documents both the proper reading of wedding banns and the burning alive of the unfortunate Kolbein for witchcraft the same year.

Management Failure and Population Extinction

In retrospect, we can see that many of the management decisions made by the Greenlandic elite were disastrous (McGovern 1981). Although the scale and timing of the climate changes that affected Greenlandic managers were beyond human control, the vulnerability of their society to particular impacts and the response to perceived challenges and opportunities were certainly subject to culturally mediated political choice. As argued elsewhere (McGovern 1981), it would appear that Norse managers simply managed badly, and their society died as a result.

As Vibe (1967) demonstrates, ocean current dynamics make the west coast of Greenland unstable on the scale of centuries, with any given point on the coast passing through repeated cycles of resource scarcity and plenty as marine resource concentrations move up and down the coast and terrestrial resources undergo boom and bust cycles. The Inuit of West Greenland have survived and prospered by maintaining locational flexibility, moving up and down the long coastline as climate changed and seasonal resource zones shifted.

The Norse were far less mobile. The domestic animal component of their subsistence economy (especially cattle) was closely tied to a few restricted pockets of low-arctic vegetation in the fjords of the southwest. The elite farmers with the richest pastures and heaviest investment in cattle were least likely to consider any adaptive strategy that would devalue these resources. While Norse sealing parties might extend their hunting ranges, the inhabitants would still be tethered to the home farms (and the stone churches) deep in the southern fjords. The politically dominant (but climatically threatened) herding component of the Norse subsistence economy thus limited the possibilities for effective development of the marine hunting component.

The elite connections to the markets and political centers of continental Europe must have proved increasingly difficult to maintain. Documentary sources describe increased East Greenland drift ice as a growing hazard to transatlantic navigation by the mid-fourteenth century. About the same time, changing fashions in Europe were replacing walrus and elephant ivory with Limoges enamels in luxury goods and religious artifacts. Demand for the main product of the costly Nordrsetur hunt was dropping just as the climate-related dangers of both the hunt and the trip across the Atlantic were increasing. We have no evidence for an attempted restructuring of trade goods production, and a late court case describes Greenlanders forcing unwanted trade goods on chance visitors looking only for provisions (Gad 1970). While other North Atlantic communities successfully shifted to commercial fishing, the Greenlanders apparently continued to offer increasingly devalued, old-fashioned goods to the few traders willing to risk the drift ice.

Since the lower-ranking Norse farmers were effectively dependent upon sea mammal hunting anyway, and seventeenth- to nineteenth-century West Greenland was to become an international center for whale, seal, and walrus exploitation, we might imagine that the prospects for enhanced Norse maritime adaptation would be considerable. Even if the Norse farms remained nailed down to the inner fjords, expansion of marine hunting efforts in the local area should have proved productive.

This strategy would almost certainly require acquisition of more Inuit technology and expertise than the Norse Greenlanders apparently were willing to absorb. As we have seen, the Norse lacked both harpoons and the ringed seals normally taken with them, despite nearly three centuries of contact with the Inuit. The complex of whaling gear (large harpoons, float valves, etc.) so successfully employed by the Thule Inuit in West Greenland for five hundred years is also absent. There is also no evidence for the acquisition of Inuit skin boats, despite the shortage of timber suitable for the keels of traditional Scandinavian clinker-built ships.

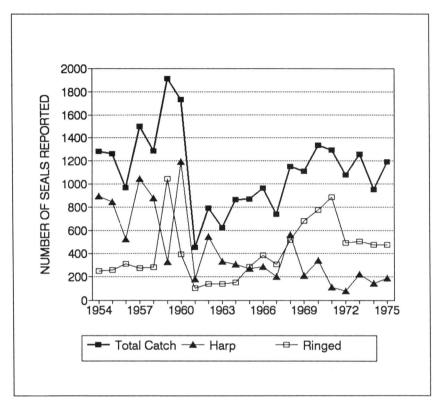

Figure 6.6. Reported seal catch, 1954–1975, Qaqortoq, Greenland.

Modern catch data from southwestern Greenland indicate that the failure of the Norse to exploit ringed seals effectively may have been increasingly costly during climatic fluctuations. Figure 6.6 presents a 21-year record of major seal species taken in one part of the former Norse eastern settlement (for a discussion of these data, see Vibe 1967; McGovern 1986). In the first third of the chart (approximately 1954–60) the total seal catch is dominated by migratory harp seals. The well-documented cooling of the early 1960s (just under 1°C) altered harp seal migrations, causing a crash in catches all along the southwest coast. Harp seal catches did not begin to recover until the 1980s. Note, however, that after a few hard years, the total seal catch reported at Qaqortoq recovered to nearly pre-crash levels—propelled by a steady increase in ringed seal hunting in the period 1960–75. Similar patterns of crash and rapid recovery through shift in target species are evident in catch records for the Narssaq and Nuuk districts in the eastern and western settlements. Because we have no reason to suspect a radical change in seal distribution since Norse times, it would appear that the Norse Greenlanders would have been able to manage a similar shift in critical resources, if they had acquired the necessary technology and skills.

More speculatively, we might also wonder what might have developed from an integration of Norse and Inuit populations and adaptive strategies. The Norse could have provided milk, wool, metal, and access to European markets in exchange for sea mammals, boats, and arctic products. Had the skraelings been properly Christianized and suitably socialized they could even have provided a welcome source of additional profit to their Norse patrons, much as the Sami of arctic Scandinavia provided income to elites in northern Norway. A variation of this pattern was actually developed by the Danish colonial administration in the eighteenth century and provided the basis for a culturally and technologically diverse society that persists to the present day in Greenland.

Speculative scenarios could be further elaborated, but it is clear that Norse Greenland did not perish in a barren wasteland devastated by the Little Ice Age. Instead, they starved in the midst of unexploited resources, with a working model for maritime-adapted northern survival camped on their doorsteps. The death of Norse Greenland was not caused by nature, but by culture.

WORLD VIEW AND MENTAL TEMPLATES

If the leadership of this tight little society did indeed manage so badly that the whole population failed to react appropriately to climate change, cultural competition, and market peripheralization, we might well ask why. After all, there is no lasting advantage to managing your own society so you have the privilege of starving last. We may assume that the managers of Norse Greenland did not intend the outcome that resulted from their self-serving, short-term choices. Why did they choose so badly, dooming themselves and their culture?

As many have observed, humans make decisions based upon culturally mediated perception and interpretation of reality and may or may not consistently observe environmental variables that other humans would find important. Some managers may be more interested in closely tracking church politics and the latest building styles than in accurately recording variability in seal catches. A variety of cognitive maladies common to all managers may have afflicted the Norse elite (discussed in McGovern et al. 1988):

1. False Analogy. The managers' cognitive model of ecosystem characteristics (potential productivity, resilience, stress signals) may be based on the characteristics of another ecosystem (Norway, Iceland) whose surface similarities mask critical threshold differences from the actual local ecosystem.

2. Insufficient Detail. The managers' cognitive model is overgeneralized and fails to allow for the actual range of spatial variability in an ecosystem whose patchiness is better measured in resilience than initial abundance (Moran 1984).

3. Short Observational Series. The managers lack a sufficiently long memory of events to track or predict variation in key environmental factors over a multigenerational period and are subject to chronic inability to separate short-term and long-term processes.

4. Managerial Detachment. The managers are socially and spatially distant from agricultural producers who carry out managerial decisions at the lowest level and who are normally in closest contact with local-scale environmental feedbacks.

5. Reactions out of Phase. Partly as a result of the last two factors, the managers' attempts to avert unfavorable impacts are too little and too late, or apply the wrong remedy.

6. SEP (Someone Else's Problem) (Buckland 1988:7). Managers at many levels may perceive a potential environmental problem but do not feel obligated to take action because their own particular short-term interests are not immediately threatened. Some adverse impacts may actually enhance the managers' position by differentially impoverishing unruly subordinates and potential rivals.

The Norse Greenlanders were probably also subject to a series of obstacles to perception and management that were far more culture-specific. The world view of a particular culture at a particular moment may be a product of both current social and environmental conditions as well as traditional knowledge of variable time depth.

The world view of the medieval Scandinavians of the North Atlantic is set out in considerable detail in law codes and sagas, and it has been the subject of a series of scholarly analyses (Andersson and Miller 1989; Byock 1988; Durrenburger and Palsson 1989; Hastrup 1985; Miller 1986; Palsson

1991). In her extended analysis of the twelfth-century Grågås law code, Hastrup describes a world view that rigidly partitions land and society into a series of dual oppositions. Law, society, home, and order lay on one side, and dangerous, lawless chaos lay on the other (Hastrup 1985:136–51).

These categories had a strong locational aspect. The farmyard and home field of the family farm were bounded by a low earthen dike (still visible archaeologically), which provided legal and symbolic security. An assault within a man's home field was legally more serious than one farther from home, and a variety of malign nonhuman beings were magically confined outside the dike. In Iceland, the center of human order and society lay at Thingvellir (the site of the major annual assembly), and the opposing center of natural chaos and evil lay in the desolate "lava field of misdeeds" in the unpopulated arctic interior. Persons sentenced to permanent exile were both literally and figuratively set outside the bounds of human society. They could be killed on sight without the need to pay for spilling their blood (blood money), and they had to live in the wilderness, where they would be exposed to weather, hunger, and the inhuman creatures that haunted such places (several mountains in Iceland are still named "Trolls-Church"). A heroic outlaw could win readmission to human society by killing other outlaws and struggling successfully against the evil creatures of the wilderness.

Clearly, this was not a nineteenth- or twentieth-century romantic world view that sees pristine nature in positive opposition to corrupting culture, but a more traditional European dichotomy of good, safe (but fragile) human culture and dangerous, potentially evil nature. Both pagan and Christian cosmology saw the natural world as potentially hostile, and both gloomily predicted a steady decline of humanity and the human world, ending in Ragnarok/Armageddon/Götterdämmerung.

Hastrup (1989) has argued that the identification of wilderness with threat and evil was so extreme in late medieval Iceland that it inhibited effective exploitation of distant saeters (shielings). Although changes in vertical zonation during the LIA probably also played a part in settlement contraction, there seems little debate over the character of this medieval nature-culture division among scholars most familiar with the Norse documentary and literary evidence.

What effect did this cognitive division have on the fate of Norse Greenland? Figure 6.7 presents the world view probably shared by medieval Greenlanders and Icelanders (categories based upon Hastrup 1985, Palsson 1991). Although some individuals (heroes, witches, and Christian clerics) could safely act as intermediaries, the passage between realms

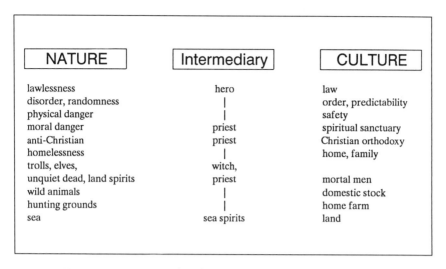

Figure 6.7. Summary of medieval Greenland/Icelandic world view.

was dangerous and uncertain. In this light, the elaborate magical buffering associated with the trips to the Nordrsetur hunting grounds becomes immediately comprehensible.

This world view also places the Inuit in an ambiguous position. Are they normal humans of a different culture (like the English, Franks, Irish, etc.) to fight, trade with, marry, and learn from? Are they instead non-human creatures of nature to be shunned? Like trolls, they did not bleed when wounded. Like many water-beings, they did not use iron weapons. Had any Norseman overcome the barriers of language he would have encountered an Inuit world view and ideology full of humanlike animals and powerful sorcery not based upon a nature-culture dichotomy like his own. It is all too easy to imagine Norsemen culturally preprogrammed to reject all innovations from the Inuit, fatally ignoring tainted technology and alien expertise and keeping closer and closer to home, hearth, and church (Hastrup 1989).

This structuralist analysis leaves many questions unanswered. As Palsson argues:

> Some scholars concentrate on the search for abstract semiotic systems, emphasizing cultural codes rather than social action-language rather than speaking. . . . The saga-people become trapped in the superorganic, as prisoners of medieval culture. . . .
> We cannot observe or participate in the praxis of the natives, but

the "world out there" presented in our second-hand field notes
is a world of active persons—not of rules and things. (Palsson
1991:17–18)

Both traditional structuralist and traditional ecosystemic cultural
ecological analyses have been criticized as overly static and unreflective
of the active role of individual humans in reshaping meaning and realign-
ing system linkages. If the Norse Greenlanders did maintain the ultimately
maladaptive world view documented in their laws and literature, maintaining cultural purity at the cost of biological extinction, we still must ask
why. It is as much of a dead end to blame their extinction on rigid cultural
programming as to resort to simple climatic determinism.

In responding to social situations, as well as to environmental
changes, the individual Norse colonist in fact had a range of potential
options open. The relative rigidity of the Norse world view and its enforce-
ment were variables that could be altered from one generation to the next.
The early pioneer settlers like Skalla-grim possessed the same cultural baggage yet showed far greater adaptive flexibility than their fourteenth- and
fifteenth-century descendants. The Norse world view was subject to conscious manipulation, reinterpretation, and alteration (as the battles over
Christian doctrine indicate). If it solidified into a rigid barrier to successful
adaptation, fatally limiting options in a changing world, then this rigidity
was a *result* of such manipulation. The choice *not* to innovate is a real choice
made by particular people in a particular political and economic context.

During the long contact period between Inuit and Scandinavian in
Greenland, many on both sides must have discovered mutual humanity,
and it is hard to imagine that Norse seal hunters never admired the sealing
skills of the kayaker. Had the Norse been a simple band-level egalitarian society, we might easily imagine that households adopting Inuit technology would gradually replace households that did not, as selection took
its toll on the overly conservative. It is hardly an accident that these life-
saving skills were so systematically rejected—it took a great deal of effort
on somebody's part.

We have seen that Norse Greenland was far from egalitarian, and
selection did not operate entirely at the level of the individual household
or kin group. Instead, a multifarm community, ritually and economically
dependent on a few large manors, was the minimal unit of survival. If
alteration of the seasonal round, labor allocation, or social contract was
proposed, its adoption or rejection would be a community decision highly

influenced by the opinions of the wealthier farmers. According to our data and models, short-term climatic stresses would tend to enhance the authority of the elites and increase the dependency of the majority. Propelled by short-term economic necessity, the Norse social units may have emphasized cohesion and communal solidarity at the expense of innovation and cross-cultural experimentation.

If increased Inuit technology transfer and a declining emphasis on inner-fjord pastures were optimal for the society as a whole, they were by no means optimal for the elites. Some Nordrsetur hunters or seal-dependent smallholders may have seen greater benefits in a more mobile existence and more merit in Inuit lifeways than did the partly clerical Norse elite, proud of their stained glass and church bells. In the contest for community support, however, there is no question who was better placed to manipulate both world view and social sanctions. Increasing the rigidity of the existing northwest European nature-culture split through sermons, thing meetings, and the occasional execution at the stake would be only one means of bolstering social control in a threatened society.

The economic hierarchy that fostered this deadly control was itself a product of pasture distribution and the initial division of land and resources. The Norse pathway to extinction was directed by the distribution of natural resources, by the pattern of climatic impact, by culture-specific cognitive patterns, as well as by divergent class interests. No single decision, but a cascade of decisions closing options and forestalling innovation made Norse Greenland one of the most conservative of the Scandinavian North Atlantic colonies. Culture, ecology, and history together provided the backdrop for the last fatal decision not to choose.

CONCLUSION

Whatever combination of unenlightened self-interest, class conflict, imperfect knowledge, and maladaptively rigid world view produced the disastrous management choices of the Greenlandic elite, the result was fatal to the whole society. Many important questions remain unresolved in Greenlandic archaeology, and more research is urgently needed to go beyond facile generalization. It seems clear, however, that like characters in a proper classical tragedy, the Norse Greenlanders contributed significantly to their own grim fate.

The case of Norse Greenland may have some disquieting parallels in the modern world. Like the Norse Greenlanders, many humans today are pursuing limited, but intensive strategies of exploitation requiring precarious balancing of distant resource zones and markets. Like the Norse, many economies have developed high levels of vulnerability to sudden change in a changing earth. Like the Norse cathedral in the arctic, there are today many monuments to peoples living beyond the means of local resources. Like the Norse elites, we are today very certain of the complete adequacy of a particular world view, and we are often willfully ignorant of alternate sources of expertise.

If modern managers of global resources respond to change and challenge no better than their predecessors in Norse Greenland, Ragnarok may yet prove more than myth. Like the Norse Greenlanders, however, we are not inevitably the prisoners of history and culture. Like them, we have many potential options. We can choose to broaden, rather than restrict, the management subculture and actively seek alternate courses. If the case of Norse Greenland can spur such efforts, then perhaps the Norse Greenlanders themselves will not have suffered and struggled and finally died in vain.

Note

I would like to thank all the people from many countries and disciplines whose hard work and kind cooperation have made field work in the North Atlantic so enjoyable over the past fifteen years. I am particularly grateful to our hosts in Greenland and Iceland, and to the field crews whose endurance and good humor were so often tested. Particular thanks are due to Claus Andreasen, Tom Amorosi, Jette Arneborg, Gerald F. Bigelow, Paul Buckland, Joel Berglund, and Christian Keller for providing practical help and constant intellectual stimulation. Thanks are also due to our hosts at the School of American Research in Santa Fe for making our stay so productive and relaxing. Funding for research reported here was generously provided by the National Science Foundation, the National Geographic Society, NATO's Scientific Grants Program, the Wenner-Gren Foundation for Anthropological Research, the American-Scandinavian Foundation, and the PSC-CUNY Research Grants Program. Anne, Daniel, and Eliza made it all worthwhile. All errors of fact or interpretation remain my responsibility.

Chapter 7

Population Ecology and Civilization in Ancient Egypt

FEKRI A. HASSAN

At a time when overpopulation and the prospects of accelerated climatic change are regarded as imminent threats to human survival and prosperity, archaeological and historical information that furthers our understanding of the long-term survival of human civilizations is indispensable. From it we can hope to gain insight into the magnitude of current problems, suggestions for ameliorative action, and clues to pitfalls in thinking and management. Egypt, with its long and eventful history, is a rich source of historical and archaeological data that may identify factors contributing to human survival under changing environmental conditions and the continuous flux of social, political, economic, and cultural forces.

The history of Egyptian civilization began seven thousand years ago when settled farming villages first appeared on the fertile banks of the Nile. Within two thousand years, the cultural landscape of Egypt was almost totally transformed. Villages and hamlets dotted the Nile floodplain from Nubia to the Delta. Towns and religious centers stood above the flat valley as vivid markers of the new era (Hassan 1988). Most of Egypt was under the rule of a single king. Within the span of three centuries thereafter, a prosperous state and a dynasty of divine kings erected the most ambitious architectural edifices of classical antiquity, the great pyramids of Giza, which remain today as striking reminders of the achievements of one of the earliest nation-states, 4600 years ago. For three millennia Egyptian civilization continued to flourish, until it was contained within the folds of the Greek, Roman, and eventually the Arab world.

Ancient Egyptian civilization may dazzle us with its monumental architecture, fascinating hieroglyphic writing, and exquisite art, but to understand its full glory we must consider the lives of the successive generations that sustained it, how they worked the land, how their fortunes changed with a changing Nile, and how they managed to maintain an ongoing social enterprise amid so many forces that worked against a cohesive, integrated social order.

CIVILIZATION, POPULATION, AND SOCIETY

Although we cannot draw ironclad historical laws from specific archaeological case studies, we can recognize structured sets of relations that crosscut regions and transcend time. The survival and prosperity of agricultural or agroindustrial populations is primarily a function of managing the production and consumption in which people of different ages, genders, occupations, and levels of wealth and power participate. Accumulation and allocation of capital, technological know-how, and inputs of labor and energy are structural elements in the dynamics of a civilization.

A "civilization" that sustains such things as monumental architecture, great cities, written culture, and fine arts is primarily a complex organization of numerous regional human groups. It is a result of diverse human interactions with the environment and the collaborative and competing interests of various social entities. Large populations, in early as well as modern nation-states, have sustained this complex organization through centralization of power and a hierarchy of social dominance and subordination. Such structures are constantly threatened by competing centers of power and power-hungry groups (Hassan 1981a).

Yet this organization is best viewed not as a homeostatic human ecosystem (see Winterhalder 1984) but as a totality of various units of production, consumption, and power (cf. Patterson 1990), held together by mutual interests, coercion, or ideological "glue" and stirred constantly to change through conflict. Conflicts often result from a clash of interests. The plurality of a large population in a state society is structured not merely on a hierarchy of power from peasants to king but also on a *heterarchy* of power centers of every variety (see Crumley 1987a, 1987b). In Egypt, coalitions and antagonisms between the military, the priesthood, and provincial rulers were as crucial in shaping the cultural landscape during the New Kingdom as was the opposition between peasants and elite. All of these might depend, to a greater or lesser extent, on local and regional economic and ecological factors, amid a host of other conflicts and allegiances.

Overall production and consumption in state-level societies are indisputably related to the size of various population sectors and their respective rates of production and consumption. Hence the dynamics of a society cannot be properly understood without knowledge of demographic conditions and factors that influence rates of production (management, capital, labor, energy, natural resources) and consumption (standard of living, values, expectations). For example, a complex state involves a relatively large number of administrators as well as individuals and groups involved in the manufacture, transport, and trade of commodities. To partake of the benefits of an integrated economy or, in later stages, to stay out of harm's reach, farmers end up supporting a non-food-producing portion of the population through taxation, exchange, or services.

Through time the size and demands of the non-food-producing sector grow. Concomitantly food production shifts from a primarily "home" economy, in which effort is directed at satisfying family or community needs, to an economy that allocates a sizable portion of production to non-food-producers. The required increase in productivity can be met only by greater labor input, a change in labor arrangements, or increasing yield per food producer. Increased labor input occurs through prolonging the duration of the workday, increasing the number of workdays per week, expanding or increasing the seasons of agricultural labor, or increasing the number of laborers. Increased productivity may also result from specialization—as, for example, in the segregation of herding, fishing, and farming activities. It may also consist of managerial or technological changes that promote an increase in yield per capita, such as improved techniques of weeding, irrigation, or fertilization, or the introduction of new crops or farm implements, or changes in landholdings, the foundation of credit unions, and so forth. Most, if not all, of these "innovations" or improvements are closely linked with natural resources in a number of ways, such as the size and pattern of cultivable land, the climate, the availability of water, soil characteristics, topography, accessibility of labor, and biotopic composition. They are also related to demographic variables, such as family size, age composition, migration patterns, population growth rate, and spatial settlement patterns.

Ultimately the effectiveness of the machinery of a state society is expressed in population and resources. In some cases interregional state organization may eventually collapse into regional social units or simply deteriorate. Ecological disasters may reduce farmers' ability to produce beyond their own subsistence needs, or the demands of a top-heavy economy may exert a degree of misery and suffering that compels farmers to rebel, desert their land, or starve. All of these outcomes are known to have happened in Egypt in historical times. During these periods the whole fabric of society, including religious practices and art, is likely to be shaken and reshaped.

The continuity of a civilization is ensured when the management sector absorbs the influx of critical goods without overloading the productive sector. In the long run the expansion of the management sector and its allied services (traders, craftspeople, police, tax collectors, clerks, military personnel, retainers) can only continue by appropriating the services of more land and labor. The additional resources thus gained permit the allocation of state revenues and labor toward technological, administrative, and military enterprises. But territorial expansion adds to overhead costs because of the requirements of investment in transport (roads, draft animals, carts, boats), an increase in the number of middlemen, the establishment of military outposts to guard transport nodes, and other military expenses necessary to maintaining annexed territories. A state pushed to the limit of its secured supply line and dependent upon the continuous flow of critical and costly goods from distant territories is in a "metastable" condition. That condition can be prolonged for a while through—singly or in combination—sound bureaucracy, technical advances in productivity, maintenance of adequate transport facilities, military superiority, and benign ecological conditions. But sooner or later environmental degradation of resources, surfacing of inner conflicts, climatic and ecological disasters, or the rise of competing states with less bureaucratic fat and more military muscle will promote rapid collapse of an "older" civilization.

In an extended military empire with a high ratio of consumers to food producers and with a high rate of managerial consumption, the native population can increase beyond the ability of interior resources and labor input to support it. As this geographically expanded state begins to crumble, non-food-producers are likeliest to suffer first. This situation leads to intolerable overexploitation of the peasants and a breakdown in social order. Various powerful sectors in the society—the king and his court, provincial chiefs, priests, and the military—begin to compete for scarce resources and for control of disintegrating power structures. This competition can accelerate the collapse. The various elites vie for power until one prevails. The skill of the new leadership, the ecological conditions, and the strength of internal opponents or foreign threats can prolong or shorten the new regime.

REGIONAL PRODUCTIVITY, DIVERSITY, AND ADAPTABILITY

Economic production driven by demands for consumption is inextricably linked to available natural resources within a regional context. The perceived political and geographical boundaries of a region, generally the ecospace in which cultural activities are habitually undertaken, both define and express social organization and modes of production and consumption, as well as transportation and communication. As societies change, this "landscape" (Crumley and Marquardt 1987) and its boundaries become altered or modified.

In my analysis, the degree of integration and mutual dependency between regions, and the degree of cooperation between producers and managers within and between regions, constitute the most critical structural nodes in the continuity and prosperity of a society. Two closely related concepts in this dynamic are *diversity* and *adaptability*. Homogenization and simplification of a society's economic base, often associated with attempts to increase production,[1] reduce diversity and place the majority of the population at great risk in times of economic or environmental perturbation. The capacity of a society to cope with adverse conditions is also a function of economic and technological diversity, including the breadth of available knowledge of alternatives for action and management. A society's capacity for revitalizing its organization and developing coping strategies can be called its adaptability.

My previous work on climate and Nile floods (Hassan 1981b, 1986) clearly indicates that climatic conditions are rarely constant or uniformly cyclic. Climate changes episodically at various time scales and with varying intensity. Most climatic fluctuations occur at time scales beyond the reach of modern records; thus scientists have increasingly turned to historical and archaeological data to reconstruct long-term time series that reflect climatic episodes. These data are also valuable for tracing variability over shorter intervals within episodes—that is, climatic phenomena that recur frequently enough to influence human perceptions of predictability over the course of a generation or two.

The effects of unexpected climatic changes can undermine the stability of a civilization, causing social disorder, famines, depopulation, or warfare. However, the impact of climatic change on a society depends ultimately on the efficacy of the socioeconomic and political organization and the rate of consumption of critical goods relative to labor input and productivity. A combination of high consumer demands, a work force pushed to its limits, and a high dependence on imports may offer the opportunity for further economic prosperity to one segment of the population, but it also places the entire society at risk of collapse within a relatively short span—a few hundred years. Ancient civilizations like Egypt survived such mishaps and were regenerated only because food production was never totally and inextricably linked to centralized authority.

The annual Nile floods have always been the vital pulse of the human ecology of Egypt. Discussion below, after some background remarks on the early human ecology of the region and the nature of the Nile flood itself, builds on estimates of the ancient population time to arrive at a historical overview of the short- and long-term effects of the Nile flood on human affairs.

THE HUMAN ECOLOGY OF EARLY EGYPT

With an initial population of ten thousand or perhaps only a few tens of thousands, the early farming communities of the Nile Valley were not wholly dependent on the cultivation of cereals. In addition to farming, they herded sheep, goats, cattle, and pigs, and they hunted, fished, fowled, and gathered wild plants (Hassan 1988). Their increasing dependence on cultivated cereals, which had become the staple food by the time of the Old Kingdom (Butzer 1976:86), was a reflection of sedentary settlement patterns and the greater productivity of cereal grains. Sedentariness, which favored stationary food-processing equipment, storage facilities, and access to fertile natural basins, reinforced agricultural strategies that minimized long-term mobility. Hunting had become an almost negligible source of food by the Middle Predynastic (Nagada I).

The decline in hunting may have resulted from the depletion or withdrawal of wild game from the proximity of early villages, which necessitated longer trips away from home base. Since domestic animals could be pastured in floodplains, herding became a more productive alternative to precarious hunting along the margins of the adjacent desert. Larger edible game would have been hunted out quickly,[2] and carnivores would have been hunted down or chased away because of the threat they posed to herds.

Fishing and fowling also provided the animal protein needed to supplement a cereal diet. Fishing in particular has been a major source of animal protein throughout Egyptian history, as other meats have become progressively more expensive. Fish have remained a renewable resource because of the high biotic potential of fish, low-efficiency fishing technology, and difficulty of locating fish.

Food intake from cattle, sheep, goats, and pigs ultimately declined, probably because of incentives for more efficient land use. A given area of land can sustain more people through a grain crop than it can through cattle: the energy conversion factor yields a ratio of close to 10:1. Over the long run grain would thus have been preferred as avoiding excessive labor input for the same amount of return. Moreover, with the emergence of a stratified society by the Late Predynastic and its entrenchment during the Old Kingdom, farmers would have had to boost production beyond family subsistence needs. The likely responses to this increased demand would have been to increase family size (to increase the labor force) and to allocate more work to the cultivation of the highly productive cereal grains.

Thus by the time of the Old Kingdom a great proportion of the natural basins in the Nile floodplain were under cereal cultivation. Land was annexed as population expanded, and villages split to form daughter villages. The grasslands of the floodplain may have been cleared for new fields. Trees such as acacia and tamarisk were cut down for fuel or to make tools, furniture, and boats. Gradually the distribution of trees was dramatically reduced.

The most important and perhaps the most ancient constructions used to control the hydrography of the Nile Valley were dikes, earthen embankments along rivers and canals that routed the Nile's northward flow downstream into natural basins. The dikes also served as roads and were the only means for connecting villages during summer inundations, when the rest of the country was under water. These embankments (*djisr,* pl. *djsour*) were of two main types: public dikes, of interregional importance, and local dikes that benefited small communities. The construction and maintenance of public dikes was under government supervision. High floods could destroy dikes entirely and thus seriously interfere with agricultural planning.

Lift irrigation was limited in ancient times. The *shaduf,* a simple water-lifting device, was introduced perhaps as late as 1250 BC, during the New Kingdom. The shaduf can water about a quarter of an acre (approximately one-tenth of a hectare) daily. Archimedes' screw (*tambour*), introduced in Hellenistic times, could irrigate three-quarters of an acre (around three-tenths of a hectare) per day. A more efficient device also used in the Hellenistic period was the *saqia,* which could irrigate one to five acres (four-tenths to two hectares) per day, depending on the depth of the water.

Agriculture, Irrigation, and Expansion

During the Old Kingdom and perhaps into the beginning of the New Kingdom, the area of the Nile Valley that could be irrigated was naturally greater
than the area under cultivation. During the Old and Middle Kingdoms,
increases in population were accommodated by simple extensification of
agriculture: unused land was simply claimed for new cultivation. The increase in population that occurred during the Middle Kingdom involved
both extensification and intensification: cultivation of new land and improved cultivation of existing arable land. Under the New Kingdom, with
the growing exigencies of costly wars and the demands of a broaden-
ing non-food-producing class (noblemen, priests, and the court), adequate
production could be sustained only through heavy taxation, more efficient
irrigation, new crops, and land reclamation at the state level. These policies characterize the Greek and Roman periods as well and account for a
continued increase in population, albeit at a slower rate than before. Ultimately, however, the hydrography of the Nile set the limit to population,
as Egypt was continually reminded.

In ancient as in modern Egypt, Nile water was a major source of prosperity or poverty. The annual Nile floods, which literally resurrected the
land, were nevertheless anticipated with apprehension: they varied considerably in strength, in some years bringing too little water and silt, in
others flooding to such extremes that canal and field systems were damaged or destroyed. Recent investigations of the historical record of these
floods from AD 645 to the present (Hassan 1981a) and of the geologic
record during the Holocene (Hassan 1986) have revealed both long-term
and short-term episodic changes in Nile floods, in addition to stochastic
changes. These changes, in the height, timing, peak, duration, and sequence of the annual summer flood, are highly unpredictable. Even today
forecasts are unreliable, and it is unlikely that ancient Egyptians could
have arrived at any reliable predictive strategy.

Changes in the volume of the Nile floods occur at several scales: over
intervals of about 35 years (20–50 years), 150 years (120–180 years), 300
to 500 years, 1000 to 1600 years, and even longer stretches of "geological" time. Except for signs notable at the shortest interval, changes in the
Nile flood operate beyond the memory span of a single human generation,
or even two generations. Variations can thus scarcely be recognized in any
orderly way to serve as a basis for reliable prediction.

Variations in annual discharge can be drastic. From the late 1800s to
the early 1900s average daily flow was roughly 129 billion cubic meters.

In 1879 a maximum of 129 billion cubic meters per day was reached. In 1913 discharge fell to a minimum of barely 44 billion cubic meters per day. Such variations were initially reported by Hurst (1957:260–62), who noted that for the periods with well-established records, 1869–98 was a period of very high floods, whereas 1899–1942 was a period of very low floods. When the Aswan flood gauge reaches 93.3, a flood is considered dangerous. In the period 1869–98, twenty-two of the total of thirty annual floods passed 93.0; sixteen of those passed 93.3. Over the next forty-four years, only two floods passed 93.3. In the first period the difference between highest and lowest annual floods (at peak flow) was 2.75 meters, which amounts to 20 billion cubic meters per day.

Despite this huge volume, water shortage is an enduring problem owing to the seasonality of the Nile flood. The flood peaks in August and September; spring drought accompanies minimum flow in April. Before massive capacity for water storage, only recently made possible by the construction of the Aswan Dam (1902) and later the Aswan High Dam (1971), cultivation of summer crops was necessarily restricted to land immediately adjacent to the river.

The impact of variations in the Nile flood on Egyptian population and economy is unmistakable. Variation directly affects agricultural productivity by changing the size of arable area. Ninety-one times during the period from AD 640 through 968 discharge fell below the requirements of irrigation. In the remaining years the Nile was anomalously high (Abu-Zayed 1987). Farmers thus had to contend with low floods three or four years of every decade. In 1877 a low flood, two meters below average height in Upper Egypt, left 62 percent of Qena Province and 75 percent of Girga Province unirrigated (Willcocks and Craig 1913).

Annual variations in the flood can have a particularly acute impact on population and economic prosperity when poor floods occur in successive years. Low floods in AD 962–68 and for a decade around AD 1059–66 had devastating effects—what might be called the "Joseph effect" after the biblical account of the seven fat and seven lean years, except that these variations have no regular periodicity (Hassan 1981a).

The indirect effects of variable annual floods can be equally dire. Historical records from the early Islamic period to the present offer instances when famine, plague, or political disorder that contributed to misery and depopulation occurred in the wake of excessively low, catastrophically high, or erratic Nile floods (tabulated below). Famines in the wake of the low Nile in AD 967 reportedly led to the death of 600,000 persons in and around Fustat (Old Cairo). In the famine of 1200–1201 people became so desperate that—according to one eyewitness, Abdel Latif Al-Baghdadi, a visiting physician from Iraq—they resorted to cannibalism among other horrors. Al-Baghdadi estimated that about one hundred to five hundred persons died daily from hunger. He also observed that, among crafts-people, of the nine hundred weavers in Cairo, no more than nineteen were left alive at the end of the famine. This estimate—that 110,000 died in the span of twenty-two months in Cairo alone—seems exaggerated, but it indicates the scale at which population disasters relating to low flood were reckoned by contemporaries. In the Terrible Famine (al-Shiddat ull-Uzmma, literally "The Greatest Crisis") of AH 447 (AD 1059), which lasted unbroken for seven years, horses, asses, dogs, and cats were consumed before people at last began to eat each other. Passersby were caught in the streets by hooks let down from windows, drawn up, killed, and cooked. Human flesh was sold in public.

Over the long run, the high frequency of one of these series of "water famines" is likely to define the ceiling for population that can be sustained given any particular mode of production. Even beneath that ceiling, annual agricultural productivity in ancient times was extremely variable. Crop yields could also vary drastically from one irrigated basin to the next, de-pending on changes in geomorphology of the floodplain as a result of silta-tion and erosion. At times, only storage coupled with regional or national integration of supplies could have prevented severe depopulation. The rural population was vulnerable to famines if regional or national manage-ment collapsed. The urban and ruling population was equally vulnerable under severe conditions, when depopulation reduced the labor force.

Egyptians overcame a high frequency of severe ecological trauma by maintaining a population sufficiently large to provide ample revenues (for the nobles, priests, and royal court) but at the same time small enough to avoid running into one disaster after another. A population was likely to suffer if its numbers rose beyond the critical carrying capacity of "average" flood stages (see Hassan 1978).

The Population Size of Ancient Egypt

With the exception of Butzer's (1976) analysis, estimates of size and fluc-tuation of the Egyptian population before medieval times have been highly speculative. Population estimates have ranged wildly from a few millions to as much as twenty million (Hollingsworth 1969). Ancient historical ac-counts themselves are conflicting. In 60 BC the Greek historian Diodorus

TABLE 7.1.
Estimation of probable population of ancient Egypt

	Old Kingdom	New Kingdom	Greco-Roman
Area in feddans	1.1 million	1.5 million	2.25 million
Yield	450 kg/feddan	600 kg/feddan	800 kg/feddan
Seeds	90 kg/feddan	120 kg/feddan	160 kg/feddan
Loss	45 kg/feddan	60 kg/feddan	80 kg/feddan
Yield to elite (tax)	70 kg/feddan	110 kg/feddan	200 kg/feddan
Net yield/feddan	245 kg	310 kg	360 kg
Consumption/capita	200 kg/yr	180 kg/yr	150 kg/yr
Total rural population	1.35 million	2.56 million	5.76 million
Urban population	67,500	154,000	403,000
Total population	1.42 million	2.74 million	6.16 million

reported a native Egyptian population of three million, a much lower figure than the 7.5 million quoted by Josephus in AD 66, under Herod Agrippa. Butzer's estimates, based on the number and size of settlements, offer attractively "reasonable" results. Yet in view of the inherently unreliable nature of primary archaeological data and the hidden fallacies of historical analogy, his careful work deserves corroboration through other methods. Thus far I have experimented with four such methods, but my focus here is on a method based on the agricultural ecology and economy of Egypt. The key variables in this method are (1) the cultivable area of the Nile Valley and the Delta before the introduction of perennial irrigation; (2) gross crop yields for the Pharaonic, Hellenistic, and Islamic periods; (3) net crop yields, after deduction of (a) seed reserved for further cultivation, (b) seed lost to pests or disease, and (c) seed allocated toward taxes; (4) rate of per capita grain consumption; and (5) ratio of urban to rural population (table 7.1). Tables 7.2 and 7.3 present the same scheme with adjustments for lower crop yield, subsistence, and variable taxation for Greco-Roman Egypt.

Cultivable Area. The total area of Upper Egypt is estimated at 10,379 square kilometers. Let us assume that about 25 percent was cultivable by natural basin irrigation in good years. Natural basin irrigation may have been expanded to 30 percent of total area during the New Kingdom through the introduction of *shaduf* water-lifting technology. During the Greco-Roman period this area could have been further expanded to 38 percent as a result of land reclamation and further improvements in irrigation technology.

TABLE 7.2.

Estimation of probable population of Greco-Roman Egypt assuming different rates of taxation and minimum subsistence levels

	25% Tax	40% Tax	48% Tax
Area in feddans	2.25 million	2.25 million	2.25 million
Yield	700 kg/feddan	700 kg/feddan	700 kg/feddan
Seeds	140 kg/feddan	140 kg/feddan	140 kg/feddan
Loss	70 kg/feddan	70 kg/feddan	70 kg/feddan
Tax	175 kg/feddan	280 kg/feddan	340 kg/feddan
Net yield/feddan	310 kg/feddan	210 kg/feddan	150 kg/feddan
Consumption/capita	150 kg/yr	150 kg/yr	150 kg/yr
Total rural population	4.65 million	3.15 million	2.25 million
Total population	4.98 million	3.37 million	2.40 million

Assuming 38 percent as the maximum, the total cultivable area amounts to 3925 square kilometers or 934,150 feddans.[3] (One feddan = 4200 square meters or 1.038 acres.)

We can also assume that the area under cultivation in the Delta likewise expanded in Greco-Roman times, after an initial phase of reclamation during the New Kingdom. An early modern estimate (AD 1840) reported that the proportion of area of cultivable land in the Delta to such land in Upper Egypt was 1.4:1. We should assign a somewhat lower ratio for ancient times, perhaps as low as 0.8:1 during the Old Kingdom and rising to 1:1 during the New Kingdom.

Crop Yield. Gross crop yield of wheat and barley in Egypt from AD 1805 to 1952 ranged from 675 to 777 kilograms per feddan (see, e.g., Selim 1940), compared with 200 to 300 kilograms per feddan in medieval Europe (Evans 1980). We may thus assume that 800 kilograms per feddan was the highest yield possible under the best conditions of marling, manure fertilization, adequate irrigation and drainage, and favorable agricultural policy from the Greco-Roman period until the 1950s of the present era. Looking backward, we may project yields during the New Kingdom at 600 kilograms per feddan and during the Old Kingdom at 450 kilograms per feddan.

To obtain net yield per unit of land area available for cultivation, the grain reserved for seeds, lost to pests and disease, and allocated to taxes must be taken into consideration. In general, from historical data we can assume that 20 percent of total yield was reserved for seeds and a further 10 percent was lost to pests and disease. Also from historical data, the rate

TABLE 7.3.

Estimation of probable population of Greco-Roman Egypt assuming different rates of taxation and adequate subsistence levels

	25% Tax	40% Tax	48% Tax
Area in feddans	2.25 million	2.25 million	2.25 million
Yield	700 kg/feddan	700 kg/feddan	700 kg/feddan
Seeds	140 kg/feddan	140 kg/feddan	140 kg/feddan
Loss	70 kg/feddan	70 kg/feddan	70 kg/feddan
Tax	175 kg/feddan	280 kg/feddan	340 kg/feddan
Net yield/feddan	310 kg/feddan	210 kg/feddan	150 kg/feddan
Consumption/capita	200 kg/yr	200 kg/yr	200 kg/yr
Total rural population	3.48 million	2.36 million	1.68 million
Total population	3.73 million	2.53 million	1.81 million

of taxation may be set at 15 percent under the Old Kingdom, rising progressively to 20 percent, then 25 percent or more under Greco-Roman and Arab rule. Average production in these later times amounted to 6 ardebs per feddan. (One ardeb = 135 kilograms of grain; 6 ardebs = 810 kilograms, approximately the high estimate of 800 kilograms per feddan given above.) The tax rate in Arab times was between one and three ardebs (135 to 405 kilograms) per feddan—that is, as low as 17 percent, but up to 50 percent under exploitative regimes.

Urban and Rural Populations. To obtain figures for rural and urban population I gauged urban population as about 5 percent of rural population under the Old Kingdom, about 6 percent under the New Kingdom, and about 7 percent in Greco-Roman Egypt—proportions generally appropriate for preindustrial agricultural systems. Total population estimates with these considerations in mind were 1.42 million for the Old Kingdom, 2.74 million for the New Kingdom, and 6.16 million in the Greco-Roman period.

The estimate of six million for Greco-Roman Egypt must be regarded as very close to the maximum and may have been approached only at rare peak periods. It is based on a very low rate of taxation, low subsistence income, maximum crop yield, and the maximum cultivable area possible before modern agricultural policies were introduced in the 1850s.

Smaller Crop Yields and Variable Tax Rates

Table 7.2, which presents a more realistic estimate of yield per acre of 700 kilograms per feddan and estimates population size under different rates of taxation, gives a range of population between 2.4 and 4.98 million. The higher figure is possible only if taxation was low.

Egypt was considered the granary of Rome. During the reign of Ptolemy II Philadelphus (285–246 BC) Egypt supplied Rome with 1.5 million artabas of grain (33.75 million kilograms, at 22.5 kilograms per artaba); by the reign of Justinian (AD 527–65) shipments had increased to as much as 8 million artabas (180 million kilograms) (Wallace 1938). Other estimates (Lewis 1983:165) state that total export to Rome in an average year was 6 million artabas (135 million kilograms). Given a cultivable area of 2.25 million feddans and setting the tax destined to Rome at the maximum of 180 million kilograms, unit tax would amount to 80 kilograms per feddan.

The most common total tax rate ranged from one to eight artabas per aroura (Lewis 1983:165), approximately 40 to 306 kilograms per feddan. (One aroura = 0.575 feddan.) An average of 170 kilograms per feddan (about 1.25 ardebs/feddan, or 4.5 artabas/aroura) would thus seem plausible. From this amount 80 kilograms per feddan would go to Rome, and 90 kilograms per feddan would go to the occupation army and to native elites and functionaries.

Given this tax rate the population subsisting at a minimal level may have been as high as 4.98 million. Alternatively, at a somewhat better level of subsistence, the population would have been close to 3.72 million. With a higher rate of taxation, including payments of bribes and protection money and other gratuities common in a corrupt system, as are documented for Roman Egypt (Lewis 1983:162–63), the population would have been close to a range of 2.53 million to 3.37 million (see tables 7.2 and 7.3, column 2). These figures are consistent with the estimates of 2.5 million for Egypt during the AD seventh century, which were exceeded only during the late thirteenth century when population reached 3.4 million to 4 million (Russell 1966).

Other Sources for Estimating Population

Population can also be estimated from land area and area required per family. According to Russell (1966), a family requires five feddans. Assum-

TABLE 7.4.
Probable population of ancient Egypt on the basis of land area and acreage
per family

	Old Kingdom	New Kingdom	Greco-Roman
Area in feddans	1.1 million	1.5 million	2.25 million
Population	1.1 million	1.8 million	3.15 million

ing family size at five persons in the Old Kingdom, six in the New King-dom, and seven in Greco-Roman times yields population estimates of 1.1 million for the Old Kingdom, 1.8 million for the New Kingdom, and 3.15 million in the Greco-Roman era (table 7.4). If family size was uniformly about six persons, population would instead be estimated at 1.2 million, 1.8 million, and 2.7 million, respectively.

These figures can be compared with others previously derived from historical sources. O'Connor (1972:80) notes that the area cultivated in Ramesside times was 6 million arouras (approximately 3.57 million fed-dans or 15,000 square kilometers). Given that land area in medieval Egypt and as late as 1820 was 1.53 to 2.5 million feddans, this estimate of 6 million arouras probably refers to total available area, not area under culti-vation. In 1961, for example, nearly 29 percent of the cultivable land was fallow, nonarable, and public land. From this figure we could assume that the area under cultivation in Ramesside Egypt was about 4.3 million arou-ras or about 2.55 million feddans—a figure congruent with the land area for medieval and premodern Egypt. If two arouras were needed to feed one person (Baer 1962), the Ramesside population can be estimated at 2.14 million persons. A different historical record states that 9 million arou-ras were devoted to agricultural land during the Ptolemaic period (Russell 1966). Here again, this figure may represent 6.4 million arouras actually under cultivation, and an estimated population of 3.2 million.

Russell (1966) also refers to a tax levied by Diocletian (reigned AD 284–305) that encompassed 400,000 men who owned plows. Given that adults constitute about 40 to 50 percent of the entire population, we can assume that adult male farmers represented about 20 percent. This figure would suggest a population of two million persons. Russell assumes a family unit of eight persons, much higher than usually assigned to pre-industrial agrarian communities. If we assume a family size of seven per-sons, the population would have amounted to 2.8 million. Lloyd (in Trig-ger et al. 1983), quoting Herodotus, estimates the strength of the Egyptian

TABLE 7.5.
Range of population estimates in millions based on various methods

Old Kingdom	New Kingdom	Greco-Roman
1.4	2.74	6.16
		4.98
		3.37
		2.4
		2.53
		1.81
1.1	1.8	3.15
1.2	1.8	2.7
	2.14	3.2
		2.8
		2.46
1.23	2.12	3.23

army at 410,000 for the Late period, from the Saitic dynasty until Herodotus' visit (450 BC). Every man was given 12 arouras. Herodotus' count most probably refers to the total number of adult males, or the total number that could be inducted into standing and reserve armies. The total cultivated area would thus have represented 4.92 million arouras, and the total population would have been 2.46 million.

From these and other estimates given above, and compiled in table 7.5, we may conclude that the population of ancient Egypt was most probably about 1.2 million persons in the Old Kingdom, 2.1 million in the New Kingdom, and 3.2 million in the Greco-Roman period. From these data, allowing for fluctuations in population in response to low Nile floods and political disorder (modeled on evidence from after AD 600, for which historical records are available), one can construct a hypothetical population curve such as that shown in figure 7.1.

The rise of the Predynastic agricultural population over two thousand years from about 10,000 to 400,000 (see Hassan 1981b) suggests an annual growth rate on the order of 0.18 percent. This rate, considerably higher than the 0.08 to 0.12 percent for the Neolithic in the Near East (Hassan 1981a), is probably a function of the great agricultural potential of the Nile Valley. Population growth during the Pharaonic period, from 400,000 to 2 or 2.5 million in the New Kingdom over a span of about seventeen hundred years, suggests an average growth rate of 0.1 percent. I also estimate rates of 0.13 percent for the Old Kingdom and 0.057 per-

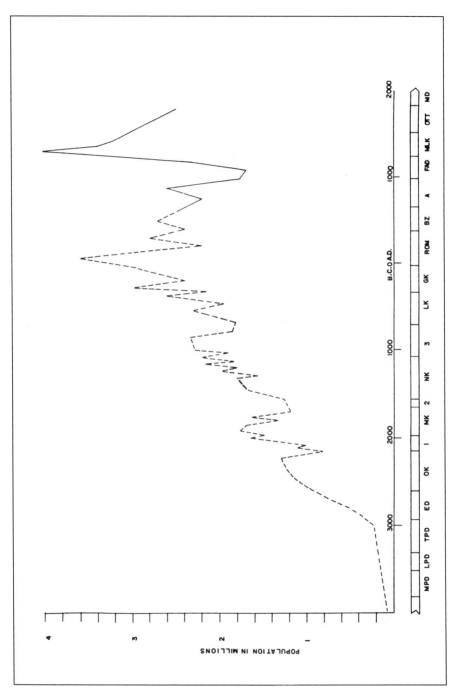

Figure 7.1. Population of Egypt from ancient to modern times.

cent for the New Kingdom. This difference between regions is primarily attributable to Egypt's freedom from the severe salinization problem that affected Mesopotamia, as well as exceptional opportunities for agricultural extensification and the exploitation of natural flood basins by minimal technological efforts, such as earth embankments (dikes) and drainage canals, that could be locally managed.

During the Late period and afterward, the population fluctuated, but given an average estimate of three million during the Greco-Roman period, the average annual growth rate from the New Kingdom to the Roman period was rather slow, perhaps in the range of 0.024 percent. The pattern of growth was probably uneven, responding to stochastic variations in the size of local populations, the effects of droughts and disastrously high floods, epidemics, and political unrest.

Ancient History and Population Ecology

We are now in a position to review what we know of population in terms of the historical record and projections of variations in Nile flood. The diachronic synopsis presented below suggests and reinforces some major points that I address in my overview and conclusion.

The low floods during the early phase of Egyptian civilization (Bell 1970; Butzer 1984; Hassan 1986) coincided with the struggle to unify Egypt and create a single political order. The population was relatively low and with the benefits of good administration could still survive low floods. Plentiful agricultural yield after 2770 BC, as a result of greater political stability, effective bureaucratic administration, and good floods, was perhaps responsible for the prosperity that culminated in the building of the great pyramids.

Low floods and the rising power of local administrators brought down the central government by ca. 2200 BC (Bell 1971; Butzer 1984). Perhaps in the same style as events associated with the low floods at the time of the original unification of Egypt, political reunification by the founders of the Middle Kingdom in 2040 saved the region from the effects of low floods in 2002 (Butzer 1984). The rulers of this founding dynasty (2040–1991 BC) embarked on ambitious programs of flood control and land reclamation, including parts of the Faiyum Depression.

By 2000 BC there was still enough pasture land (Baer 1962, cited in Butzer 1976:86) to equal the amount of cropland. According to O'Connor (1972), cropland was close to the towns and grazing land lay farther afield, a pattern that may also have prevailed around smaller settlements. (Pas-

TABLE 7.6.
Years (AD) of low Nile River levels associated with high grain prices and famines

706	1200	1420	1803
726	1201	1426	1807
	1231	1428	1821
952	1263	1450	1877
962–968	1294	1468	
997	1295	1484	
	1297	1485	
1007–1008		1486	
1052–1054	1304		
1056	1307	1641	
1059–1066	1338	1694	
	1350		
1123–1124	1363	1704	
1181	1383	1722	
1184	1395	1783	
1191		1792–1793	

turage remained more or less stable thereafter, until the introduction of perennial irrigation in the nineteenth century of the present era enabled the extension of cultivation beyond the flood basins.)

Perhaps coincident with the arid period in the adjacent desert region northeast of Egypt, aridity in the Egyptian Sahara is recorded from 1930 to 1230 BC. As low Nile floods are strongly correlated with dry climate in the Egyptian Sahara, the weakening of central government during the twelfth and thirteenth dynasties (1991–1640 BC) and the rapid succession of some seventy kings within 144 years (1783–1640 BC) may have been caused in part by low flood conditions and concomitant famine and disease. At least twenty-seven inscriptions from the Cataracts of Nubia record floods eight to eleven meters higher than present levels during the period from 1840 to 1770 BC (Bell 1975).[4] High floods during a general phase of low floods are not uncommon (see above and table 7.6) and can only add to economic devastation if they are exceptionally high. The invasion of Egypt by the Hyksos, who achieved control of the Delta by 1640 BC, was perhaps facilitated by the region's weakness owing to the era's low floods and low crop yields. The desire of the Hyksos to move into new territory may itself have partially been precipitated by a peak dry period.

When new Egyptian leaders reorganized the army into a professional force and regained native sovereignty, the New Kingdom (1550–1070 BC) inaugurated a military society and an era of empire-building justified by the need to prevent further foreign aggression and to secure national stability. Despite manifestations of a golden age during that period, the foundations of Egyptian society were shaken by (1) ideological conflicts (Akhenaten, 1353–1335 BC), (2) the ascent of commoners to the throne via military careers (e.g., Horemoheb, 1319–1307 BC), and (3) after the reign of Ramesses II (1290–1224 BC), low Nile floods, weak pharaohs, and powerful aspirants.

Low floods in Egypt at that time coincided with a dramatic drop in lake levels in East Africa ca. 1260 BC, the abandonment of agriculture in Nubia after 1224, and the accumulation of aeolian and salt crusts on the floodplain in Nubia (Butzer 1984:107). After a period of prosperity, and coinciding with the demands of a vast empire and a standing army, these low floods were likely to have weakened Egypt. Poor floods were probably behind the failure of the food supply in 1153 and the eight- to twenty-fourfold increase in grain prices in 1110 (Faulkner 1975). Low floods co-inciding with the end of a short moist interval and with a resumption of aridity may have caused the famines in Libya that are reported (in texts from the reign of Merenpetah, 1224–1214 BC) to have led to successive invasions from that quarter and to a countering campaign by Ramesses III (1194–1163 BC) (O'Connor, in Trigger et al. 1983). This historical event suggests a new reduction of Nile floods in 1260–1150.

Continued warfare against the Libyans and against rising centers of power in Asia, along with increasing demands of a pervasive bureaucracy and the military machine, required and forced increased productivity, which seems to have been achieved both through increasing the size of the labor force and by technological improvements. The increase in the labor force is likely to have been accomplished by increasing the number of laborers per family, causing a marked rise in the Egyptian population. The peasants are likely to have had large families (averaging six to seven persons), to have worked harder, and to have retained little for themselves after taxes. The standing army and the war industry also drew away a sizable component of the most able-bodied food producers and further burdened the peasantry with demands for food production.

Under the preexisting state of technology the population must have dangerously approached critical carrying capacity. This capacity was somewhat increased with the introduction of *shaduf* irrigation, which expanded the cultivable area, especially in the delta, where the differential between floodplain and water was not too great. The new capital in the eastern Delta (Pi-Ramesse), established with an eye toward the troublesome eastern frontiers of the empire, must have benefited from these agricultural developments.

The demise of Egyptian civilization during the Third Intermediate (1070–712 BC) and Late (712–332 BC) periods may have been caused in part by ecological factors, as Egypt entered a new phase of progressively lower flood discharge, and in part by expansion of government and military functions—the latter overtaxing the temples, the nomarchs (the rulers of administrative districts or nomes), and ultimately the peasantry. Pushed to the limits of maximum labor input and minimum subsistence, the peasants became increasingly vulnerable to ecological catastrophes and crop failures. This dimension of the Late period may partly explain the collapse of Egyptian institutions under the additional burden of foreign occupation.

The expansion of Egypt's population and the increase in its grain exports during Hellenistic and Roman times were apparently primarily the result of land reclamation (as in the Faiyum); excavation of new canals; the spread of water-lifting devices (the *saqia*), which in some places enabled the harvesting of two crops per year with sorghum as a summer crop; the use of a *qanat* system to exploit agricultural land in the desert; and a rigorous system of administration, riverine and maritime transport, and tax collecting. Broad-scale improvements under Roman rule are exemplified by programs under Augustus (30 BC–AD 14), who ordered his army to repair and deepen canals so a flood of 12 cubits (6.48 meters), compared to the previous minimum of 14 cubits (7.56 meters), would guarantee a bumper harvest (Bell 1948). But again, by AD 200 an overextended population and a despotic and brutal tax-collecting system led to social disorder and the flight of many peasants from the land.

In the late Roman era and through the Arab conquest the deterioration of state management of canal clearing and reclamation projects, together with the spread of political corruption and still heavier taxation, plunged Egypt into a state of severe depopulation and disorder. Farmers became increasingly vulnerable to the vicissitudes of Nile flooding, and famines and plagues followed in one of the saddest chapters in Egyptian history. Except during the reigns of a few insightful rulers, who managed to counteract the effects of a poor flood, population fell until it reached a low of about 1.6 million by the tenth century AD (Russell 1966). After 1100, commerce with the west via Venice and Genoa, under some able rulers, led to a transient peak before population was set back again by excessive taxation, corruption, and mismanagement of agriculture and the economy under the Ottomans. Population totaled about 4 million in 1348 but had dropped to 2.5 million by 1799–1802, when Napoleon's expedition defeated the Mameluke regime appointed by the Ottomans.

Only after 1820 did the population begin its unprecedented modern climb toward tens of millions. This rapid increase was primarily related to improvements in water management, tied in turn to changes in administration and technology and new infusions of capital. These developments, initially inspired by the agricultural policies of Mohammed Ali (Viceroy of Egypt, 1805–48), included the spread of perennial irrigation, which both increased cultivated area overall and enabled the cultivation of new types of crops. Demographically the increase was a result of reduced mortality rates at all age levels, though especially for infants.

Egypt's population today is more than twenty times that in ancient times. The population almost doubled between 1820 and 1859 (from 2.54 million to 5.125 million), doubled again by 1907 (to 11.3 million), and more than doubled again by 1960 (to 26 million), nearly doubling again (to 50 million) by the late 1980s (see fig. 7.1). Despite an increase in cultivable land from 6.8 million acres in 1897 to 10.2 million acres by 1960, per capita acreage fell from 0.81 to 0.38 during the same interval. Egypt, a primary grain-exporting region in antiquity, has since World War II been heavily dependent on food imports of grain, flour, meat, fish, oil, fat, vegetables, and fruits. By the 1960s about half the per capita grain supply was imported.

Overview and Future Outlook

Pharaonic civilization survived for about three thousand years, and under it Egyptian peasants continued to pursue their agricultural activities in more or less the same tradition until the introduction of dramatic agricultural innovations in AD 1820.[5] The longevity of this ancient society was a result of the weak connection between food production and central administration. Regional or national authorities could only partially protect the peasantry from ecological or economic disasters. Peasants continued to eke out a living and rebound from depopulation as dynasties came and went and as political systems rose and collapsed. Only under the most dire ecological events—which are rare and operate at the scale of hundreds of years—and only under the most oppressive regimes did they experience excessive morbidity and mortality. A system of deliberate population controls (e.g., minimum age for marriage, enforced abstinence, and abortion) must have regulated the population in order to meet the demands of subsistence and taxation without incurring excessive misery. In addition, it was sound administrative policy to keep taxation at a level that did not starve the peasantry or cause them to desert their land.

From the Late Predynastic period onward, communities had to deal with variations in flood levels and drainage as well as destruction of natural levees by floodwater. Likely responses must have consisted of fortifying natural levees, building artificial dikes, and digging extension canals and drainage ditches. These efforts were primarily local, as was the case well into the nineteenth century of the present era. The key activities that required collective labor and organization on the regional level were seasonal participation in the reinforcement of natural levees along the channel of the Nile itself. None of this required central management by the pharaoh.

Changes in the land use of the floodplain, the disappearance of wild game animals, and greater reliance on grain crops as staple foods by the time of the Old Kingdom were thus most likely a response to the economic and political changes that accompany the advent of an agrarian subsistence pattern. The concomitant increase in population was a response to decisions made to increase efficiency of food production (minimize excessive labor input) and meet the demands of a growing sector of non-food-producing town dwellers, including managers, priests, and craftspeople.

The changes in land use were most probably associated with changes in territorial activities and land ownership. Common grazing lands probably came increasingly under village or subregional jurisdiction. Flood basins, because of their importance to grain production, must have come under village ownership or control very early. With the rise of petty kings, land was probably seen as royal property that could be allocated to local chiefs, who in turn controlled access to it. The king, nobles, and priests owned large estates as well.

Egyptian peasants today are no longer directly in control of their fortunes, since water is allotted by the government. The government also decides what to grow and when. Farmers also depend on fertilizers and machinery provided by the government. Political instability under these circumstances can lead to traumatic economic experiences. In the 1980s Egyptians watched the declining water level in Nasser Lake, behind the Aswan High Dam, with great apprehension. Nile flood discharge had declined from 82 billion cubic meters per day in the 1970s to 42.5 billion cubic meters per day in 1987 (Arafa 1988): Egypt might soon lack the water minimally essential for irrigation, drinking, and hydroelectric power generation. Reserves in the dam averted a devastating water shortage, but they were severely depleted. In 1983 the water stored behind the High Dam amounted to about 100 billion cubic meters. By 1987 as much as 70 billion cubic meters had been withdrawn to withstand the crisis.

Centralized administration and participation in a world economy can and have allowed the population of Egypt to expand well beyond the region's ecological capacity. But this expansion only courts disaster at a national scale if unanticipated, albeit inevitable, long-term climatic/ecological changes occur, such as the low floods in the 1980s. These natural events can be especially disastrous if they coincide with poor political or economic leadership or adverse world economic conditions—including shortages of raw materials or industrial machinery, accumulated debt, or costly armed conflicts.

Unlike Pharaonic Egypt, Egypt today requires centralized government not only to sustain an unprecedentedly large population but also to counteract the projected increase in population over the coming decades. Paradoxically, though this long-lived society survived for millennia because of weak connections between central administration and production, that loose balance is no longer a viable alternative. Yet the idea of the state as an engine for social justice, expressed in the ancient concept of *ma'at,* is now more than ever an essential ingredient for the continuity of Egyptian life. Riots, unrest, and fanatical ideologies proliferate in an atmosphere of poverty, ignorance, and social frustration. Energy that should be allocated for development may have to be diverted for discipline and control, which in turn creates an atmosphere of apprehension, resentment, and alienation. Under these social conditions, development projects are likely to flounder because the hearts and minds of the people are not behind them. This situation can only perpetuate economic problems, especially if in the meantime population continues to grow as expected.

In this context it is appropriate to note that the Malthusian predicament can only be averted through technological breakthroughs. In ancient Egypt the limits of production under available technology were reached by Greco-Roman times. Thereafter, for more than a thousand years, the population hovered at about 2.5 million. Only when modern technology enabled a dramatic increase in the availability of water did the capacity of the land to feed more people increase well beyond previous limits. The increase in population set in motion since the 1820s has been further sustained by nonagricultural sources of national income (tourism, the Suez Canal, petroleum, revenues from Egyptians in petrodollar countries, and loans). Egyptian industry remains underdeveloped. Because the sources of nonagricultural income are highly dependent on the geopolitical climate, agricultural and industrial development projects are indispensable to the well-being of present and future generations of Egyptians. As an essential element for this development, vocational education and efficient management must be given the highest priority. A calculated plan for replacing an obsolete, underfunded, and overburdened educational system and an outdated, overextended, inefficient bureaucracy is critical to any future amelioration of economic conditions.

Egypt is in a good position to leap forward into a new age by virtue of its geopolitical position and its human resources. The human resources are not simply a matter of numbers—after all, ancient Egyptian civilization was the work of a few million people who would all fit into any of the populous neighborhoods of Cairo today. The place of Egypt in the modern world has primarily been made by an educated sector tied historically to the modern educational system. It is precisely by expanding the educational base, to serve rather than to flood the development sector, that potential flash points may be averted.

The dramatic increase in the size of the Egyptian population since 1820 has been predicated upon factors that have become increasingly dependent on international relations. Egypt has also outgrown the limits of its natural (agricultural) bounty under current technological practices. The projected increase in population and development is expected to lead to greater demands for water that will exceed Egypt's current share of Nile waters as fixed by international treaties (Egyptian Ministry of Irrigation 1981; Markaz el-Bihouth el-Arabia 1988; Waterbury 1982). These increasing demands, set against the prospect of exacerbated climatic fluctuations that may affect the volume of Nile floods, place the prosperity of Egypt once again at the mercy of good management of the Nile.

CONCLUSIONS

In the historical contexts discussed above, and in the context of the current situation of governmental control over production and involvement in the world economy, the prospect of extreme global climatic changes and their effects on ecological resources provide a strong incentive for the promulgation of a global economic and political policy. Issues of ecology are inseparable from government. They have been ever since the Neolithic, but ecology and society have never been so saliently intertwined as they have recently become.

The key developments in the population history of Egypt have been

(1) a slow increase in yield per unit of land area that stabilized at about 1.6 tons per hectare, about the same as the yield for England in 1800 (Evans 1980), until it began to increase again after 1929 (Selim 1940:142); and (2) an increase in cultivated area that continues to the present. The expansion of arable land is a function of waterworks: water-lifting devices, canals, dikes, reservoirs and barrages (small dam systems), and the recent technology of the great modern dams. From the Ptolemaic period until the early 1800s of the present era, the population of Egypt reached the limits of agricultural productivity under preindustrial technology and high taxation at an average of about 2.7 million persons from ca. AD 635 to 1821, ranging between a maximum of 4 million in 1348 and a minimum of just under 1.7 million in 1090. The variation of population size in this "stationary" state was a response to stochastic variations, volume of Nile floods, control and maintenance of waterworks, and taxation. The upward spiral in population after 1821 was linked to an increase in crop yield, the introduction of new crops, and expansion of cultivated area through the application of "industrial" technology, which is closely linked to a centralized style of government and a world market economy.

Although reclamation projects are still under way today, water remains a limiting factor in the survival and welfare of Egyptian society. A "water famine" today would mean poor crop yield, shortage of drinking water, and a drastic cutback in electric power. The danger of drastic climatic change today is perhaps greater than ever before. A recent series of droughts in the Sahel have already placed Egypt on the brink of disaster. The greatest famines in the historical era occurred in the period from AD 980 to 1200. On that basis, and given cyclical scales of 300 to 500 years and 1000 to 1600 years, adverse climatic transitions thereafter may be roughly predicted for the years 1430–1630, 1830–2030, and 2130–2730. (We should also recall that the population of Egypt fell from 3.2 million in the fifteenth century to less than 2.4 million by the turn of the nineteenth.)

Although I do not have great faith in the precision of these predictions, the reality of episodic variations cannot be ignored. Any predictions for the future are also complicated by the effects of our own time on the earth, which are likely to increase both the unpredictability of climate and the severity of its fluctuations. As in Egypt, where water is a finite and critical resource, climatically controlled resources are closely linked with human welfare in many areas of the world. It thus seems prudent to minimize our present massive assault on world climate, with its unforeseeable consequences (in addition to global warming); to develop benign technology for *long-term* nondestructive agricultural and industrial productivity; and to manage the planet with compassion, respect, and a sense of justice in the hope of minimizing war, terrorism, and disastrous competition for cheap production at the cost of human and environmental life and well-being. I hope that in this effort the ancient concept of *ma'at* will continue to inspire the sustenance of our global civilization.

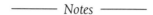 *Notes*

1. Relevant examples might include the aftermath of the rise of the early Egyptian state, or the modern Egyptian policy of growing cash crops.

2. In the Nile Valley wild game cannot support more than one person per square kilometer (Hassan 1974, 1981b). It would not have taken very long for a population of 120,000 persons in Upper Egypt (about 12 persons per square kilometer) to have annihilated the wild cattle and hartebeest.

3. Willcocks (1899) gives the total cultivable area of Qena Governate as 342,936 feddans, and the area of its basin as 129,700 feddans. The basin thus represents about 38 percent of the total available acreage.

4. These records strike me as not entirely trustworthy. They imply flood surges not merely two to four meters higher than normal in the northern Nile Valley (Butzer 1984:107), but considerably higher, since aggradation has caused recent floods to rise at a higher level above the channel than in Pharaonic times. Nevertheless the Nubian inscriptions may have been based on a floodplain that had aggraded to a higher level than at present.

5. It is interesting to note that Egypt's agricultural revolution occurred within the same general era as the Industrial Revolution in Europe, which was well begun by 1800.

Chapter 8

The Ecology of Conquest

Contrasting Agropastoral and Agricultural Societies' Adaptation to Climatic Change

CAROLE L. CRUMLEY

States such as China and Rome constitute only one type of complex society: spatially and socially hierarchical, urban, agrarian. Archaeologists have recognized other states (such as the Maya, Celtic polities, and the medieval Sahel kingdoms), which are not characterized by dual social/spatial hierarchies, cities, and a monocultural form of agriculture (Crumley 1976, 1987a, in press; Friedl 1986; Gamst 1970). Nonetheless, most archaeologists assume that pastoral and agropastoral societies are less complex—perhaps not even "true" states—even when they are class-based legislative democracies with money economies, taxation, and other markers of state societies. Pastoral and agropastoral states, although socially hierarchical, display a landscape "footprint" that corresponds to the heterarchical distribution of natural resources—what ecologists term *patchiness*. Urban states display a hierarchical city-town-village footprint, in keeping with the necessity of supporting concentrated populations through monocropping and long-distance bulk transport of comestibles.

In this chapter I wish to dispute the supposedly greater "simplicity" of nonurban states by exploring two contrasting examples from Europe; the research is based on archaeological, literary, and environmental evidence. I argue that complexity in human societies should not be defined in terms of the overlap of spatial and social hierarchies, or by the presence of particular features, such as cities. Complex systems—human, environmental, or mechanical—are characterized by their relations as much as by their structure. An alternative definition would focus on the ability of the system to respond to diverse phenomena. Thus, by contrasting a state fitting the more traditional urban definition (Rome) with agropastoral states (Celtic), the focus is on their relative flexibility in economic, spatial, and sociopolitical organization during times of marked environmental change.

Temperate Europe's climate was dramatically warmer between ca. 300 BC and the third century AD. The Mediterranean-Temperate ecotone moved far to the north of its present position, and the characteristically variable climate of western Europe was relatively stable for five centuries. There are considerable implications for the latter half of the Iron Age (La Tène), the late Republican and Roman Empire expansion, and the time of resurgent rurality and agropastoralism known as the Dark Ages or Migration period. One such implication is that climatic stability/instability and the concomitant necessity of environmental and economic adjustments are at least as explanatory of Roman expansion (and subsequent decline) as any claim to greater cultural "complexity" might be.

STUDYING SOCIAL COMPLEXITY

The task of characterizing the social structure, ecology, and political economy of Celtic society in the half-century before the Roman conquest has long been a central theme in European studies (e.g., Childe 1925, 1926; Dechelette 1927; Fustel de Coulanges 1908; Grenier 1924; Hubert 1934). Culture-historical and cultural evolutionary approaches to state formation (e.g., Childe 1934, 1951; Steward 1949) have been particularly popular in Anglophone countries but have found only limited favor in France, Germany, and elsewhere.

In particular, post–World War II and especially post-Sputnik scholars throughout North America found inspiration in the cultural evolutionism of Leslie White (1949, 1959). White's macroscale analysis of human history in terms of increasingly efficient energy capture found a ready audience among positivist social scientists who were eager to find historical confirmation that technology is the key to human progress. In like fashion, the assumption of Childe (1951), Adams (1966), and others that complex societies are civil (i.e., urban, from the Latin *civis*) has become paradigmatic in the archaeology of the state.

The roots of such assumptions are deep in Western philosophy. The idea of progress—that is to say, the identity of human evolution and history as gauged by the increasingly complex transformation of materials— is not only the cornerstone of so-called modern thought (Nisbet 1980). The notion can be traced at least from the eighth-century BC Greek philosopher-farmer Hesiod, through medieval Christianity's Great Chain of Being and the Danish museologist Worsaae's Three Age System, to Morgan and Spencer, its best-known nineteenth-century proponents. By disassembling the fabric of societies into autonomous temporal (Stone Age, Bronze Age, Iron Age) and structural-functional units (kinship, government), the theme of increasing complexity could be focused on technology and urbanization as indicators of sophisticated social and political organization. This analytic structure not only harkened back to supposed influences on Europe of the Mediterranean city-states, it also mirrored the preferred interpretation of nineteenth- and twentieth-century industrial capitalists, who saw both advances in technology and the global penetration of a centralized free-market (*laissez-faire*) economy through urbanization as a cure for social and political backwardness. Thus high-density population centers supported by rural agriculturalists and an intricate technology under the control of elites were adopted as the hallmarks of complex societies, past and present. This reading of the history of society set the agenda for Western colonialism and tied the future of much of the world's peoples to a particular economic, social, and spatial definition of progress.

Contemporary cultural evolutionists have eschewed improved technology and population growth as indicators of increasing complexity, embracing instead the role of finance, control, and ideology in the empowerment of emerging elites (Earle 1989). Although this change represents a laudable increase in the sophistication of evolutionary models, value continues to be placed on the state's stability despite a growing literature to the contrary (Paynter 1989). The underlying assumption remains intact: polities without both spatial and social centralization (that is to say, settlement hierarchies and urban elites) are still widely considered inherently unstable, transitional, and incomplete, and their trajectories unfinished until such time as they become states or their instability leads to collapse. Such polities are termed *chiefdoms*.

I have pointed out elsewhere (Crumley 1976) that many societies universally termed civilizations or states are patently not urban; however, most archaeologists are willing to see the Classic Maya, dynastic Egypt (Hoffman, Hamroush, and Allen 1986 notwithstanding), and the medieval states of the Sahel (Gamst 1970)—not to mention the early modern period in the British Isles—as exceptions that prove the rule.

Although a corpus of literature examines the relation of social differentiation (inequality) to spatial patterning (Paynter 1989; Wenke 1989), most workers continue to assume that the correlation is always positive: societies with rank-size settlement distributions (cities) are states. It is quite possible for elites to govern without benefit of nested settlement hierarchies, however, and for marked class distinctions to be played out without leaving the spore of cities.

Finally, although evidence from every major culture area points to environment as playing a crucial enabling role in the choice of subsistence strategies, few sustained examinations of the implications of environmental change have been undertaken by cultural evolutionists (an exception is Maya prehistory). This lack of study is in keeping with an approach that prefers technological over environmental change and the rhetoric of collapse over the evidence for accommodation.

What, then, constitutes complexity? I have argued elsewhere (Crumley 1987a:160ff.) that many archaeologists erroneously conflate complexity with order, order with hierarchy, and hierarchy with power (e.g., McGuire 1983:91).[1] Others (Johnson 1982:395ff.) have equated complexity with the increased decision-making effectiveness of leadership hierarchies. This latter definition of complexity has encouraged the importation of mechanical models of social stratification from engineering and business, which effectively obviates other definitions of power as well as the role of individuals. Ironically, these hierarchical models have recently been replaced in management by more flexible and inherently more complex heterarchical structures, which link individual responsibility and accomplishment with corporate success.

I define *heterarchy* as a system in which elements are unranked relative to one another or ranked in a variety of ways depending on conditions (Crumley 1979, 1987a); the term is borrowed from cognitive psychology (McCullogh 1945) through artificial intelligence (Minsky and Papert 1972) and refers explicitly to a heterarchy of *values;* an individual might ignore conflicting personal values (such as simultaneous opposition to abortion and support of the death penalty) or an awareness might precipitate a crisis. This situation is similar to what Bateson refers to as the "double bind" (1972).

The implication for the values of an entire society is that an intricate net of power relations—*counterpoised* power, in which negotiating individuals operating in varying contexts play a critical role—can not only support state apparatus but give rise to suprastate confederacies as well. To understand so-called complex societies, we must recognize that hierarchy is invariably a temporary solution to the problem of maintaining order (Paynter 1989:375); furthermore, generalized heterarchical structures—both cultural and environmental, which are always present though not necessarily dominant—lend flexibility in the negotiation of power relations. Perhaps most important, the individuals who interpret, explain, and integrate values in a society (religious practitioners, lawgivers, philosophers) always play a pivotal role in maintaining order.

Gamble (1986:29) has argued that complexity must have both diachronous (scheduling) and synchronous (alliances) referents, adding important temporal, cognitive, and (potentially) ecological considerations to a definition of complexity. Ecological parameters would seem to be particularly important, since the distribution of resources and the stability of the system as a whole would necessarily add to the complexities of scheduling and alliances for sedentary as well as more mobile populations. It follows that societies with value systems more likely to retain democratic heterarchical institutions would include individuals and groups able to respond effectively to both environmental and cultural change (Crumley and Marquardt 1987; Gunn, this volume). Cultural knowledge, termed *capturing* (Gunn, this volume), would be extensive and highly valued in such societies.

Johnson (1982) has struggled with reconciling egalitarian values with evident inequality, distinguishing *simultaneous hierarchies,* where a single group of people rule (states), and *sequential hierarchies,* where power does not always rest with the same people (chiefdoms). I think that Johnson's difficulties would be eased if he abandoned the term *egalitarian* (implying as it does an equal distribution of resources and power) and substituted *democratic,* which maintains the *value* of egalitarianism while admitting the inequities of electoral praxis.

A totally value-free meaning for the term *complexity* is obviously impossible; however, a minimalist definition would focus on the number of elements in a system and the variety of ways the elements are related to one another. While retaining hierarchies, this definition admits the concept of heterarchy and addresses the need to identify and describe nonhierarchical as well as hierarchical relations in complex systems. This is demonstrably true of Celtic polities, the salient points of which are reviewed below.

ELEMENTS OF CELTIC SOCIETY

Literary and archaeological evidence plentifully support a remarkably detailed picture of Celtic society at two scales: continental and regional. From Hungary to the Atlantic, and from the British Isles to Spain and northern

Italy, there is evidence of the pervasiveness of the Celtic pantheon (Green 1986). Although major deities were shared, there are abundant indicators of the considerable importance of regional gods and goddesses as well (Green 1986; Oaks 1987). Successively more magnificent and unifying art styles link the whole area during the Iron Age (Megaw 1970; Powell 1966); certain polities, such as the Aedui with their enameling *ateliers,* exhibited particular virtuosity in craftsmanship and design (Bulliot and de Fontenay 1875).

Contemporary Greek commentators favorably compared druidic philosophy with Egyptian, Assyrian, Persian, and Indian thought; Diogenes Laertius reports that many considered the study of philosophy to have begun among the Celts. Caesar and Ammianus report that the Druids themselves, while fulfilling governmental, educational, and moral responsibilities to their respective polities, were linked more broadly in fraternal organizations which met yearly near Chartres to hear interpolity grievances. Tacitus and Caesar note that polities designated kings (who acceded to the higher authority of the Druids) or elected officers (*vergobrets*) on the basis of explicit criteria for fixed terms (for classical references see Crumley 1974, 1987b; Hubert 1934:220). Ample evidence exists for political parties based on the patron-client relation, which crosscut class and kin lines and had a structure that was essentially the same as those found in contemporary Rome (Crumley 1974, 1987b; Taylor 1966). It is clear that these polities were democratic monarchies and participatory democracies with senates and polity and suprapolity high courts guided by pansocietal law.

Polities exhibited class-based social differentiation, including an aristocracy of religious and governmental leaders, a landed equestrian class (*equites*) with explicit military responsibilities resembling a similar formation in the antebellum American South, and free and unfree agriculturalists, skilled tradesmen, entrepreneurs, and laborers (Crumley 1987b).

The economies of larger and wealthier polities were based on a monetary system from at least the beginning of the second century BC (La Tène III) (Lengeyel 1969). Main sources of wealth were taxation, the import and export of raw and finished materials, and four main types of commercial production: stockbreeding (horses, cattle, sheep, pigs), metal mining operations, artisans' activities (especially weapons production), agricultural production, and, as a service to other wealth-producing operations, protection.

In the early 1930s, Hubert (1934) advanced the theory that some Celtic polities were primarily pastoral, others primarily agricultural—depending on both the environment and the length of time the group had occupied their region—and all were rural. His "leapfrogging" theory of Celtic colonization was meant not only to refute the wave theory of population movement then current, but to offer a model of Celtic society implying considerable social, political, and ecological sophistication.

Briefly, Hubert argues that increasing population resulted not in centralization but in fission, with wealth divided between group members who stayed on the ancestral lands and others who received their share in animals (horses, cattle, pigs) and other portable wealth and then moved on. These colonizing groups would have been remarkably flexible, able to adapt to a wide range of environments using agricultural, pastoral, horticultural, and artisans' skills as needed. They are not without parallel: during the nineteenth century, the western portion of the American continent was settled in similar fashion by peoples of temperate European origin.

THE LANDSCAPE FOOTPRINT

Hubert's argument is supported by recent archaeological evidence. Many excavated *oppida* (an oppidum is a hill fort or fortified town) resemble towns engaged in administered trade (Goudineau and Peyre 1993; Wells 1984) or armories, not cities, and lack evidence of a large resident population. Audouze and Büchsenschütz (1989) support a view of the late Iron Age landscape as essentially rural, with isolated farms, villages, and oppida—reinhabited earlier Iron Age sites—in response to the penetration of economic forms and urban styles from the Mediterranean. They argue that this commercial penetration was the first element of the Roman conquest in place; the second was the military action itself, and the third was the abandonment of oppida and the establishment of Gallo-Roman cities. Yet even in subsequent times, when Gaul became a part of Roman or Frankish or Carolingian empires, much of its indigenous political and social power was still firmly rooted in the countryside. Powerful figures can always do their work in spaces other than urban: sacred groves, castles, the graves of ancestors, council grounds, fairs. Implantation of the urban form on this profoundly rural society necessitated twin tactics of forced hillfort abandonment and urban construction and the eradication of the Druids (Clavel-Levêque 1989; Crumley 1987b). The more uniform Celtic pattern of power distribution throughout the landscape was replaced by the urban-rural duality; the suppression of the Druids broke the thread of knowledge from generation to generation. Both were calculated to alienate Celtic society from the practice of democratic, heterarchical power relations and foster acceptance of a centralized, autocratic Mediterranean society whose emblem was the city; Celtic-Roman interaction in the late Iron Age offers an early, well-documented case study: an urbanized, mono-cultural agrarian society engaged in the economic and military penetration of agropastoral legislative democracies linked, through the Druids, in a religious and judicial federation that spanned a continent.

CLIMATE, BIOTIC PROVINCES, AND SHIFTING ECOTONES

Three dominant climatic regimes affect Europe (fig. 8.1): the Atlantic, which carries moisture inland from the ocean; the continental, which carries dry air south and west from the Eurasian (Siberian) steppes; and the Mediterranean, which transports dry air from the North African (Sahelian) desert.[2]

Rainfall occurs when moisture-laden Atlantic air collides with colder air masses (Siberian), or when it reaches the western slopes of mountain-ous areas (Massif Central, Alps, Pyrenees). In general, both the continental and Mediterranean regimes bring dry conditions to Europe.

During the winter, the Sahelian system shrinks in size, allowing the Atlantic system to dominate the Mediterranean littoral, bringing winter rains. The continental system expands, bringing cold, dry air into central and western Europe. In the summer, the Atlantic system penetrates farther into continental Europe, bringing moisture. Dry summers in continental Europe may be brought on by dominance of either continental or Medi-terranean regimes.

Changing dominance of the various regimes is due to the shifting loca-tion of the Westerlies (sometimes referred to as the jet stream). Differential heating by the sun of the earth's surface strengthens or weakens the three systems relative to one another to produce frontal (daily, weekly), seasonal, and yearly variations. A number of other factors (e.g., orbital movements, volcanism, anthropogenic trace gasses) also affect the sun's intensity and thus the annual duration of a particular regime's dominance. All atmo-spheric climate, ranging from tomorrow's weather to the entire Pleistocene, can be understood by reference to these global and regional systems.

Appropriate time scales for the discussion of *climatic* change (as op-posed to daily meteorological—weather—changes) are from weeks to mil-lennia, because it is at these scales that circulation systems are identifiable

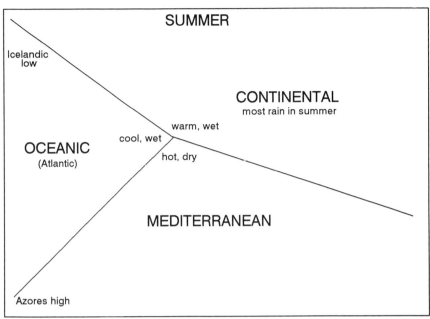

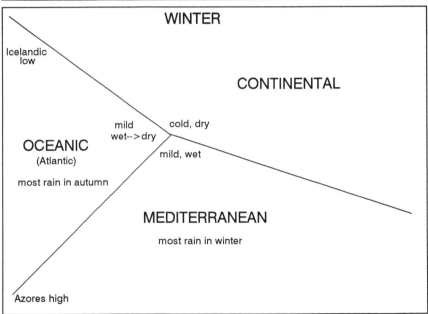

Figure 8.1. Dominant climatic regimes of Europe.

and tractable. Although the *duration* of the climatic change is important, the *frequency* of the change is particularly important in evaluating human adaptation. Weeks of unsettled weather are bothersome and may reduce yields; years to decades of unpredictable climate can destabilize elites whose authority is tied to climatic regularity; centuries of highly variable conditions favor flexible spatial, socioeconomic, and political organization. Stable climate, I argue here, tends to favor relatively inflexible forms of governance. Furthermore, the *rapidity* with which climate can change is especially relevant to its impact on human populations (Bryson 1988); the position of the Westerlies (except as impeded by topography or high pressure ridges) is fluid and sensitive to a suite of factors.[3]

The major climatic regimes and the major biotic provinces of Europe, while not a perfect match, are nonetheless strongly related (Daget 1980; Denizot and Sauvage 1980; LaFontaine, Bryson, and Wendland 1990). Palynology, paleoethnobotany, and living vegetational communities existing well outside their range are some of the categories of evidence paleoclimatologists use to determine the historical locations of climatic regimes. The position, width, and permanence of boundaries between biotic provinces (termed *ecotones*) associated with particular climatic regimes may similarly be derived; the relative sluggishness with which biota respond to climatic change does, however, pose a problem. Thus it is fortunate that other proxy evidence enables us to infer historical climatic change. Perhaps the most sensitive indicators are human beings, who are mobile, observant, and communicative.

The collection and transmission of cultural knowledge about environmental parameters has been termed *capturing* (Gunn, this volume); the quarry is the needed information about how best to survive certain environmental conditions, and for the most part this information is transmitted as long as traditional authority is valued. Periods of stable climate (whether hot or cold, wet or dry, or even consistently unpredictable) allow humans the opportunity to experiment and convey the results to succeeding generations in the form of successful strategies given a particular set of conditions. Strategies captured under conditions that no longer pertain may eventually fail to be transmitted, but the multigenerational longevity of such information is nonetheless remarkable. Periods of unpredictable climate require much greater flexibility on the part of human populations in their utilization of resources; also required is a much larger store of potentially useful information. In these periods, individuals who curate and transmit cultural information about a wide range of subsistence strategies are particularly valuable to the group as a whole. When unpredictable conditions persist, sociopolitical structures emerge that are more amenable to changes in population size, pattern of authority, and locale.

THE CLIMATE OF LATE PREHISTORIC
AND EARLY HISTORIC EUROPE

It is relatively well established that the world went through significant cooling and warming episodes between 1200 BC and AD 900 (Denton and Karlen 1973). I will document the regional effects of three major temporal episodes in western and central Europe and then discuss cultural changes relative to those episodes.[4]

From ca. 1200 to about 500 BC, vegetational and literary evidence from everywhere in Europe indicates a cold period of particularly severe winters (fig. 8.2). While the Atlantic climatic regime continued to bring moisture to northwest Europe, dominance of the continental regime in central Europe resulted in severe drought (Jäger and Ložek 1982). Particularly wet conditions are indicated for northwest Europe between 750 and 500 BC, which points to the continued dominance of the Atlantic regime in that more circumscribed area. It is suggested that the ecotone between dry central Europe and wet northwest Europe was somewhere in what is now southern Germany, perhaps at the Swabian and Franconian Jura, perhaps farther north at the Vosges west of the Rhine or the Hunsrück near Frankfurt. In any event, the southeast German Bavarian Plateau and the modern or recent countries of Czechoslovakia, Hungary, Romania, northern Yugoslavia, and Austria suffered severe cold and drought. Because the Sahelian system was much reduced in extent, even the Po Valley and Greece would have been affected; for the inception of this period Bell (1975) has documented a climate-related cultural disruption all around the Mediterranean Sea, including Egypt (Hassan 1981a; Hassan and Stucki 1987). Europe northwest of the Alps would have been chilly but well watered.

By 300 BC, and until at least AD 300, conditions were drastically changed (fig. 8.3). The Mediterranean climatic regime dominated year-round over a large portion of southern Europe, resulting in hot, dry summers and winter rains. Although it is difficult to pinpoint the ecotone between temperate European (that is, Atlantic and continental) regimes and the Mediterranean regime, I suspect that the ecotone was as far north as northern Burgundy in France and had fully mediterraneanized the climate of the Po Valley in Italy, the Yugoslavian and Hungarian plains, and the lower Danube.

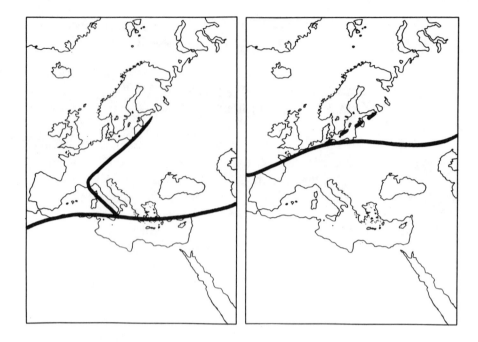

Figure 8.2. Relative position of
air masses, 1200–300 BC.

Figure 8.3. Relative position of air masses,
ca. 300 BC–AD 300.

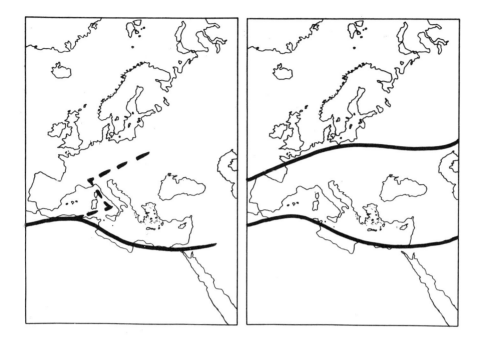

Figure 8.4. Relative position of
air masses, AD 500–900.

Figure 8.5. Late Holocene range of the
Temperate-Mediterranean ecotone.

By AD 500, and until about AD 900, the climate could be characterized as neither stable nor salubrious (fig. 8.4). The Atlantic regime frequently triumphed over the continental in spring and fall throughout the period, and in summers too except for mid-period. Thus in Europe there were cold, snowy winters; cool, wet summers; frosts; and floods: Alpine glaciers advanced between AD 450 and 700, and the Nile had ice on it in AD 829. Again the ecotone between the Sahelian-derived Mediterranean system and the Atlantic and continental systems was far to the south, along the northern fringe of the African continent.

In summary, the relative position of the bioclimatic ecotone between the southerly (Mediterranean/Sahelian) and northerly (continental/ Siberian and Atlantic) systems demonstrates that they have ranged in geographic position from approximately 48 to 36 degrees north latitude in the period ca. 1200 BC–AD 900 (late Bronze Age to the end of the early Middle Ages) (fig. 8.5). The dominance of one regime over another imposed limitations and afforded opportunities to species in the respective biotic communities; similarly, certain human adaptive strategies proved more effective than others.

IMPLICATIONS FOR PEOPLES OF THE ECOTONAL REGION

From approximately 300 BC to AD 300, continental Europe experienced a markedly warmer and drier climate; the period is termed the Roman Climatic Optimum (Denton and Karlen 1973; see also Crumley 1987c; Gunn and Adams 1981). During this period, the relatively narrow overlap zone between temperate Atlantic/continental and semiarid Mediterranean climatic and biotic regimes moved north of its average twentieth-century position in southern France. Precisely how far north Mediterranean conditions prevailed is not certain, but today the maximum northerly extent of commercial viticulture is in the Champagne region of France (about 49 degrees north latitude). MacKendrick (1987) reviews classical sources that report flourishing vineyards as far north as England (southern England is ca. 51 degrees north latitude), which suggests a shift of the ecotone at least one hundred kilometers north of its present position.

This does not, of course, mean that Mediterranean climate dominated as far north as the British Isles; the most important effect of the warmer period was that northwest Europe experienced extreme climatic events only rarely. Viticulture and the cultivation of other Mediterranean flora (e.g., olives, figs, dates) are practical when late spring or early fall freezes are rare and rainfall is predominantly in winter (Lamb 1977); these conditions are characteristic of a Mediterranean climatic regime. In contrast, temperate European vegetation is supported by an Atlantic regime, which brings rain in the summer, and a continental regime, which threatens inopportune frosts (Ladurie 1971). For hardier northern species, such conditions are not problematic in the long term.

Today the ecotone can be seen most dramatically at the crest of the Montagne Noire, at the southern edge of the Massif Central, where the vegetation changes in less than a meter from Mediterranean to temperate flora. Equally remarkable is the transformation that can be observed along a north-south trajectory in the Rhône-Saône corridor; here such cultural indicators as roof tiles and culinary preferences, although hardly the empirical data of botanical surveys, give the strong sensory impression of moving from central to southern Europe. This shifting ecotone has been studied hydrologically by Gunn and Crumley (1991); they explore Burgundian microclimates through the relationship between stream discharge and global temperatures.

Burgundy has long been the locus of this shift, although (as explained above) not the sole region to feel its effect. Guinot (1987) notes that the region's enduring central position between north (*langue d'oeil*) and south (*langue d'oc*) is reflected in its dialectical history. Burgundy serves as both historical and contemporary microcosm of the effect of dramatic shifts in the position of the ecotone, and more generally, global-scale climatic change (Gunn and Crumley 1991).

What are the implications for the Celtic realms of a marked change in the dominant climatic regime? In periods when Atlantic and continental regimes dominated (as in the first half of the Iron Age) a flexible suite of economic strategies, drawing on diverse species of flora and fauna, would have been superbly suited to those regimes' extremely variable conditions. An agropastoral economy, such as that practiced by the Aedui in their highly tessellated landscape, has enormous advantages when climatic regimes marked by extremely variable conditions predominate. Druids, among other members of Aeduan society, would have been repositories of considerable economic and environmental lore, enabling the society to adjust to almost any exigency.

The advent of warmer, more stable conditions would have created considerable economic pressure to profit from the lucrative Mediterranean wine and olive industries (Clavel-Levêque 1989) and the ready urban grain market. More conservative strategies would have been abandoned,

first in the drier valleys, then in rolling uplands. In Burgundy, high elevations (e.g., the Aeduan hillfort of Bibracte) were the only locales in which
the old rainfall patterns continued, which, as much as any other factor, can
explain the reflorescence of oppida in La Tène III times. With the forced
abandonment of the hillforts and the attempted eradication of the Druids,
the Romans were able to complete their economic penetration of Burgundy
and much of northwest Europe. A stable climate facilitated urbanization,
the homogenization of the landscape through the commoditization of rural
produce, and the devaluation of the intergenerational transmission of environmental lore.

Burgundy became a cow tethered at Rome's northern door. As long as
climatic conditions were stable, the attenuated economy was viable; when
conditions again became variable at the end of the warm period, key elements of Burgundy's successful Iron Age economic and social adaptation
had been swept away.

During the first millennium BC, the people archaeologists refer to as
Urnfield, Hallstatt, and La Tène—and historically identified (by 500 BC)
as Celtic—occupied the northern half of the range of the Mediterranean-
Temperate ecotone. South of the Celts along the north Mediterranean lit-
toral were great sea-trading polities, among them Greeks, Etruscans, and
Romans.[5]

Although Celtic peoples had been advancing on settlements in Italy
and Greece since at least the fifth century BC, by the end of the second
century BC the tables had turned dramatically: Romans had come to dominate previously Greek-controlled shipping lanes and trade enclaves and
had made a province of the southern fringe of Celtic polities in France. By
the end of the next century, Rome was in possession of the entire Mediterranean region and of continental western Europe as far as the Rhine.
The extent and duration of Pax Romana was greatly facilitated by climatic
conditions that favored Roman—as opposed to Celtic—economic, social,
and political organization (Gunn and Crumley 1991).

Not only were Roman patterns of settlement and land use in marked
distinction to those of Celtic polities, they were especially suited to the
mediterraneanized climate of Europe. As Audouze and Büchsenschütz
(1989) suggest, commercial penetration was critical in preparing the way
for conquest, and everywhere Roman agriculture and horticulture flourished. The use of space, class relations, patterns of inheritance, and forms
of government associated with Mediterranean ecosystems all moved north
along with (Clavel-Levêque 1989), but not entirely because of, the Roman
conquerors.

What was gained was an agricultural strategy that featured extensive production of relatively few crops, supported large urban populations, and was well suited to a semiarid climatic regime; what was lost, over the centuries of stable, Mediterranean-type climate, was the flexibility of the more independent, spatially diffuse Celtic system of multiple-species agriculture and pastoralism, much more suited to periods of uncertain climate.

The reappearance of the more characteristically European climatic pattern (of Atlantic and continental dominance) and the subsequent retreat of Roman hegemony did not result in the simple restoration of the European pattern of exploitation whose legacy the Celts had inherited; the information—passed from individual to individual and generation to generation—the social, political, and spatial relations, even many of the species themselves had been lost. Instead, the Roman system's inadequacies in the face of climatic uncertainty ushered Europe into a period when peoples to the east and north found their fortunes much improved as compared with those of their southern neighbors. By then, the elites of ecotonal Europe had been introduced to Christianity and Latin; the unfree and the destitute farmed a lord's land or feared pestilence in the faltering cities.

CONCLUSIONS

To sum up, hierarchical models, such as those routinely employed in the evolutionary sciences, both biological (see note 1) and social, are inherently no more complex (and may be less so, by the working definition offered above) than nonhierarchical (heterarchical) models; more important, they are employed in the service of a progressive cultural evolution. As distinguished from "chiefdoms," the term *state* focuses attention on only one type of complex society: hyperhierarchical, urban, agrarian. Pastoral and agropastoral societies, even when they are legislative democracies, are therefore, by definition, less complex. The dominant paradigm of cultural evolutionary theory, concerning how the structural elements of society have changed through time, obscures the dynamic social relations (complex by any definition) among and within many polities for which ethnography, written accounts, and archaeology give us evidence.

Beginning around 300 BC and for the next century or so, the climate of temperate Europe changed dramatically, leading to the period climatologists call the Roman Climate Optimum, which lasted until about the AD third century. The most notable effects were the northward movement of the Mediterranean-Temperate ecotone and the stabilization for more than five centuries of the characteristically variable climate of Europe. The time of resurgent rurality and agropastoralism known to us as the Dark Ages is rendered more comprehensible when set in a frame of major environmental change and broken cultural links.

I believe a lesson can also be applied to contemporary environmental change. The message is this: environmental uncertainty necessitates economic, social, political, and structural flexibility as well as the preservation of species diversity. The European Economic Community, while facing many challenges, will find none greater than planning for the effects of marked environmental change: drought, flooding, species extinction, population movements, market instability. EEC planners would do well to consider the social, economic, and environmental price of agribusiness, and the associated urbanization of heretofore rural populations. As Hassan argues (this volume), flexibility is best maintained by agropastoral populations relatively free of standardized central planning and distributed in a variety of environmental settings. Free-market measures, which are intended to standardize production throughout the EEC, drive small producers out of business, reduce the genetic variability of agricultural products, and increase the risk to the food supply.

Finally, we must reassess the premises on which we investigate and give value to the various organizational structures which characterize human society. Control hierarchies generally impose standardized solutions that fail to differentiate among cultures and regions and their collective histories; heterarchies of scale and value increase the complexity of the planning effort but also its likelihood of success. Thus, although a global-scale plan to safeguard the environment is clearly desirable, it is equally important that decisionmakers safeguard cultural and genetic diversity by valuing local knowledge and maintaining distinct traditions of animal and plant husbandry. To effect this, the historical ecology of regions must be undertaken on a global, case-by-case basis. It may be that regions whose populations are still largely agropastoral (and this includes many European as well as Asian, African, and Central and South American states) are already better able to withstand markedly different environmental conditions than urban states. Inasmuch as Western philosophical traditions systematically favor the urban victor over the rural vanquished, our flawed understanding of the significant ecological costs of urbanization, industrial agriculture, and the top-down decision making characteristic of hierarchies may prove an instrument of self-destruction.

——————— *Notes* ———————

1. This misunderstanding is not confined to archaeologists or even social scientists; many natural scientists make the same error (Allen and Starr 1982; O'Neill et al. 1986; Pattee 1973; cf. Ricklefs 1987).

2. LaFontaine, Bryson, and Wendland (1990) correctly term this North African air mass the Cyrenaican airstream; for emphasis herein I have referred to it as Mediterranean, in order to remind readers of its importance to the Mediterranean basin in all periods. Technically, however, the Mediterranean lands affected by the Cyrenaican air mass are at the northern edge of its region of dominance and might be considered ecotonal in their entirety at a more macro scale.

3. Other important factors are ocean currents, topography, and precession (seasonal and longer-term changes in the axial and orbital position of the earth relative to the sun [Gunn and Crumley 1991]).

4. The following climatic data are derived from Beug (1982), Ladurie (1971), LaFontaine et al. (1990), and Rotberg and Rabb (1981) unless otherwise indicated.

5. Leagues and federations of peoples in the ecotonal region as a whole (e.g., Celts, Greeks, Etruscans) could profitably be compared.

Chapter 9

The Role of Archaeology in Raising Environmental Consciousness

An Example from Southwest Florida

WILLIAM H. MARQUARDT

The present drains the past to irrigate the future.
—Henri Bergson

One focus of historical ecology is on formulating culturally sensitive responses to environmental challenges, global and regional. In this paper I assert that archaeologists are in a position to provide a long-term, broad-scale perspective on culture and environment and that this perspective can be translated to the lay public with salutary effect on environmental problems. I illustrate this process by describing a case from southwest Florida, where some success has been achieved in promoting awareness and understanding of Florida's bountiful but fragile environment in the context of archaeological investigations into the region's prehistory and history.

In southwest Florida these understandings have crossed class and political lines and been translated into a vocal and well-informed regional constituency for historic preservation and habitat conservation. The southwest Florida situation may not be typical, as discussed below, but I maintain that the approach merits consideration in other areas. The historic preservation and environmental protection movements have vested interests in common, although they have different histories and class identifications. These interests can be focused clearly and pursued effectively by archaeologists.

THEORETICAL POSITION

My overall orientation is critical and comparative, utilizing dialectical analysis and applying the results of dialectical understandings (Marquardt 1992a:104–13). I take historical ecology to be the multiscalar and multitemporal study of the dynamic relations between people and the physical environment. Historical ecology goes beyond human ecology, cultural ecology, and environmental anthropology in elucidating the relations between effective scales of human-environment interactions and pointing the way toward constructive transformation of these relations. For me, as perhaps for a number of the authors represented in this book, historical ecology is that aspect of dialectical analysis and practice that deals specifically with human-environment interactions.

At a broader scale, the historical study of human-environment relations cannot be divorced from the study of human-human relations because the environment is cognized, and decisions about how to relate to the environment are made, and actions are taken, in specific sociohistorical contexts (Marquardt 1992a:106–8; Marquardt and Crumley 1987:4–7). In these specific contexts, contradictions and conflicts arise in the course of cognizing the environment and in the emergence of power relations. Because physical structures are determinative and because the actions of humans can also alter physical structures, it follows that explicit attention to historical relations between humans and the environment is an important aspect of a broader dialectical study. This aspect, which is called historical ecology, is the subject of this book.

I have set forth a dialectical approach to processual archaeology elsewhere (Marquardt 1992a) and argued that "anthropologists'/archaeologists' understandings of cultural processes can be put to use in attempting to improve the communities in which they live" (Marquardt 1992a:112). In this chapter, I describe one such application of historical-ecological knowledge in a contemporary context. Before doing so, I introduce the case study by framing an argument for the special qualifications of anthropological archaeologists in helping to educate people about the biosphere and their relationships with it.

AMERICANIST ARCHAEOLOGISTS AS MESSENGERS OF ENVIRONMENTALISM

Archaeologists trained in the United States are particularly well suited to transmit a historical-ecological perspective to policymakers and to the public. We are trained in the scientific method yet steeped in the critical, comparative discipline of history. We use the methods and techniques of empirical science, yet we ultimately produce narratives of what happened, how, and when. Our field is inherently fascinating to many nonarchaeologists, and people are predisposed to consume stories of the unknown, potentially adventurous past.

With few exceptions, neither cultural nor economic geographers have had much success in making the connection between people and their environments meaningful to the public. Even in an era of tantalizing televised travelogs, and of satellites that can read over our shoulders from thousand-kilometer-distant orbits, American school children still don't know where Kansas is, much less Kuwait, nor do their parents adequately appreciate the connection between the American economy's dependence on fossil fuels and the price of their children's food and clothing.

Biologists have probably done better in getting their concepts across, but in American schools the most lasting effect of biological education may be the naturalization of hierarchy. Taught by a generation of teachers trained in the 1960s cybernetics of the Biological Sciences Curriculum Study (BSCS), systems-oriented biology is derived ultimately from Cell Theory, in which differentiation and interaction are countered and orchestrated by centralized control. BSCS biology implies that an overriding trend of evolution is an inevitable increase in complexity, which makes it hard to grasp as even plausible the wholesale elimination of hundreds of species in a distant rain forest.

Economic models have had more influence on policymakers than they have on the general public, but the presidential election of 1992 showed that disaffection with the American economy can be decisive at the polls. I suspect that the choice between Bush, Clinton, and Perot was based very little on the details of the candidates' economic plans. The voting public's reaction was not for a particular economic model or strategy, but against the perceived failure of the economy at large. Economists, like all empiricists, often disagree, further adding to public confusion.

If geographers, biologists, and economists have failed to educate the public about the relations between themselves and their environments, one might imagine that ecologists would stand a better chance of success.

Every politician is now in favor of environmental protection, or so they would have us believe, yet environmental problems worsen each year. A poll taken today would undoubtedly reveal that the person on the street now believes that "protecting the ecology" (sic) is a high priority, but most would not favor higher taxes or a lower standard of living, if "cleaning up the environment" entailed such personal sacrifices. Most ecologists are not environmental activists. Many believe that ecology is not a separate scholarly discipline, but simply a set of concepts and techniques. Others still practice the systems ecology approach that dominated 1960s and 1970s biology and ecology. This approach promoted a notion of orderly and natural succession in nature and focused attention of the ecosystem itself as the basic object of study (see Winterhalder, this volume). Ecologists generally come from natural science and natural history backgrounds, in which the actions of humankind are either considered irrelevant to their studies of ponds and prairies or regarded as egregious insults to the "natural" ecosystems they are so fond of studying.

Archaeologists have not fared any better than geographers, biologists, economists, and ecologists in improving the general public's understanding of environmental problems, but I want to argue that Americanist archaeologists have the appropriate training and are better placed to be effective environmental messengers than many others. This situation stems from the position in which anthropological archaeologists find themselves: on the boundary between natural science, social science, and history.

Anthropological archaeology is best conceived as a social, not merely a natural, science (Marquardt 1985:67–68), and it is most productive when pursued critically and comparatively (Marquardt 1985:68–70, 1992a; Marquardt and Crumley 1987:4–6), which links it methodologically to history. Whereas natural scientists tend to conceptualize behaviors as either natural or cultural (see Ingerson, this volume), the anthropologist is more inclined to see all animal behavior, including that of humans, as natural. Anthropologists recognize that some behavior is cultural and some noncultural, however, and find insight in the studies of natural scientists (such as ecologists) and social scientists (such as economists).

American archaeologists have traditionally worked for the government or for universities, so their audiences have often been other professionals. Findings reported to the Army Corps of Engineers and articles in *American Antiquity* do not reach the public, so we should not be surprised at the lack of widespread sympathy for or broad understanding of what archaeologists do. This is not going to be another plea to archaeologists to write popular books or to seek favorable publicity for our field, although

these goals are laudable and there is an emerging literature and set of successful case studies. Instead, I want to focus on ways to transmit cultural
and environmental awareness to the public on a region-by-region basis. To
illustrate, I describe an archaeological program that I began in southwest
Florida in 1983. I first provide a brief introduction to what is known of the
native American populations that are the focus of our archaeological investigations (for more detailed accounts, see Hann 1991; Marquardt 1987a,
1988b; for archaeological and paleoenvironmental background, see Marquardt, ed. 1992).

THE WORLD OF THE CALUSA

When Europeans arrived in southwest Florida in the sixteenth century
they found a complex and powerful society. The Calusa were divided into
nobles and commoners, supported an elite military force, and received
tribute from towns hundreds of kilometers away. They possessed a belief
system that encompassed daily offerings to ancestors and a notion of an
afterlife. Elaborate rituals included processions of masked priests and syn-
chronized singing by hundreds of young women. They painted, carved,
and engraved. The walls inside the temple were covered by carved and
painted wooden masks. The head chief's house was said to be able to
hold two thousand people without being crowded (Fontaneda 1944; Hann
1991; Solís de Merás 1964; Vargas Ugarte 1935; Zubillaga 1946).

The Calusa were a complex, tributary, fisher-gatherer-hunter society.
They are considered enigmatic because almost all the people known to
have achieved a similar measure of complexity are agriculturalists who depend on one or more staple crops for their subsistence and are thus able to
produce and distribute a surplus. So far as we can tell from our study of
both historical and archaeological data, the Calusa and their south Florida
neighbors raised no crops.

One part of an explanation for Calusa prosperity is the remarkable
productivity of coastal estuarine marine meadows. Some scholars conclude that rich inshore food resources sufficed to fulfill the role usually
played by agriculture (Goggin and Sturtevant 1964:207).

A cultural materialist model for Calusa development has been proposed by Randolph Widmer, who argues that the complex Calusa political
organization was a result of efforts to provide subsistence for a growing
population (Widmer 1988:262–63). Widmer thinks that the population
steadily increased between 500 BC and AD 800, until by about AD 800 the

carrying capacity of the environment had finally been reached. Arrival at this threshold led to the establishment of a centralized political structure in order to resolve disagreements and to distribute food and other materials. Widmer believes that this structure was maintained until European contact in the sixteenth century (Widmer 1988:261–76).

But perhaps the Calusa complexity noted by the Spaniards was not the result of a slow, steady process of cultural evolution. Could it not have been a development of the historical period, stimulated by European arrival in the present-day southeastern United States and circum-Caribbean (Marquardt 1991)? South Florida natives were in both direct and indirect contact with Europeans as early as the first few years of the sixteenth century (Marquardt 1988b:176–79).

Significant changes in Calusa social and political organization may have occurred as a result of the broader European-dominated mercantile/imperial economy. We know the European goods that found their way into traditional exchange networks were accorded high value by the natives, at least initially. Those on the periphery of the Calusa sphere of influence may have tried to control the distribution of these goods in their own areas, leading to the threat of a decentralization of Calusa authority. The response to such a challenge may have been new power and tributary relations (Marquardt 1987a:103–10, 1991).

Among the Calusa, spiritual and political authority seems to have been mediated in the person of the paramount chief (Laudonnière 1975:110). If this was the case, then the sudden availability of metal, cloth, foods, inebriating drink, and other exotics would have had a spectacular effect. Local chiefs on the peripheries of the Calusa domain could have tried to increase their own authority by serving as intermediaries between their constituents and the Spaniards.

Such a challenge to the authority of the paramount chief would have to be met (Marquardt 1988b:187–88). A successful reassertion of authority would require a demonstration of the paramount's capacity not only to control European goods but to amass the resources necessary to support a military force and to distribute largess to loyal supporters. Only in this way could he assert his paramountcy against regional pretenders. In short, I speculate that it was in the early 1500s, not at ca. AD 800, that the Calusa social formation shifted from a chiefdom to what Gailey and Patterson (1988:79) would call a "weak, tribute-based state."

Whatever the origin of their complexity, the eighteenth-century demise of the Calusa is as perplexing as it is poignant. Franciscan records (Hann 1991) show that the Calusa still resided in their homeland and exerted influence on neighboring polities as late as 1698 (Hann 1991), long after the ravages of European diseases, forced labor, and militarism had devastated north Florida populations. By the early 1700s, however, the Calusa had been overrun by Creek Indians from present-day Georgia and were under pressure from Yamassee Indians from South Carolina, who wanted to sell them into slavery (Parks 1985:52–55). These Indians from the north had themselves been displaced by slave raiding, colonization, and military activities of the British, French, and Spanish. By 1711 remnants of Calusa and other groups were living in the Florida Keys, under continuing pressure from Creeks and Yamassees. The Spanish tried belatedly to rescue some of the Indians, but most died of diseases en route to Cuba; a few remnant groups in the Florida Keys were contacted by Jesuits in 1743 (Hann 1991:325–33; Parks 1985:56–65; Sturtevant 1978).

Why did the Calusa, who had held out for so long, suddenly crumble between 1698 and 1711? One telling factor may have been the effect of a devastating hurricane that apparently slammed into the southwest Florida coast ca. 1710. Geological evidence in the form of distinctive sediment facies documented in core samples, along with radiocarbon dates, indicate that cataclysmic storm surges occurred at ca. 1710 and at least at two other times, ca. 320 BC and AD 630 (Davis, Knowles, and Bland 1989).

If the authority of the Calusa chief depended at least in part on his ability to manipulate the environment, and guarantee its bounty, what would be the political effect of such a disastrous event? A loss of faith? Accusations of witchcraft? At the very least, a thousand-year storm would sweep away the villages in the Calusa heartland, disrupt communications, and make the natives even more susceptible to diseases. We know from historical sources that the Calusa did succumb to invasion and that they had been displaced from southwest Florida by 1711. The coincidence of the geological data and historical evidence invites further investigation.

Equally intriguing is the seventh-century storm, radiocarbon-dated to ca. 630. In the Calusa area, AD 600–650 marks the transition from the Caloosahatchee I to the Caloosahatchee II period, recognized by the establishment of numerous villages, the construction of substantial shellworks, and the greatly increased presence of Belle Glade pottery, a ware first manufactured in the Lake Okeechobee area some two to four hundred years earlier (Marquardt 1992b:13–14; Widmer 1988:78–81). This cultural transition is also reflected in the circum-Glades area to the south of the Calusa heartland in a dramatic increase in incised wares, which stand in sharp contrast to a plainware tradition many centuries old.

Did the surprising level of Calusa complexity result from a gradual process of cultural evolution, or was it something that happened suddenly in the first half of the sixteenth century? What roles did natural resources, climate, and weather play in the rise and fall of the Calusa, and how were these physical structures mediated by sociohistorical ones? It was these historical-ecological questions that first led to my interest in southwest Florida, heartland of the historic Calusa, where virtually no detailed chronological and environmental data were known. These data were needed if we were to shed light on the central issue of how and when the Calusa attained such remarkable complexity.

The gathering of basic background information, both archaeological and historical, is now finished (Hann 1991; Marquardt, ed. 1992). Admittedly, we are far from understanding the emergence of Calusa complexity or the causes for the rise and fall of their fortunes. We have, however, made some progress using a historical-ecological approach. We have approached the Calusa region at a number of scales, gaining understandings at certain effective scales only to move beyond them to others. This approach challenges the traditional culture-area approach by successively transcending boundaries of study.

As but one example (see Marquardt, ed. 1992 for additional discussion), the archaeological sites in and around the Charlotte Harbor estuarine system (Charlotte Harbor, Pine Island Sound, and Estero Bay) seemed initially to be an adequate unit of study, since it is the heartland of the historic Calusa, and its productivity was thought to be a major determinant of Calusa prosperity. But Walker's (1992) zooarchaeological studies reveal significant heterogeneity within the estuarine system in the past, a heterogeneity that still exists to a certain extent today, in spite of modern disturbances. Furthermore, an emerging corpus of data on sea-level fluctuations (e.g., Stapor, Mathews, and Linfors-Kearns 1991; Walker 1992) shows that the boundaries of the estuarine system itself, as well as the location of various habitats along a salinity gradient, fluctuated significantly through time. Archaeobotanical, geologic, topographic, ceramic-technological, and artifact analyses have added further to our multiscalar comprehension of the Caloosahatchee area.

This understanding has also reinforced the realization that the Charlotte Harbor estuarine system is slowly but surely dying, and that this process is a result of modern development of the past two generations. Although this process has local causes, it is part of a broader-scale phenomenon. Charlotte Harbor is part of the larger system known as the Gulf of Mexico, the environmental health of which has declined drastically in the past few decades, and which has only recently begun to receive attention in the popular press (e.g., Lee 1992) and in government programs (the Environmental Protection Agency declared 1992 the "Year of the Gulf").

One aspect of our archaeological research program in the Charlotte Harbor area has been to try to transmit to contemporary people our multi-scalar understanding of the estuarine system, its intricate interconnectivity, and its importance to the Calusa—and their own—quality of life. I next provide some background information on Florida's political economy, describe the contemporary economic and social context of our project, and conclude with some comments about the usefulness of public involvement in transmitting environmental awareness.

POLITICS AND THE ENVIRONMENT IN TWENTIETH-CENTURY SOUTHWEST FLORIDA

Southwest Florida began to undergo broad-scale development less than a century ago. Most south Florida towns only recently celebrated their centennials, but only since World War II has population increase reached levels three and four times the national average (Fernald 1981:82).

Florida has never had a state income tax, and in fact the Florida constitution expressly forbids one, but Florida was one of the first states to impose a tax on gasoline. Its penny-a-gallon tax in the 1920s helped to quadruple Florida's paved highways, making it easier to attract tourists. Not until 1949 did Florida institute its first sales tax. That tax is now 6 percent on consumer purchases, but groceries, medicine, and a wide range of services are exempt from taxation (Judd 1991c). The first $25,000 of one's personal residence is exempt from real estate taxes, and property taxes are undervalued throughout the state. In 1991, Florida ranked seventeenth in the nation in per capita income, but thirty-sixth in the amount that the average citizen is taxed by the state (Hill 1991). Indulgent regulations on development, including a surprising dearth of impact fees, along with a virtual absence of trade unions and the presence of a sizable "reserve army" of laborers who have recently migrated to Florida, have fueled a boom in real estate and development.

Some of the most extraordinary population increases have occurred in what was formerly open countryside. For example, the southwest Florida town of Cape Coral began in 1957 when the Gulf Land Corporation cleared some 2000 acres of previously undeveloped land in what was once the

Calusa heartland. By 1980 Cape Coral's population had reached 32,103; in 1990 it was 74,991, a density of about 658 persons per square mile.

Most of peninsular Florida's population increase is in the form of in-migration. Nearly one thousand people move permanently to Florida each day, and fewer than two hundred move out. Without going into great detail, it can be simply stated (perhaps understated) that Florida's natural resources cannot long sustain such increases, and that water quality, ecological diversity, pollution control, and other environmental issues loom large in Florida's future.

Water is perhaps the most critical factor in Florida's quality of life. Every day, each Florida resident and visitor uses an average of 175 gallons of water, compared with averages of 110 gallons in the United States as a whole, 52 in Great Britain, 39 in France, 35 in Israel (Bair 1991). The users of about half of Florida's water are agriculturalists, but lawn care accounts for millions of gallons per day and discharges pesticides and fertilizers into aquifers and waterways throughout the state. Urbanization exacerbates the water problem because demand for water per acre increases as former wetlands and citrus groves are turned into subdivisions and mobile home communities. The Governor's Commission on the Future of Florida's Environment estimated in 1990 that during the next ten years "each hour, approximately 19 acres of forests, wetlands, and agricultural lands will be converted to urban uses as a result of growth" (Bair 1991:4A).

Florida has a system of five virtually autonomous water management districts with the power to tax residents within their districts. The districts are overseen by political appointees. Twenty years after the state mandate, the districts have yet to prepare a comprehensive statewide water management plan (Judd 1991a:1A). The five districts combined have a budget of nearly $500 million, or $38.12 per resident. This immense bureaucratic structure stands in sharp contrast to those of other states. For example, in Oregon, where a centralized state water-management plan is rigidly enforced, the water management department operates at a cost of only $2.45 per resident (Judd 1991b:1A).

Unbridled growth threatens to undermine and obliterate the very attractions that have always drawn people to Florida. Florida's abundant and diverse wildlife is endangered by loss of habitat; the panther, manatee, and gopher tortoise are only the best publicized of numerous plant and animal species threatened with extinction. Runoff saturated with pesticides and fertilizers from south Florida farmlands is slowly killing the Everglades. Channelization projects that drained the region earlier in this century profoundly altered the nature and functioning of the famed "river of grass."

In short, Florida's environment is the issue of the 1990s. I believe that decisions made in the next ten to twenty years will determine the quality of life in Florida for centuries to come. While such issues as water resource management are best solved on a statewide and interstate basis, the effective locus of political action is neither at the state nor at the local community level, but at a scale in between. I now turn to a case study to illustrate archaeology's role in raising environmental awareness at the regional scale.

THE SOUTHWEST FLORIDA PROJECT

Assisted by Alan May and several members of the Southwest Florida Archaeological Society, I began the Southwest Florida Project by mapping a shell midden site on Josslyn Island in the summer of 1983 (Marquardt 1984). This effort was funded by Josslyn's owners, Donald and Patricia Randell. Preliminary visiting and testing of various sites on the islands of Charlotte Harbor and Pine Island Sound were done intermittently over the next two years, with volunteer assistance and meager university resources.

A grant from the National Science Foundation in 1985 enabled us to begin gathering seasonality and paleoenvironmental data, including geological coring and the monthly collection of marine samples (clams, three species of fish) to establish ways of reading paleoclimatic and paleoseasonality data from ancient faunal remains. We also collected plant seeds, wood, and fibers to form the first comprehensive archaeobotanical comparative collection for the area.

In an attempt to tap some of the obvious wealth in the area, I received some seed money from the University of Florida's College of Liberal Arts and Sciences. We planned a number of small parties, produced a four-color brochure complete with a pledge card, and in effect tried to sell the project to some of the area's wealthy residents. This initiative failed, thoroughly and miserably. In retrospect, a large part of the failure can be blamed on the fact that we were not local, and no one really had any idea of what we were up to. We had nothing tangible to show, nor any way of demonstrating that our commitment to the area was sincere and long-term. Neither the Florida Museum of Natural History (then known as the Florida State Museum) nor even the University of Florida had any significant established community involvement in the area.

Small gifts and volunteer assistance from private citizens were all that sustained the project in its early years. I entered the names of those who had supported the project into a data base, and kept track of gifts, willingness to volunteer, and history of work with the project. Those who had been particularly helpful with publicity, volunteer labor, or cash contributions were sent occasional updates about our progress, conveying in straightforward language the excitement of the anthropological questions we were beginning to try to answer, and informing them of significant advances in our knowledge (new radiocarbon dates, results of the geological coring and why it was important, etc.).

People seemed so appreciative of these periodic updates that I sought funds from the Gannett Foundation to produce a project newsletter. In 1986 we received a $3000 grant to produce the first issue of a two-color, sixteen-page project magazine I called *Calusa News* (Marquardt 1987b). In it I explained anthropological interest in the Calusa and the importance of preserving and learning from their sites, summarized the findings thus far, and reproduced and expanded the "updates" I had been sending out to donors and volunteers, covering the calendar years 1985 and 1986. I enclosed a return envelope that people could use to be put on the *Calusa News* mailing list (free) or to send in a contribution. I also published the names of all people and organizations who had contributed more than $10 in a given year.

The fund-raising plan was never formal, although I did establish six contributor's categories from "member" ($10–99) to "patron" ($100,000 and above). Although the newsletter was (and still is) free, people were asked to contribute at least $10 per year to become a member of what I called the "Calusa Constituency." It seemed to me that if the prehistoric Calusa and their predecessors were to be investigated and understood, a group of people from the Calusa area itself would have to participate actively.

I set about the task of raising awareness about the Calusa at the regional scale. I felt I had to try to forge a link between today's residents and the Calusa on the basis of a regional-scale awareness of the environment. It was not that people did not care individually about the environment or about historic preservation, but existing mechanisms were insufficient to sustain discourse and cooperation at a scale beyond the individual community. I perceived my task as one of fostering both synchronic linkage (education about the characteristics of the contemporary environment for contemporary people) and historical linkage (identification with the previous inhabitants of the same environment).

I gave numerous public talks, showing slides and artifacts that portrayed the special qualities of the area. I found that environmental, wildlife, and archaeological societies were sympathetic to my message because they saw that I and they were interested in the same thing—protecting/conserving resources and learning more about them for the benefit of all. Some also realized that the key to success lay in reaching beyond their own neighborhoods and communities to seek a broader, regional consensus. Members of service clubs and chambers of commerce welcomed the message about the distinctiveness of their region (synchronic linkage). I suggested to them that they were the local inheritors of an area once populated by a truly remarkable Native American culture and that they had something in common with the Calusa: they lived in or had chosen to move to southwest Florida because they recognized, appreciated, and benefitted from the bountiful coastal environment (historical linkage). Some developers understood that historical values could be assets to their properties and sought advice and help in planning for land modification. County planners, accustomed to operating at a supracommunity but subregional scale, yet articulating with broader-scale regional planning authorities, state agencies, and so on, appreciated having someone with the appropriate expertise to help them assess the significance of archaeological sites.

The second issue of *Calusa News* was mailed in March 1988 (Marquardt 1988a). A third followed in May 1989 (Marquardt and Blanchard 1989), a fourth in December of that year (Blanchard 1989). Contributions and the size of the mailing list steadily increased. We began to attract some gifts in the $5,000 to $20,000 range from private individuals and foundations. I also added to the mailing list the names of about two hundred professional archaeologists who I thought might be interested in seeing results of the project.

Although research results were promising, the project had no permanent and reliable funding until 1988–89. Until that time my own salary came entirely from soft money. From January 1984 through June 1988, I drew about one-third of a normal professional salary from the grants and contributions; most of the budget was allocated to research expenses. The Florida Museum of Natural History hired me as a full-time curator on 1 July 1988, and we received several significant contributions toward a permanent archaeology endowment in 1989 (Marquardt and Blanchard 1989:3).

By 1993 the *Calusa News* mailing list contained more than four thousand names, and the list of volunteers numbered more than one thousand. What happened between 1986 and 1993 was (1) a greatly increased involvement of the public in archaeology, by means of visible, well-publicized local excavation projects; and (2) the sharing of the findings with broad segments of the local community.

Ironically, it was the initial lack of support for the project that led us to rely so heavily on volunteers. But what we found was that volunteers do excellent work under supervision, and that southwest Florida has many people of all ages willing to work conscientiously and carefully without any compensation other than the excitement of participation in a dig. The most important factor in sustaining this level of interest and dedication is, in my opinion, communication—of the findings, the importance of the work, and our appreciation of their help.

One innovation that has added particularly to our productivity is the institution of the field laboratory. At the Pineland site in May 1988, then-graduate research assistant Karen Jo Walker suggested that we ask volunteers to help us wash, label, and catalog the artifacts in the field, as well as process the flotation samples. I was dubious but agreed to try the idea. My doubts were quickly erased by the enthusiasm with which many people took to the tasks. Under Walker's supervision, a dozen people were soon sitting cheerfully at makeshift plywood tables in the shade, meticulously washing, labeling, and cataloging. Some found that they preferred lab work to digging and sifting, while others wanted to do some of both.

Many of our volunteers are retired persons who work one to several days per week. Many are in fine physical condition, but others cannot endure long hours in the bright sun or do heavy labor for prolonged periods. For these people the lab is the perfect situation because it provides interesting and productive labor as well as social stimulation.

The Pineland site lends itself to the employment of many volunteers at once because it can be reached by car; many of the sites we tested in the first years of the project were on remote islands. During a fourteen-day period in May 1988, eighty-four different people worked 1782 hours, and we were able to take clean, catalogued, and numbered artifacts and completely processed flotation samples back to the university. We repeated the volunteer experience at Pineland a year later, in May 1989. This time, 170 volunteer excavators and lab workers worked a total of 2438 hours over a two-week period.

Encouraged by the community involvement, we began to think of bringing the project even more to the attention of area residents. Local supporter Jan Brown conceived the idea of an archaeology/education project that would bring the Nature Center of Lee County, the Fort Myers Historical Museum, the Lee County school system, and the Florida Museum of Natural History together in a team effort to tell the Calusa story to a broader public (Blanchard 1989:2).

The project, which we called "The Year of the Indian: Archaeology of the Calusa People," was funded in 1989 by a major historic preservation grant-in-aid from Florida's Bureau of Historic Preservation, Department of State; a second grant for the project was received in 1991, a third in 1993. Volunteer laborers, under our direct supervision, excavated at two prehistoric sites: Useppa Island (fall 1989) and Pineland (spring 1990 and spring 1992). The public was encouraged to visit the excavations. One hundred thirty different individuals worked a total of 2985 volunteer hours at the Useppa Island dig between 15 October and 15 December 1989; 334 different people put in 7906 hours at Pineland between 7 March and 30 April 1990; and 337 people worked 11,037 hours at Pineland between 7 March and 30 May 1992.

Under the direction of education coordinator Charles Blanchard, more than 5400 elementary school students participated in hands-on classroom demonstrations and visits to the Pineland site in 1990 and 1992, and more than six hundred teachers received special training. Public response has been overwhelmingly positive.

In addition to the school program, a summer program focusing on the Indian heritage of southwest Florida was held at the nature center and a multimedia show on the Indian past opened at the nature center's planetarium in April 1991.

Exhibits on "Indian Use of Native Plants" and "Europeans and Indians" were created for the nature center and the historical museum, and we assisted the Museum of the Islands Historical Society in establishing a "Calusa Room" in their new building on Pine Island. Indian artifacts were duplicated for use in the exhibits and in the summer program. Publications were prepared for both academic and lay audiences, and a public lecture series brought prominent speakers to talk to the community in 1991.

I believe that whatever success we have had in building a long-term project in southwest Florida is largely a function of public outreach. We were able to convince people that there are very special archaeological resources in their area—resources worth protecting and learning about—and furthermore that they are welcome to participate in the investigation. We have worked with responsible developers in Lee and Collier counties to identify archaeological sites so they can be protected or avoided. As a result of working on our projects, many local citizens have joined the Southwest Florida Archaeological Society, supported local museums (e.g., Museum of the Islands, Useppa Island Historical Museum), and appeared at public hearings to voice their support for historic preservation.

Lee County has adopted a historical preservation element for its comprehensive plan and conducted a countywide archaeological survey, which speaks well for the level of public involvement in one of Florida's fastest-developing coastal counties. Neighboring Collier County was slower to adopt an ordinance, but it finally did so in the summer of 1991. During the consideration of the ordinance, every public hearing was attended by vocal and articulate advocates of archaeological and environmental preservation, many of whom had become involved in archaeology through our project.

I make no claim that our project generated all of this citizen advocacy; certainly such groups as the Southwest Florida Archaeological Society, the Audubon Society, and the Sierra Club also promote local awareness of environmental and historic preservation issues, and they did so long before we came upon the scene. I do believe that learning about the Calusa and their environment has provided many southwest Florida residents with a broader, regional-scale link to the past, and that their purposeful political actions derive to some significant degree from a supracommunity perspective and a broader environmental understanding that is partially a result of our presence.

Even our empirical archaeological findings carry implicit and explicit messages of environmental preservation. The story of the Calusa is also the story of the Charlotte Harbor estuarine system, a marvelously productive, shallow, grassy estuary fed by three major rivers and surrounded by geologically young barrier islands. We teach both adults and children about the mangrove detritus food chain. As we dig and process artifacts, and when we give public talks, we draw connections between the quality of life for humans and animals and the quality of the water, land, and air.

Furthermore, our educational efforts reach beyond the typical profile of those who join archaeological and nature societies. In 1990, school buses brought 1473 elementary school children to Pineland in eight weeks; in 1992, 2232 visited the dig over a ten-week period. Many were blacks, Hispanics, and whites from underprivileged backgrounds. Our site tours started at the water's edge, where we oriented the children geographically and talked to them about the mangroves and sea grasses and how the estuarine environment provides nutrition for so many fish. We were astonished to learn that many of the children of this coastal area had never seen the coast before! For many—including a number of middle-class children—our archaeological walking tour was also their first close look at a cow, a woodpecker, or a strangler-fig tree.

The lessons of archaeology and the lessons of nature seem to blend well and are easily taught in the out-of-doors and in hands-on classroom demonstrations. We like to think that a number of southwest Florida children now have a better understanding of their environment as well as their cultural heritage.

In teaching about the environment, we do not represent the ancient Calusa as consummate conservationists, nor do we allow them to be portrayed as ignorant and violent savages. We try to represent the Calusa way of life as the result of a long succession of human decisions, human relationships with each other, and human relationships with the physical surroundings. We emphasize that only concerted, purposeful human activity will ensure that the region continues to grow in a way that does not destroy the very resources that make it such an attractive place in which to live.

Note that the "Year of the Indian" project funds have come from a historic preservation "special category" grant-in-aid. Special category funds are traditionally disbursed for the renovation or adaptive reuse of historically significant buildings. Only one archaeologist sits on Florida's ten-member Historic Preservation Advisory Council, which ranks the funding proposals each year. We not only received full funding for the 1989–90 project, but these historic preservationists ranked our second-phase proposal second out of fifty-four special-category grant proposals recommended for funding. More than half of our budget is for analysis, conservation, curation, laboratory equipment, and publication—items and activities notoriously hard to fund properly in cultural resource management and National Science Foundation contexts.

What chord did the "Year of the Indian" strike with Florida's historic preservationists? Again, I suggest it is one of public outreach. Historic preservationists realize the appeal of archaeology and are committed to historic preservation for public benefit. When they make their case for the rehabilitation of buildings, they emphasize (1) heritage, that is, the value of "pride of place" for local citizens, and (2) fiscal responsibility, in other words, rehabilitation and reuse of an old building is less expensive than building a new one. I believe that they see archaeologists as building even more appreciation for the past by reintroducing a lost part of local history and providing, as the historic preservationists believe they do, a nonradical but effective counterbalance to powerful and potentially undisciplined forces of economic development.

REGIONAL HISTORICAL ECOLOGY AS
ENVIRONMENTALIST PRAXIS

I believe that the southwest Florida experience can be generalized to situations elsewhere. It would be a delusion to imagine that we have reached everyone in southwest Florida with a message about Indian heritage and environmental preservation. Certainly we have not reached and will never reach many people in the area. There was little or no public awareness of the prehistoric past when we began the project, however, and I know that our message has reached hundreds of people in the form of meaningful, personal interactions with archaeology and the environment and that many hundreds more have had at least some casual contact by visiting museums, touring our digs, or watching our multimedia show at the planetarium. This has happened in an area in which the economy is one of booming development and the politics are heavily Republican, conservative, and business-oriented.

Could this much have been accomplished without a large part-time population of active retired people? Could the cultural and natural resource preservation message have been transmitted as effectively in a county that lacked an already established environmental education program in its school system? I admit that retirees contribute significantly to our work force, and that the educational and economic resources of Lee County have facilitated the project in many ways. However, I think that pride in local cultural heritage can be promoted anywhere interesting questions are posed and an archaeological record exists to be investigated. Our volunteers are from all walks of life and all ages. (Our work week is Wednesday through Sunday, to encourage the visits and participation of working people.) People interested in local history and environment can be found even in communities where the population is sparse or the economy weak.

Although contemporary Floridians and the ancient Calusa are in no way related, they both have had to face environmental and sociopolitical dilemmas in the same environmental setting. Among the sixteenth-century Calusa, the authority of the paramount chief was tied in part to his ability to ensure continuous bounty from the environment. Both environmental and sociopolitical factors contributed to the rise and fall of the Calusa. In twentieth-century Florida, people are beginning to demand of their elected representatives an account of efforts to ensure that the environment continues to produce its fruits and that there are adequate resources for all. Both environmental and sociopolitical factors have also contributed to the booms and busts of Florida's economy. The recession of 1991–93 wreaked havoc in state government, and even the governor conceded that a state income tax could not be ruled out in Florida's future.

As the Calusa learned, resources may seem infinite, but there is no accounting for an unexpectable catastrophic event. Even the Calusa kingdom could not exist in isolation, though it held out for far longer than most native Florida societies did. Ultimately, the Calusa fell victim to political struggles that originated in the broader-scale reality of European colonialism. Today, Floridians are finding that their own political economy is tied inextricably to the economy of the nation. Dependent on tourists and development for money to provide basic services to its permanent residents, it is constrained to attract hundreds of new residents per day, steadily eroding the very environmental advantages that make Florida such an attractive place in which to live. There are limits to growth, even in the Sunshine State. The more we can draw a link between today's and yesterday's Floridians and help today's Floridians to understand the connections between their environment and the quality of their lives, the better equipped today's Floridians will be to cope with environmental challenges in the future.

It is too early to say how well the environmental lessons have been internalized by the several thousand young people who have visited our sites and learned about the environment of their own area, nor whether their awareness will be reflected in altered behavior as they reach adulthood. If their behavior is anything like the political commitment of some of their elders in Lee and Collier counties, there is reason for optimism.

The important factors in successfully forging meaningful links between present and past and stirring an environmental awareness, it seems to me, are (1) a regional focus; (2) a long-term commitment to the region; (3) mutually beneficial relations with local historical, environmental, conservation, and other like-minded societies; and (4) public outreach in a variety of settings. It is always a happy circumstance when everyone gains from a situation. People now look forward to our public presentations, digs, and newsletters. Meanwhile, we are obtaining the detailed understanding of the Calusa heartland that is essential for answering the broad anthropological questions we have posed about the complexity and collapse of the Calusa.

A historical-ecological orientation guides both our archaeological research and the practice of the insights that we gain from that research. Our motto might be "As we learn, we teach." The lessons of regional historical ecology can be learned and taught at the same time, to the benefit of all concerned.

Chapter 10

Toward a Properly Historical Ecology

Thomas C. Patterson

The whole Darwinian theory of the struggle for existence is simply the transference from society to animate nature of Hobbes's theory of war of every man against every man and the bourgeois economic theory of competition, along with the Malthusian theory of population. This feat having been accomplished . . . the same theories are next transferred back from organic nature to history and their validity as eternal laws of human society declared to have been proved.

—Frederick Engels, letter to Lavrov, 12–17 November 1875 [1]

Let me preface my examination and analysis of historical ecology and historically contingent totalities with an account that reflects certain elements of truth and illustrates many of the points I wish to discuss.

About a century ago, industrial capitalists began to build factories and power plants around the eastern Great Lakes. These factories burned bituminous coal to heat the forges and turn the turbines that powered the machines. Fumes laden with sulfuric acid and other contaminants spewed from tall smokestacks, and great plumes containing these particles were carried several hundred miles northeastward. The contaminants eventually fell to the ground as dust particles or mixed with raindrops. They settled on buildings and statues, fell on trees and lakes, and were inhaled by people and animals far from where they originated.

The factory owners made enormous profits. They used inexpensive raw materials, and with the aid of legislators and powerful friends in government, they paid their workers low wages to toil under difficult and frequently dangerous conditions. More often than not, the workers were acutely aware of the dangers that lurked in the factories; however, they continued to work under these circumstances because they had no other means to support themselves and their families. In some instances, the workers succeeded in organizing unions that pursued various strategies to improve their working conditions and quality of life. These tactics put them in direct opposition to the goals of the factory owners, who wanted profits and docile workers who would merge their knowledge, skills, and energies with those of inanimate machines. When the workers undertook various kinds of job actions to improve their lot, the factory owners often retaliated by calling in the police, by seeking the aid of like-minded judges and politicians, or by threats to fire the workers, to replace them with scabs, or to relocate the factories to another region or to another country where labor power, right-to-work laws, and political allies could be purchased for less money.

After a decade or so, people living downwind from the factories began to complain. "Acid rain," they said, "is destroying the marble buildings and statues in the cities."

The conservationists told the press and their legislators, "It's killing the fish in the lakes."

"That's not important," the legislators replied. "It's just one kind of fish. There are still plenty of species that are not being disturbed, so go fish somewhere else."

Native Americans claimed, "The factories are killing us and our way of life. Acid rain is polluting the lakes and streams and killing the fish; it is destroying the forests where deer live and the nut trees we harvest in the fall."

The lumber companies asked the state, "Let us cut down the forests before they die so we can make a profit. The Indians and their neighbors can move somewhere else or get a job."

The conservation lobby spent a lot of money proclaiming the value of fish and trees and the need for legislation to protect them. Other political action committees—such as those representing the factory owners or the coal and nuclear industries—also spent hundreds of millions of dollars to protect and promote their interests. A few politicians were eventually voted out of office and new ones were elected; in the wake, regulations were enacted that provided some protection to the environment.

Factory owners were told to install scrubbers on their smokestacks to remove the pollutants from the emissions. Others were told to build taller smokestacks so the pollutants would be borne much greater distances before they settled; they no longer damaged the lakes and forests people were complaining about, but they began to damage those farther downwind. In five or ten years, the inhabitants of those areas voiced complaints about their trees dying, the diminishing numbers of fish in their lakes and rivers, and the increasing numbers of people who suffered from respiratory ailments and other afflictions related to air pollution. It was difficult to show that these illnesses were caused by the pollutants, as the tobacco and petrochemical companies well knew. They argued that "statistical correlations do not necessarily indicate causation." Many legislators believed them.

After World War II, factory owners in the region learned about a new product that everybody—the manufacturers of refrigerators, air-conditioners, spray cans, and even the government—seemed to want. It was a chlorofluorohydrocarbon (CFC) compound with a thousand and one uses. The market for this commodity had enormous growth potential and opportunities for high profit margins. What an investment opportunity! A number of companies sought to meet the existing demand for CFCs and to create new markets for their product.

There were a few problems. CFCs were almost indestructible at sea level, but that was okay since they accumulated and disintegrated in the ozone-rich upper atmosphere. There was a little problem with the chlorine released during this reaction. Each atom destroyed tens of thousands of ozone molecules. They resembled tiny video-game pacmen gobbling up billions and billions of oxygen atoms; they were slowly destroying the ozone layer, a filter that reduces heat and prevents dangerous ultraviolet radiation from reaching the earth's surface.

In the late 1980s, the president's science advisor claimed, "This is not a serious problem. Yes, of course, the ozone layer blocks heat and the ultraviolet radiation that causes sunburn and skin cancer. However, since most of the ozone destruction has occurred over Antarctica, which is inhabited mostly by seals and penguins, there is no real threat to human beings." What he meant was, "At worst, some plankton might be destroyed, and a few penguins will get sunburned. A small cost for economic progress. Anyway, if the ozone layer gets thin somewhere else, the inhabitants under that hole can always buy hats or chemical sunblocks manufactured by one of the pharmaceutical or petrochemical companies."

In December 1991, scientists reported evidence suggesting that a large hole was developing in the ozone layer over eastern North America and Europe. The hole continued to grow, and the incidence of various kinds of skin cancer, including lethal melanomas, increased almost immediately. Many of the early cases were individuals, such as farm and construction workers, who toiled in the sun. Other cases occurred among the spouses and children of the factory owners, who frolicked in the sun at high-altitude ski resorts and on ocean beaches. Ultimately, exposure became entirely democratic, affecting those who stayed inside as well as the ones who wore hats and used chemical sunscreens.

The story does not, of course, mean that factories in capitalist regimes were the only ones that polluted the environment in this century; for several reasons, those in the socialist countries have no better or worse records in this regard. First, the factories built during and after the 1930s in the Soviet Union were often modeled after those in the Great Lakes region; hence, the organization and techniques of production were similar, even though the relations of production—that is, the interrelations among the factory workers, their managers, and the state—were fundamentally different (Nove 1969; Lewis 1979). Second, it is essential to consider the historical contexts in which industrialization occurred in the USSR, the Eastern Bloc, and China: the civil war and invasion following the Russian Revolution, the embargo of the following decades, the threat of war in the 1930s, World War II, the Cold War initiated by National Security Council Resolution 68, and the wars in Korea and Vietnam, all of which diverted enormous resources, resulted in wanton disregard for the environment in the name of national security, and created a "climate of fear" that was just as real as the one fueled by the paranoid distortions of the industrial-military complex in the West.

I

In the opening story, we saw that the social and natural worlds are inextricably intertwined. Changes in one dimension led to changes in the others. Since the 1970s, the environmental movement has focused attention on ecology and made ecological destruction a social issue. It understands current global ecological problems in terms of their linkage to human activity. However, as Mellos (1988) observes in his important analysis of the theoretical underpinnings of the ecology movement, these understandings of human-nature connections are typically portrayed in terms of neo-Malthusian, expansionist, eco-development, or radical ecological perspectives, each of which makes certain assumptions about human nature and posits a direct, socially unmediated relation between the individual and nature. The presuppositions simultaneously link the various perspectives and differentiate them. They affect how the advocates of each standpoint comprehend the association between environmental destruction and human action, how they constitute ecology, and what kinds of political action they prescribe to rectify ecological problems. Let me briefly summarize some of the main points of Mellos's analysis.

The *neo-Malthusians* view the world in terms of a late eighteenth-century theory of crisis based on scarcity: misery occurs when the size of a population, with a given level of development of its productive forces, exceeds the capacity of nature to provide an adequate food supply. Crises occur when the finite resources of nature are overused by undifferentiated masses of people with insatiable appetites and desires. The condition of the biosphere is a consequence of the relationship between the almost-unfettered consumption of nature and the limited or deteriorating capacity of nature to replenish itself in the face of overexploitation and pollution.

Neo-Malthusian explanations gained momentum during the 1960s—at roughly the same time various Third World countries proclaimed their political and economic independence from colonial powers and the United States undertook wholesale environmental destruction in Southeast Asia (Coontz 1957; Ehrlich 1968; Ophuls 1977). In this perspective, population growth is limited by wars, epidemics, famines, and other controls and by various preventive checks—for example, birth control, abortion, infanticide, or abstinence—which lower birth rates.

Since the neo-Malthusians view human societies as undifferentiated masses of people, their understanding of the relationship between nature and society is unmediated. This prevents them from asking questions about social relations, class structures, or the impact that various culturally informed practices have on the environment. In their view, ecological crises are resolved by restraining population growth, reducing the demand for raw materials, and diminishing waste and pollution. Thus, a political theory rooted in neo-Malthusian thought is concerned with restraining consumption.

Expansionists—like Kahn (1979), Boserup (1965), and the World Bank (1972) in its report on the limits to growth—believe that the infinitely expandable appetites of people are not a problem, because there is no contradiction between unfettered consumption and the capacity of nature to reproduce itself. They emphasize the enormous extent of nature's wealth and assert that scarcity must always be understood in terms of the limitations imposed by particular socioeconomic contexts and levels of development. Throughout history, they argue, people have repeatedly overcome shortages and created new needs through technological innovation.

From their perspective, ecology is ultimately crisis free. The appearance of problems in the relationship between nature and society—like the contamination or destruction of nature—creates the conditions for future solutions because of the steadily increasing tempo of technological innovation. For example, the manufacture of antipollution devices and the provision of services—such as automotive emission control devices or the clean-up of toxic waste sites, like buildings with asbestos or the severely damaged nuclear reactor at Three Mile Island—became major growth industries in the 1980s. Expansionist political praxis claims that the proper role of government is not to regulate the activities of innovative individuals but rather to protect those conditions that permit them to pursue the private appropriation and accumulation of capital with as little interference as possible.

The critical notions of Schumacher (1973) and other *eco-developmentalists* are (1) that human beings produce and consume in order to satisfy basic needs, which are constituted at the level of the asocial individual; (2) that the relationship between a community and nature is a consequence of technologies that embody different ways of appropriating nature rather than an effect of social relations; (3) that the centralization of economic and political power at a global level distributes individuals, societies, and states along a rich-poor axis; (4) that, as a result of the concentration of power, the activities of the rich are guided by the desire to accumulate and expand, while those of the poor are driven by concerns about subsistence; and (5) that the activities of the rich and poor destroy or modify the environment in different ways. They advocate self-reliance—severing connections with other communities and decentralizing political and economic power in order to eliminate the distinctions between rich and poor and to restore the viability of the environment (Mellos 1988:60).

Production, consumption, and self-reliance are the critical and problematic features for the eco-developmentalists. They view production and consumption as a single undifferentiated activity (need satisfaction) which involves the appropriation of nature either as a directly consumable object or as the source of raw materials for producing usable objects. Since the consumption of nature is not mediated by social relations, the relationship between a community and nature is determined exclusively by its technology of appropriation. Hence, technology is the source of social and ecological problems. These problems are resolved when communities become self-reliant and satisfy their needs in ways that are compatible with a stable ecological order and do not involve external assistance. The difficulties encountered by a theory of action based on this perspective are twofold: it lacks a theory of community beyond one defined merely as an aggregation of individuals, and it does not consider how such aggregates assert their political and economic autonomy from the existing world order (Mellos 1988:60–74).

Radical ecologists—like Bookchin (1980), Gorz (1980), or Leiss (1976) —are concerned with the devastating effects of hierarchical social relations and the tendencies toward accumulation generated by industrial capitalism. Hierarchical social relations simultaneously create artificial wants and degrade the environment; at the same time, they prevent individuals from realizing their human potential, from satisfying their authentic needs, and from establishing harmonious relations with nature. The radical ecologists explore the contradictions between exploitative social relations, on the one hand, and environmental destruction, on the other. They understand these contradictions in terms of a connection, an exchange, between aggregates of asocial individuals and nature that is not mediated by social relations (Mellos 1988:75ff.).

In their view, the satisfaction of authentic needs and self-sufficiency or self-management are critical; these capabilities derive from the species essence of human beings or when the efforts of individuals are free from outside interference or intervention. Authentic needs are satisfied by the individualized activities of persons who are self-sufficient managers of their own destinies. This means that those individuals, who aggregate to constitute a community, relate to nature in a variety of ways. By producing use-values, which satisfy genuine needs, rather than commodities for exchange, which create artificial wants, they establish diversity and equality. Such activities replicate the structure of nature and, thereby, restore balanced relations with it. Like the eco-developmentalists, the radical ecologists have not adequately explored how aggregates of asocial individuals assert their autonomy and self-sufficiency.

The important contribution of the theories outlined above is that they make environmental transformation and destruction global social issues. However, they leave us with two problems. First, they do not permit us to theorize and comprehend fully the complexly mediated, continually shifting relations, reciprocal interactions, and contradictions that occur within and among the various levels of both society and the natural world. Second, they do not allow us to begin dealing with the issue of what is to be done.

II

How can we conceptualize, analyze, and comprehend those relations and determinations and the consequences of these linkages? I suggest that this is best accomplished by conceptualizing both society and nature in terms of a realist ontology. Unlike empiricists, who claim that the world is accurately reflected by its appearance, realists argue that the observable elements of the world are actually structured by unobservable processes and relations.

For realists, then, society and nature are intertwined and interconnected totalities. A *totality* is a dialectically structured and historically determined unity that exists in and through the diverse interpenetrations, connections, and contradictions that join its constituent parts regardless of whether the components are observable or unobservable (Mészáros 1972:63–64, 1983). This means (1) that the whole is always greater than the sum of its parts, and (2) that it is impossible to understand a totality merely by studying the parts.

The opening story describes a large totality composed of smaller totalities—capitalist society in the eastern Great Lakes, plant and animal communities, atmospheric circulation patterns, and chemical reactions in the irradiated, ozone-rich upper atmosphere—that are both semiautonomous and subordinated to it; each totality is simultaneously subject to multiple sources of determination by the other entities with which it is linked and by the more encompassing totalities of which it is a part. For example, the acid rain pollution that emanates from the Great Lakes area and falls in both the United States and Canada has led to the enactment of different kinds of national and provincial- or state-level legislation in the two countries as well as to heated exchanges between high-level political representatives at several international summit conferences. For the past five years, federal officials have actively opposed the proposals to ban the production of CFCs, which the governments of Canada and several capitalist states in northern Europe have supported. As a result, American manufacturers continue to produce large quantities of CFCs; these compounds are subsequently released into the atmosphere, mostly by the United States government itself, while industrialists in other countries are reducing their production levels and seeking alternative commodities.

The configuration of a totality—the interconnections of its parts—is always historically contingent, confined to a particular moment in time, and changing. That is, the interconnections between the production and release of CFCs, on the one hand, and the destruction of the ozone layer, on the other, began about fifty years ago. It has proceeded at an accelerated pace since then. Thus far the process is unidirectional, and awareness of it has yielded different responses. The process may be reversible; however, if ozone depletion were stopped today, it might take a century or more before any ameliorative effects would be noticeable.

A social totality, like the modern world system or one of the ancient civilizations studied by archaeologists, also has two dimensions: what we can actually see, and the largely unobservable processes and relations that are simultaneously revealed in and concealed by everyday life. The first appears as a historically constituted, internally differentiated set of communities, linked together and organized by the institutions and practices of state structures and by class struggle. The communities are defined in relation to each other and to their positions in economic and power structures, which they variously support or challenge.

The communities themselves are organized groups of individuals with relatively homogeneous value systems; some recognize the shared positions they occupy and, consequently, the commonality of their interests. Men and women are born into communities whose organizational patterns and ethics shape how they live and how their lives are reproduced or modified through time. However, the forms of everyday life may vary from one to the next, since the various communities occupy different places in class-based structures of power; they may even be opposed, especially when states and their ruling classes differentially extract goods, labor power, or surplus value. This means that communities are culturally and historically constituted categories and that their members have explicitly or implicitly different viewpoints or standpoints about their position in the existing social order (Harding 1986:136–62; Lukács 1967). In the United States, for instance, Navajo or Winnebago communities struggling to maintain their traditional ways of life, the unskilled and professional fractions of the largely working class African-American community, the white working-class groups currently reinventing ethnicity, and the increasingly internationalized ruling class of the country have different understandings of and commitments to the status quo. In other words, the cultures of the communities are diverse and refract in complex ways the differences in their relations to concrete structures of power; their members often view the totality through lenses differentially formed by commitment, compliance, acquiescence, resistance, or opposition to those structures (Gailey and Patterson 1988).

Besides the dimension of appearances and experiences, a social totality is also composed of the unobservable, underlying relations and processes that both generate and are expressed in the observable phenomena and events of everyday life and history. This is the domain of modes of production—the economic bases and corresponding superstructures—that shape and constrain concrete specific totalities (Jameson 1981:32–58); these enable or facilitate the appearance of certain courses of development and impede or prevent others from taking place. The complex interrelations between the various levels are most adequately described by terms like reciprocal interaction, semi-autonomy, overdetermination, and uneven development (Kellner 1989:18).

In social totalities, everyday life and history are intertwined. Kosík

(1976:46) describes the connection dialectically: everyday life is the raw material of history, the stage on which it is enacted, whereas history is the disruption of everyday routines and practices. Williams (1977:121–27) portrays it as the interpenetration of residual, dominant, and emergent elements of culture and modes of production. Residual strands from past history are variably incorporated to support, cross-examine, or resist the dominant social order of the present. They potentially generate new understandings and practices for actors who occupy different places in power structures, and whose routine conduct and perceptions are contingent on, but not completely determined by, their positions within the existing framework of social relations (Callinicos 1988:76–91). Whether existing institutions and practices are reproduced or new ones are constituted rests on the capacities of groups of actors to overcome the constraints and contradictions that exist and are revealed at particular moments. From time to time, history presents real alternatives in which the actions of actors occupying particular places in structures do make a difference.

Levins and Lewontin (1985:133–42, 272–85) conceptualize nature as a multileveled totality, "a [historically] contingent structure in reciprocal interaction with its own parts and with the greater whole of which it is a part." In their view, the heterogeneous parts of the totality acquired their characteristic properties in the interactions that constituted the whole. The various elements of a totality—its parts and levels—as well as the whole itself are continually changing, though at different rates; as a result, at any given moment, one element might appear to be fixed in relation to another. The fact that totalities are continually in flux means (1) that they may destroy the very conditions that brought them into existence in the first place and (2) that the transformations create possibilities for new historically contingent structures that did not exist previously. The changes that occur in a totality and its components arise from the internal heterogeneity of the parts, the diversity of their interconnections, and their development in relation to larger totalities which influence and are influenced by those changes. In this view, the totality is shaped by the intersection of various internal and external dynamics.

Nature, as Levins and Lewontin (1985:278–85) point out, is also a totality. It is a unity of contradictions characterized by the interplay of elements and dynamics that operate at different levels of ontological reality—local species populations, communities, and biogeographic regions. Consequently, natural totalities exhibit (1) spontaneous activity and change, which have been conceptualized in terms of positive and negative feedbacks, (2) the interpenetration and interaction of categories from different levels of reality, and (3) the "coexistence of opposing principles (rather than processes) which, taken together, have very different implications or consequences than they would have if taken separately" (Levins and Lewontin 1985:285).

In their view, a community is historically specific, historically contingent, and dialectically constituted—the product of the reciprocal interactions of populations of different species residing in the same biogeographic region. It is the locus of the interactions between higher- and lower-level wholes. Although the local demographic interactions of the various species populations in a community take place against a backdrop of biogeographic and population genetic parameters, the community level is not epiphenomenal. Instead, it has its own distinctive properties and dynamics that are incompletely determined by its connections with other dimensions of reality (Levins and Lewontin 1985:137–42).

The composition of a community depends to some extent on the origin of the biota. It is linked to the biogeographic region by the dynamics of colonization and local extinction and to the particular biological characteristics of the constituent species, by the rates at which they enter the region, and by their interactions with each other and with various ecological parameters. The interconnections of the communities and their constituent populations are composed by a variety of many-to-one and one-to-many linkages. Many-to-one linkages indicate that many configurations preserve the same qualitative properties of the community. One-to-many connections between parts and wholes and between the various levels of the totality indicate indeterminacy or randomness. The existence of distinct forms of linkage ensures that examples of the same kind of community are not identical (Levins and Lewontin 1985:140–42).

Juxtaposing realist conceptualizations of social and natural totalities implies that the two are interconnected. It suggests a continuity between nature and culture, evolution and history. Such a formulation stands in opposition to several important social theoretical traditions—deriving inspiration from Descartes, Locke, Rousseau, and Kant, among others—which claim that there is a rupture between the human and natural realms and, consequently, that they must be understood or explained in different terms.

The basis for arguing that there is a connection between social totalities and natural ones is this: human beings, at the most fundamental level, engage in socially constituted, contingent, culturally meaningful activities to produce the necessities required to ensure the maintenance, demographic replacement, and social reproduction of life in the community.

They do so by interacting with nature, by appropriating its raw materials for consumption, and by transforming nature itself into a means of production. Human history documents the requisite creation of culture—the ability to symbol and to use tools for appropriating and transforming the environment; this capacity developed several million years ago among the members of at least one early hominid lineage. Human interactions with nature have been social and cultural phenomena for a long time. Consequently, they need to be considered in light of social totalities and their interpenetrations with the natural world viewed in different dimensions and at different scales and levels of inclusion.

III

The second problem is concerned with what we should do. Everyday life in today's world is shaped by a series of intersecting contradictions: among capitalist and socialist states, among the industrialized and Third World states, among competing capitalist states, and among those classes that own or control the means of production and those that do not. These contradictions affect not only how people with different relations to power interact with and understand each other, but also how their activities impinge on nature and are influenced by the environmental changes that are taking place. In this context, it is crucial to confront politics—to understand power and how it is constituted and wielded. In other words, the decision to use bituminous coal or to manufacture CFCs is not made or agreed to by every class or community in a social totality. These decisions are often complied with or contested; their implementation ultimately reflects power.

Power, as Lukes (1986:9–12) observes, is not merely an issue of force or coercion. It is also about who can affect the interests of others; who can limit the freedom of others by interfering with their choices, by structuring the options available to them, or by limiting their capacity to make decisions; and who can achieve goals or advance interests in a context of competing claims. Power is a potential that appears when classes interact; it is instantiated in their actions. It works to maintain inequalities by protecting the powerful and by depriving the powerless of political resources and promoting compliance or acceptance of the established order among them (Gaventa 1980:vi–ix).

Lukes (1974) points out that political theorists have discussed the issue of "who can affect the interests of whom" in three different ways, each of which presupposes a particular understanding of "interest" and political activity. He calls these the one-, two-, and three-dimensional views of power. In the traditional pluralist, one-dimensional perspective, interests are preferences revealed in the political activity of decision-making, and power is understood in terms of who participates in the process and whose views about the important issues ultimately prevail. In the two-dimensional perspective, power is exercised not only in the decision-making process, "but also by controlling the agenda, mobilizing the bias of the system, determining which issues are 'key' issues, indeed which issues come up for decision, and excluding those which threaten the interests of the powerful" (Lukes 1986:9). Adversely affected interests are revealed in the decision-making activity and by extrapolitical grievances and concerns that the powerful prevent from entering the political arena where decisions are made. In the three-dimensional perspective, power operates not only in the arenas of agenda setting and decision making, but also in ways that shape and modify the perceptions of the powerless about the nature and extent of inequalities, that subvert their interests, and that ultimately limit their capacity for political action.

Gaventa (1980) explores the interplay of the three dimensions of power in his widely and deservedly acclaimed study of political quiescence and rebellion in an Appalachian valley. He suggests that

> Through processes of coercive power, those most likely to challenge inequalities may be prevented from challenge, while those least likely to challenge maintain the political game as a ritual whose rules are clearly understood by all parties. Over time, there may develop a routine of non-conflict within and about local politics-a routine which may, to the observer, appear a fatalism found in "backwardness" (Gaventa 1980:161).

Gaventa (1980:vii) also examines the ways in which relatively powerless people have challenged power structures, and their varying success at transforming existing power relations. Coercion, power, and patterns of powerlessness have often combined to prevent "issues from arising, grievances from being voiced, and interests from being recognized."

The first step, he suggests, involves what Freire (1972:68, 81; 1973:21–31) has called "conscientization," the emergence and deepening of awareness. It is a process of politicization and mobilization that begins when the members of a subordinated group identify for themselves grievances and aspirations around which concrete, *self-determined* action is thought possible. These grievances and aspirations exist in the present, in the everyday experience of the people who are becoming aware how historically constituted, spatially organized, social structures and processes shape and constrain their lives. Common information about injustices and inequities, once shared, gradually becomes public knowledge and a basis for recognizing shared grievances.

Thus, the process of conscientization involves historical analyses of the institutions and practices that underlie current power relations. These analyses must occur in order to discover whether or which of the present-day patterns and routines of nonchallenge have been shaped by power and how these tendencies and habits of nonconflict are maintained. Comparisons of the extent and kinds of participation by the powerless during normal and exceptional times helps to show what subordinated groups might think or do were it not for the control exerted in one or more of the three dimensions of power by the dominant groups. Comparisons provide examples of instances when agendas and decisions were made differently and times when the powerless possibly had different understandings of their interests and different views about their capacities to shift the arena of political debate or to initiate meaningful changes. Critical, historical investigations of how power relations came to be structured the way they are in the present have the potential of exposing the hidden faces of power and the continually shifting interconnections of power and powerlessness (Gaventa 1980:253–56).

The process of conscientization must also incorporate analyses of spatiality—the socially produced spaces where social relations within and between communities are concretized and reproduced (Soja 1985). Such inquiries must take place, because the institutions and practices in which power is materialized are unevenly constituted and distributed. As a result, there are inequities within and between neighborhoods, communities, and states. Uneven development also produces externalities in which the problems confronted by the members of one community are not of their own making but rather are constituted by the inhabitants and producers of another region. In order to address the difficulties created by externalities, they must first be recognized and accurately situated in space (Harvey 1973:86–93). In other words, the landscapes, which mark the interface between the social and natural totalities described above, are often contested terrains, sites where power relations are instantiated, complied with, or disputed.

Challenging existing practices and changing human-nature interactions are intensely political acts that must necessarily begin by disrupting and breaking down patterns and routines of nonparticipation. This creates conditions where conscientization can occur, where the members of a community can share information, discover common grievances, and examine ways of remedying or overcoming what they perceive as their plight. Conscientization allows them to conceptualize situations and to carry out actions that address and resolve the issues they raised. The experience, successes, and hope gained in these initial challenges to prevailing practices and routines have the capacity to enhance the confidence that the members of a community have in their ability to address collectively and to bring about meaningful changes regarding successfully introduced issues.

The process of conscientization is potentially transformative. It has the capacity to shift the political arenas in which community members act. In the initial stages of the process, the community gains an awareness and appreciation of real issues; they begin to deal with the third dimension of power, to reshape their perceptions about the inequalities that subvert their interests and limit their capacity for political action. As these are revealed, they begin to enter a new political arena, where they can confront how agendas are established and how bias is mobilized. As the real power relations are increasingly unmasked, the terrain and nature of the struggle between the community and the powerholders become progressively more transparent, especially as this politically dominant group becomes increasingly aware of the challenges to its power and position. Under certain conditions, these controversies can spill into the arena defined by the first dimension of power, the one where power is exercised and contested by the participants in political decision-making processes, who attempt to control agendas, mobilize bias, and organize extrapolitical activities that limit the effectiveness of their opponents and prevent them from carrying out political action.

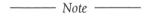

——— Note ———

1. The epigraph is from Marx and Engels 1970(3):477–80.

Epilogue

Carole L. Crumley

During the week of our advanced seminar on historical ecology, we concentrated on showing, through the discussion of shared concepts, some rational links among emotive explorations of the human condition and the more detached environmental sciences. Each of us presented a working paper which represented years of investment in particular issues and parts of the world. Egypt, France, Florida, Greenland, the Amazon, Tanzania, Yucatan: we traveled together through both space and time. One evening we each showed a few favorite slides. By week's end, our emotional involvement as individuals was fused into a spontaneous, collective desire to draft something together. What? An accord, we decided. It was not easy; we have some fundamental differences of opinion. Finally, Winterhalder and Hassan produced a draft of our "Santa Fe Accord." We debated it, adjusted the wording, and signed the document— a statement about which we could feel both foolish and a little proud.

We have begun to explore the implications and applications of an explicitly historical ecology. We are, neither collectively nor individually, finished with that task. We recognize the problems that face us at the close of what may be the most environmentally destructive century in human history. We are capable of studying intricate chains of causation and untangling them. Most importantly, however, we wish to make a difference: to affect the human future by effecting humane environmental policy.

We wish to stress that a false dichotomy between "natural" and anthropogenic causation glorifies a nonexistent "pristine" nature. No spot on the earth is unaffected by humans. The juxtaposition of a pure, natural environment with a sullied human one promotes negative attitudes toward culturally informed local and regional solutions to global problems.

Multiple causes, only one of which is human agency, produce environmental variation.

Throughout their history, human populations have both effected and been affected by environmental change. Human evolution is commonly portrayed as a triumph of increasingly sophisticated technologies over the vicissitudes of nature. But although sophisticated technologies enable short-term palliatives, technology alone—especially in circumstances where expense, availability of materials, or training make applications daunting—does not offer a lasting resolution of environmental problems and their attendant social, economic, and political woes.

Events that affect the environment can occur at a variety of temporal and spatial scales; thus, periodicity, duration, and severity of particular conditions may have separate historical and geographical distributions. Human activities play a greater role in some events than in others. Useful lessons, applicable to current problems, may be derived from studies of past and present interaction between humans and their environments, but the specifics of regional environmental and cultural history must be understood. Local and regional knowledge about the environment, transmitted through culture, can be the source of appropriate adaptive strategies in times of marked environmental change. Conversely, unfamiliarity with environmental parameters can lead to disastrous choices and actions.

Lévi-Strauss (1966:257) argues that there is no history that is not "history *for.*" The practice of historical ecology is for this: to explore our options as a species in changing times while protecting the cultural diversity that makes humans remarkable. Our concern is that a holistic approach be adopted for the study of human-environment relations. Thus far, in the rush to snare funds to study global environmental change, solving the problems of tomorrow has taken precedence over untangling those of yesterday. We argue that pattern recognition must be practiced historically—both temporally and spatially—if it is to inform policy.

How this should be done requires a much broader constituency than a few colleagues treated to a week of one another's company; it must be addressed at many scales and in many dimensions by researchers with multiple skills who are broadly trained to cooperate. Since 1989 I have been a member of the Committee for the National Institute for the Environment (CNIE), a proposed agency that is predicated on the need for a research unit capable of treating national environmental problems as they relate to global, regional, and local conditions. During the 1993 legislative session, bills will be introduced into the United States Congress to appropriate funds for the creation of the NIE; it is in such a research context that long-term coordination and cooperation can take place.

Whether or not the NIE is funded, individual and collective efforts to mold regionally, culturally, and historically sensitive policy must continue. May we enter into lively debate over their structure and content.

Santa Fe Accord

Advanced Seminar in Historical Ecology

SCHOOL OF AMERICAN RESEARCH
13–19 OCTOBER 1990

We are alarmed at the current peril to humanity and the biosphere.

Historical understanding is essential to enable present and future generations to live with dignity on a changing earth. To achieve this, we must appreciate both global connections and the diversity of local knowledge.

We question habits of thought that pit nature against culture and science against history, that assume human interaction with the environment can be characterized by mechanistic principles, and that ignore the dynamism of human ecology.

We underscore the importance of historical antecedents, of cognition and communication, of human agency, and of rich human experiences with different landscapes.

We call for research and management options that draw on the lessons from the human past to guide and promote a sustainable quality of life.

Carole L. Crumley   Thomas H. McGovern
Joel D. Gunn   Christine Padoch
Fekri A. Hassan   Thomas C. Patterson
Alice E. Ingerson   Peter R. Schmidt
William. H. Marquardt   Bruce P. Winterhalder

References

Abu-Zayed, M. M. Ali
  1987   The Nile and Egypt (Arabic edition). Cairo: Dar el-Hidaia.
Adams, R. E. W.
  1977   Prehistoric Mesoamerica. Boston: Little, Brown.
Adams, Richard Newbold
  1988   The Eighth Day: Social Evolution as the Self-Organization of Energy. Austin: University of Texas Press.
Adams, Robert McC.
  1966   The Evolution of Urban Society. Chicago: Aldine.
Allen, T. F. H., and Thomas B. Starr
  1982   Hierarchy: Perspectives for Ecological Complexity. Chicago: University of Chicago Press.
Amorosi, Thomas
  1989   Contributions to the Zooarchaeology of Iceland: Some Preliminary Notes. In The Anthropology of Iceland, E. Paul Durrenburger and Gisli Palsson, eds., pp. 203–27. Iowa City: University of Iowa Press.
Anderson, Robert S., and Walter Huber
  1988   The Hour of the Fox: Tropical Forests, the World Bank, and Indigenous People in Central India. Seattle: University of Washington Press.
Andersson, Theodore M., and William Ian Miller
  1989   Law and Literature in Medieval Iceland. Stanford, CA: Stanford University Press.
Angell, J. K.
  1991   Changes in Tropospheric and Stratospheric Global Temperatures, 1958–1988. In Greenhouse-Gas-Induced Climatic Change: A Critical Appraisal of Simulation and Observations, M. Schlesinger, ed. Amsterdam: Elsevier Science.
Angell, J. K., and J. Korshover
  1983   Global Temperature Variations in the Troposphere and Stratosphere, 1958–1982. Monthly Weather Review 111:901–21.
Arafa, M.
  1988   African Droughts and Nile Floods. Al-Akbar (Egyptian daily newspaper), 19 May, p. 3.
Arneborg, Jette
  1991   The Roman Church in Norse Greenland. In The Norse of the North Atlantic, G. F. Bigelow, ed., pp. 142–50. Acta Archaeological (Copenhagen) 61 (special issue).
Audouze, Françoise, and Oliver Büchsenschütz
  1989   Villes, villages et campagnes de l'Europe celtique. Paris: Hachette.
Baer, K.
  1962   The Low Price of Land in Ancient Egypt. Journal of the American Research Center in Egypt 1:25–45.

Bailes, K.
1985   Critical Issues in Environmental History. *In* Environmental History: Critical Issues in Comparative Perspective, K. E. Bailes, ed., pp. 1–21. Lanham, MD: University Press of America.

Bailey, F. G.
1970   Stratagems and Spoils: A Social Anthropology of Politics. New York: Oxford University Press.

Bair, Bill
1991   Floridians among World's Worst Guzzlers of Water. Gainesville Sun, 3 March, pp. 1A, 4A.

Barry, R. G., and R. J. Chorley
1968   Atmosphere, Weather and Climate. 3d ed. London: Methuen.

Bateson, Gregory
1972   Steps toward an Ecology of Mind. New York: Ballantine.

Batey, Coleen
1987   Freswick Links, Caithness: A Reappraisal of the Late Norse Site in Its Context. British Archaeological Reports 179. Oxford: BAR.

Bell, Barbara
1970   The Dark Ages in Ancient History, I: The First Dark Age in Egypt. American Journal of Archaeology 75:1–26.
1971   The Oldest Records of the Nile Floods. Geographical Journal 136:569–73.
1975   Climate and History of Egypt: The Middle Kingdom. American Journal of Archaeology 79:223–69.

Bell, H. Idris
1948   Egypt from Alexander the Great to the Arab Conquest. Oxford: Clarendon Press.

Bennett, John W.
1969   The Northern Plainsmen: Adaptive Strategy and Agrarian Life. Chicago: Aldine.

Berglund, Joel
1982   Kirke, hal, og status. Grønland 8–9:310–42.
1991   Displacements in the Building-over of the Eastern Settlement: A Sketch. *In* The Norse of the North Atlantic, G. F. Bigelow, ed., pp. 151–57. Acta Archaeological (Copenhagen) 61 (special issue).

Bergthorsson, Pall
1969   An Estimate of Drift Ice and Temperature in Iceland in 1000 Years. Jokull (Journal of the Icelandic Glaciological Society) 19:94–101.

Bernabo, J. C.
1981   Quantitative Estimates of Temperature Changes over the Last 2700 Years in Michigan Based on Pollen Data. Quaternary Research 15:143–59.

Beug, Hans-Jürgen
1982   Vegetation History and Climatic Changes in Central and Southern Europe. *In* Climatic Change in Later Prehistory, Anthony Harding, ed. Edinburgh: Edinburgh University Press.

Bigelow, G. F.
1989   Life in Medieval Shetland: An Archaeological Perspective. Hikuin 15:183–92.

Bigelow, G. F., ed.
1991   The Norse of the North Atlantic. Acta Archaeologica (Copenhagen) 61 (special issue).

Blanchard, Charles
1989   Calusa News 4. Gainesville: Institute of Archaeology and Paleoenvironmental Studies, Florida Museum of Natural History, University of Florida.

Boer, M. M., and R. S. DeGroot
1990   Landscape Ecological Impact of Climatic Change. Amsterdam: IOS Press.
Bongaarts, John, P. Reining, P. Way, and F. Conant
1989   The Relationships between Male Circumcision and HIV Infection in African Populations. AIDS 3:373–77.
Bookchin, Murray
1980   Towards an Ecological Society. Montreal, Quebec: Black Rose Press.
Boserup, Ester
1965   The Conditions of Agricultural Growth: The Economics of Agrarian Change under Population Pressure. Chicago: Aldine.
Botkin, D. B.
1990   Discordant Harmonies: A New Ecology for the Twenty-first Century. New York: Oxford University Press.
Botkin, Daniel B., and M. J. Sobel
1975   Stability in Time-Varying Ecosystems. American Naturalist 109:625–46.
Braudel, Fernand
1972   The Mediterranean and the Mediterranean World in the Age of Philip II. New
–73   York: Harper & Row.
Broeker, Wallas S., and George H. Denton
1990   What Drives Glacial Cycles? Scientific American 262:48–56.
Brooks, C. P. E.
1949   Climate through the Ages. Ernest Benn, Ltd. (New York: Dover Edition, 1970)
Bruun, Daniel
1918   The Icelandic Colonization of Greenland and the Finding of Vineland. Meddelelser om Grønland 57(3).
Bryson, Reid A.
1986   Late Quaternary Volcanic Modulation of Milankovitch Climate Forcing. Paper presented at the symposium on Mechanisms of Climate and Culture Change, J. Gunn and A. Paulsen, organizers. Annual meeting of the American Anthropological Association, Philadelphia.
1988   Civilization and Rapid Climatic Change. Environmental Conservation 15:7–15.
Bryson, Reid A., and B. M. Goodman
1980   Volcanic Activity and Climatic Changes. Science 207:1041–44.
Bryson, Reid A., and Thomas J. Murray
1977   Climates of Hunger: Mankind and the World's Changing Weather. Madison: The University of Wisconsin Press.
Buckland, Paul C.
1988   North Atlantic Faunal Connections: Introduction or Endemics? Entomologica Scandinavica, 1988 supplement:8–29.
Bulliot, J.-G., and Henri de Fontenay
1875   L'art de l'emaillerie chez les Eduens avant l'ère chrétienne. Paris: Champion.
Butzer, K. W.
1976   Early Hydraulic Civilization in Egypt. Chicago: University of Chicago Press.
1980   Civilizations: Organisms or Systems. Scientific American 80:517–30.
1984   Long-term Nile Flood Variation and Political Discontinuities in Pharaonic Egypt. In The Cause and Consequences of Food Production in Africa, J. D. Clark and S. A. Brandt, eds. Berkeley and Los Angeles: University of California Press.
Byock, Jesse
1988   Medieval Iceland: Sagas, Society, and Power. Berkeley and Los Angeles: University of California Press.

Caldwell, Joseph R.
  1958   Trend and Tradition in the Prehistory of the Eastern United States. American
         Anthropological Association Memoir 10. Washington, D.C.: American Anthro-
         pological Association.
Callinicos, Alex
  1988   Making History: Agency, Structure and Change in Social Theory. Ithaca: Cor-
         nell University Press.
Capistrano, A. Doris, and Clyde F. Kiker
  1990   Global Economic Influences on Tropical Broadleaved Forest Depletion, 1967–
         1985. Paper presented at the International Society for Ecological Economics,
         12–13 May, Washington, D.C.
Carneiro, Robert
  1988   Indians of the Amazonian Forest. In People of the Tropical Rain Forest, Julie
         Sloan Denslow and Christine Padoch, eds., pp. 73–86. Berkeley and Los Ange-
         les: University of California Press.
Chang, Kwang-chih
  1986   The Archaeology of Ancient China. 4th ed. New Haven: Yale University Press.
Chatwin, Bruce
  1987   The Songlines. New York: Penguin Books.
Childe, V. Gordon
  1925   The Dawn of European Civilization. London: Kegan Paul.
  1926   The Aryans: A Study of Indo-European Origins. London: Kegan Paul.
  1934   New Light on the Most Ancient East: The Oriental Prelude to European Prehis-
         tory. London: Kegan Paul.
  1951   Social Evolution. New York: Schuman.
Christensen, K. M. B.
  1991   Aspects of the Norse Economy in the Western Settlement of Greenland. In The
         Norse of the North Atlantic, G. F. Bigelow, ed., pp. 158–65. Acta Archaeologi-
         cal (Copenhagen) 61 (special issue).
Churcher, C. S.
  1978   Did the American Mammoth Migrate? Canadian Journal of Anthropology
         1:103–6.
Clarke, David L.
  1968   Analytical Archaeology. London: Methuen.
Clavel-Levêque, Monique
  1989   Puzzle gaulois: les Gaules en mémoire, images-textes-histoire. Centre de Re-
         cherches d'Histoire Ancienne, vol. 88. Annales Littéraires de l'Université de
         Besançon, 396. Paris: Les Belles Lettres.
Clay, R. Berle
  1976   Tactics, Strategy, and Operations: The Mississippian System Responds to Its En-
         vironment. Midcontinental Journal of Archaeology 1:137–62.
Clements, F. E.
  1916   Plant Succession: An Analysis of the Development of Vegetation. Publication
         No. 242. Washington, D.C.: Carnegie Institution of Washington.
  1936   Nature and Structure of the Climax. Journal of Animal Ecology 24:252–84.
Clements, Kendrick A.
  1984   Herbert Hoover and Conservation, 1921–33. American Historical Review 89
         (February):67–88.
Colwell, R. K.
  1974   Predictability, Constancy and Contingency of Periodic Phenomena. Ecology
         55:1148–53.

Coontz, Sydney H.
1957 Population Theories and Their Economic Interpretation. London: Routledge & Kegan Paul.

Cordell, Linda S.
1984 Prehistory of the Southwest. Orlando, FL: Academic Press.

Cory, Hans, and M. M. Hartnoll
1945 Customary Law of the Haya Tribe. London: International African Institute.

Crosby, Alfred W.
1990 A Renaissance Change in European Cognition. Environmental History Review 14 (Spring/Summer):19–32.

Crumley, Carole L.
1974 Celtic Social Structure: The Generation of Archaeologically Testable Hypotheses from Literary Evidence. Anthropological Papers, no. 54. Ann Arbor: University of Michigan Museum of Anthropology.

1976 Toward a Locational Definition of State Systems of Settlement. American Anthropologist 78:59–73.

1979 Three Locational Models: An Epistemological Assessment of Anthropology and Archaeology. In Advances in Archaeological Method and Theory, vol. 2, Michael B. Schiffer, ed., pp. 141–73. New York: Academic Press.

1987a A Dialectical Critique of Hierarchy. In Power Relations and State Formation, Thomas C. Patterson and Christine Ward Gailey, eds., pp. 155–68. Washington, D.C.: American Anthropological Association.

1987b Celtic Settlement before the Conquest: The Dialectics of Landscape and Power. In Regional Dynamics: Burgundian Landscapes in Historical Perspective, Carole L. Crumley and William H. Marquardt, eds., pp. 403–29. San Diego: Academic Press.

1987c Historical Ecology. In Regional Dynamics: Burgundian Landscapes in Historical Perspective, Carole L. Crumley and William H. Marquardt, eds., pp. 237–64. San Diego: Academic Press.

1989 The Role of Regional Histories in the Study of Climatic Change. Paper presented at the Fifty-fourth Annual Meeting of the Society for American Archaeology, 5–9 April, Atlanta.

In press A Critique of Cultural Evolutionist Approaches to Ranked Societies with Particular Reference to Celtic Polities. In Celtic Chiefdom, Celtic State, D. Blair Gibson and Bettina Arnold, eds. Cambridge: Cambridge University Press.

Crumley, Carole L., and William H. Marquardt
1990 Landscape: A Unifying Concept in Regional Analysis. In Interpreting Space: GIS and Archaeology, Kathleen M. Allen, Stanton W. Green, and Ezra B. W. Zubrow, eds., pp. 73–79. London: Taylor & Francis.

Crumley, Carole L., and William H. Marquardt, eds.
1987 Regional Dynamics: Burgundian Landscapes in Historical Perspective. San Diego: Academic Press.

Daget, Philippe
1980 Un élément actuel de la caracterisation du monde méditerrannéen: le climat. In La mise en place: l'évolution et la caracterisation de la flore et de la végétation circumméditerrannéennes, M. Denizot and Ch. Sauvage, eds., pp. 101–26. Actes du colloque organisé à l'Institut de Botanique de Montpellier les 9 et 10 avril 1980 par la Fondation Louis Emberger. Special unnumbered issue, Naturalia Monspeliensia: Revue Botanique Générale et Méditerrannéenne.

Davis, Richard A., Jr., Stephen A. Knowles, and Michael J. Bland
1989   Role of Hurricanes in the Holocene Stratigraphy of Estuaries: Examples from the Gulf Coast of Florida. Journal of Sedimentary Petrology 59:1052–61.
Dean, Jeffrey S., Robert C. Euler, George J. Gumerman, Fred Plog, Richard H. Hevly, and Thor N. V. Karlstrom
1985   Human Behavior, Demography, and Paleoenvironment on the Colorado Plateaus. American Antiquity 50:537–55.
Dechelette, Joseph
1927   Manuel d'archéologie préhistorique, celtique, et gallo-romaine, vol. 4. Paris: Picard.
Deevey, E. S., Don S. Rice, Prudence M. Rice, H. H. Vaughan, Mark Brenner, and M. S. Flannery
1979   Mayan Urbanism: Impact on a Tropical Karst Environment. Science 206:298–305.
Denizot, M., and Ch. Sauvage, eds.
1980   La mise en place: l'évolution et la caracterisation de la flore et de la végétation circumméditerrannéennes. Actes du colloque organizé à l'Institut de Botanique de Montpellier les 9 et 10 avril 1980 par la Fondation Louis Emberger. Special unnumbered issue, Naturalia Monspeliensia: Revue Botanique Générale et Méditerrannéenne.
Denslow, Julie Sloan, and Christine Padoch, eds.
1988   People of the Tropical Rain Forest. Berkeley and Los Angeles: University of California Press.
Denton, George, and Wibjorn Karlen
1973   Holocene Climatic Variations: Their Pattern and Possible Cause. Quaternary Research 3(2):155–205.
Devall, Bill, and George Sessions
1985   Deep Ecology: Living as if Nature Mattered. Salt Lake City: Gibbs M. Smith.
Drury, W. H., and I. C. T. Nisbet
1973   Succession. Journal of the Arnold Arboretum (Harvard University) 54:331–68.
Durrenburger, E. Paul
1991   Production in Medieval Iceland. In The Norse of the North Atlantic, G. F. Bigelow, ed., pp. 14–21. Acta Archaeological (Copenhagen) 61 (special issue).
Durrenburger, E. Paul, and Gisli Palsson, eds.
1989   The Anthropology of Iceland. Iowa City: University of Iowa Press.
Earle, Timothy
1989   The Evolution of Chiefdoms. Current Anthropology 30:84–88. Ecological Society of America
1991   The Sustainable Biosphere Initiative: An Ecological Research Agenda. Ecology 72:371–412.
Egyptian Ministry of Irrigation
1981   Water Master Plan. 17 vols. UNDP/EGY/73/024.
Ehrlich, Paul R.
1968   The Population Bomb. New York: Ballantine Books.
Engleberg, J., and L. L. Boyarsky
1979   The Noncybernetic Nature of Ecosystems. American Naturalist 114:317–24.
Evans, L. T.
1980   The Natural History of Crop Yield. American Scientist 68:388–97.
Fallows, James
1981   Living on the Fault Line. Atlantic Monthly (October):29–37.

Faulkner, R. O.
1975   Egypt from the Inception of the Nineteenth Dynasty to the Death of Rameses III. *In* The Cambridge Ancient History, 2.2:217–51. 3d ed. Cambridge: Cambridge University Press.

Fayter, Paul
1990   Senses of the Natural World: Recent Works in the Philosophy and History of Science. Forest and Conservation History 34 (April):85–92.

Fernald, Edward A., ed.
1981   Atlas of Florida. Tallahassee: Florida State University Foundation.

Fitzhugh, W. W.
1985   Early Contacts North of Newfoundland before A.D. 1600: A Review. *In* Cultures in Contact: The Impact of European Contacts on Native American Cultural Institutions, A.D. 1000–1800, pp. 19–22. Washington, D.C.: Smithsonian Institution.

Flannery, Kent V.
1972   The Cultural Evolution of Civilizations. Annual Review of Ecology and Systematics 3:399–426.

Fletcher, Laraine Anne, Jacinto May Hau, Lynda M. Florey Folan, and William J. Folan
1987   Un analysis estadistico preliminar del patrón de asentiamiento de Calakmul. Campeche: Universidad Autónoma del Sudeste, Centro de Estudior Historicos y Sociales.

Folan, William J.
1985   Calakmul, Campeche, su centro urbano, estado y región en relación al concepto del resto de la Gran Mesoamerica. Información 9:161–85.

Folan, William J., Joel Gunn, Jack D. Eaton, and Robert W. Patch
1983   Paleoclimatological Patterning in Southern Mesoamerica. Journal of Field Archaeology 10:453–68.

Fontaneda, Do. d'Escalante
1944   Memoir of Do. d'Escalante Fontaneda Respecting Florida, Written in Spain, about the Year 1575. Translated by Buckingham Smith, with editorial comments by David O. True. Coral Gables, FL: Glades House.

Forbes, S. A.
1925   The Lake as a Microcosm. Illinois Natural History Survey Bulletin 15:537–50. [First published in 1887]

Forman, Richard T. T., and Michel Godron
1986   Landscape Ecology. New York: John Wiley & Sons.

Fowler, Melvin L.
1974   Cahokia-Ancient Capital of the Midwest. Reading, MA: Addison-Wesley.

Frayer, David W.
1992   Could Neanderthals Talk? Paper presented at the Annual Meeting of the American Association of Physical Anthropologists, Las Vegas.

Fredskild, Bent
1986   Agriculture in a Marginal Area: South Greenland, A.D. 985–1985. *In* The Cultural Landscape, Past, Present, and Future, H. J. B. Birks, ed., pp. 28–41. Bergen: Botaniske Institut.

Freire, Paulo
1972   The Pedagogy of the Oppressed. Harmondsworth: Penguin.
1973   Education for Critical Consciousness. New York: Seabury Press.

Friedel, David A.
1986   Maya Warfare: An Example of Peer Polity Interaction. *In* Peer Polity Interaction

and Socio-Political Change, Colin Renfrew and John F. Cherry, eds., pp. 93–
108. Cambridge and New York: Cambridge University Press.

Fustel de Coulanges, Numa Denis
1908   Histoire des institutions politiques de l'ancienne France: la Gaule romaine.
Paris: Hachette.

Gad, Finn
1970   A History of Greenland, vol. 1. London: D. Hurst.

Gailey, Christine W., and Thomas C. Patterson
1988   State Formation and Uneven Development. In State and Society: The Emergence and Development of Social Hierarchy and Political Centralisation, John
Gledhill, Barbara Bender, and Mogens T. Larsen, eds., pp. 77–90. London and
Boston: Unwin Hyman.

Gamble, Clive
1986   Hunter-Gatherers and the Origin of States. In States in History, J. A. Hall, ed.,
pp. 22–47. Oxford: Basil Blackwell.

Gamst, Frederick C.
1970   Peasantries and Elites without Urbanism: The Civilization of Ethiopia. Comparative Studies in Society and History 12:373–92.

Gaudreau, Denise C.
1988   The Distribution of Late Quaternary Forest Region in the Northeast. In Holocene
Human Ecology in Northeastern North America, G. Nicholas, ed., pp. 215–53.
New York: Plenum.

Gaventa, John
1980   Power and Powerlessness: Quiescence and Rebellion in an Appalachian Valley.
Urbana: University of Illinois Press.

Goggin, John M., and William T. Sturtevant
1964   The Calusa: A Stratified Non-Agricultural Society (with Notes on Sibling Marriage). In Explorations in Cultural Anthropology: Essays in Honor of George
Peter Murdock, Ward Goodenough, ed., pp. 179–219. New York: McGraw-Hill.

Goldsmith, Edward
1985   Ecological Succession Rehabilitated. The Ecologist 15:104–12. [Responses in
The Ecologist 16 (1986):50–56.]

Golley, F. B.
1984   Historical Origins of the Ecosystem Concept in Biology. In The Ecosystem
Concept in Anthropology, E. F. Moran, ed., pp. 33–49. Boulder, CO: Westview Press.

Goodall, Jane
1990   Through a Window: My Thirty Years with the Chimpanzees of Gombe. Boston:
Houghton Mifflin.

Gorz, André
1980   Ecology as Politics. Boston: South End Press.

Goudineau, Christian, and Christian Peyre
1993   Les Eduens: Découverte d'un Peuple Gaulois. Paris: Errance.

Gould, Stephen Jay
1980   The Episodic Nature of Evolutionary Change. In The Panda's Thumb, chap. 17.
New York: W. W. Norton.

Gramsci, Antonio
1975   The Modern Prince and Other Writings. New York: International Publishers.

Green, Miranda
1986   The Gods of the Celts. Totowa, NJ: Barnes & Noble.

Green, Stanton W., and Stephen M. Perlman
1985   The Archaeology of Frontiers and Boundaries. New York: Academic Press.

Grenier, Auguste
1924   Les Gaulois. Paris.
Gross, D. R.
1984   Ecosystems and Methodological Problems in Ecological Anthropology. *In* The
       Ecosystem Concept in Anthropology, E. F. Moran, ed., pp. 253–63. Boulder,
       CO: Westview Press.
Guardreau, Denise C.
1988   The Distribution of Late Quaternary Forest Regions in the Northeast. *In* Holo-
       cene Human Ecology in Northeastern North America, G. Nicholas, ed. New
       York: Plenum.
Guinot, Norbert
1987   Position of the Dialects of the Morvan and Charolais in Linguistic History. *In* Re-
       gional Dynamics: Burgundian Landscapes in Historical Perspective, Carole L.
       Crumley and William H. Marquardt, eds., pp. 387–98. San Diego: Academic
       Press.
Gulløv, H. C.
1983   Nuup kommuneani qangarnitsanik eqqaassutit inuit-kulturip nunaqarfii.
       Kalaallit Nunaata Katersugaasivia and Nationalmuseet, Nuuk, Greenland.
Gunn, Joel
1975   An Envirotechnological System for Hogup Cave. American Antiquity 40:3–21.
1979   Occupation Frequency Simulation on a Broad Ecotone. *In* Transformations:
       Mathematical Approaches to Culture Change, C. Renfrew and K. Cooke, eds.,
       pp. 257–74. New York: Academic Press.
1982   Analysis of Modern Climate Data. *In* A Study of Late Quaternary Environments
       and Early Man along the Tombigbee River, Alabama and Mississippi, G. Muto
       and J. Gunn, eds., pp. 2-19–2-26. Atlanta: National Park Service.
1987   Middle Pecos Culture Sequence and Holocene Climate. *In* Advances in Middle
       Pecos Archaeology, S. Katz and P. Katz, eds., pp. 65–86. Proceedings of the
       Middle Pecos Symposium at the fourth Jornada Mogollon Conference, Tularosa,
       New Mexico. Amarillo, TX: Bureau of Reclamation, Southwest Region.
1991   Influences of Various Forcing Variables on Global Energy Balance during the
       Period of Intensive Instrumental Observation (1958–1987) and Their Implica-
       tions for Paleoclimate. Climatic Change 19:393–420.
Gunn, Joel, and Richard E. W. Adams
1981   Climatic Change, Culture, and Civilization in North America. World Archae-
       ology 13:85–100.
Gunn, Joel, and David O. Brown
1982   Form and Environment: Historical and Cultural Landscape Study of the San
       Antonio Missions. San Antonio: ECS Corporation.
Gunn, Joel, and Carole L. Crumley
1989   Global Energy Balance and Regional Hydrology: A Burgundian Case Study. *In*
       Proceedings of the Conference on Landscape-Ecological Impacts of Global Cli-
       matic Change. Utrecht, The Netherlands: University of Utrecht.
1991   Global Energy Balance and Regional Hydrology: A Burgundian Case Study.
       Earth Surface Processes and Landforms 16:579–92.
Gunn, Joel, with G. Muto, ed.
1982   Analysis of Modern Climate Data. *In* A Study of Late-Quaternary Environments
       and Early Man along the Tombigbee River, Alabama and Mississippi. 3 vols.
       Atlanta: National Park Service.
Gunn, Joel, William J. Folan, and Hubert R. Robichaux
1990   An Analysis of Discharge Data from the Candelaria River System in Mexico: In-

sights into Paleoclimates Affecting the Ancient Maya Sites of Calakmul and El Mirador. Submitted for publication.

Guthrie, R. D.
1978   Bison and Man in North America. Canadian Journal of Anthropology 1(1):55–73.

Hamilton, A. C., D. Taylor, and J. C. Vogel
1986   Early Forest Clearance and Environmental Degradation in South-West Uganda. Nature 320 (6058):164–67.

Hann, John H.
1991   Missions to the Calusa. Gainesville: University Presses of Florida.

Hansen, J., D. Johnson, A. Lacis, S. Lebedeff, P. Lee, D. Rind, and G. Russell
1981   Climate Impact of Increasing Atmospheric Carbon Dioxide. Science 213:957–66.

Harding, Sandra
1986   The Science Question in Feminism. Ithaca: Cornell University Press.

Harms, Robert
1987   Games against Nature: An Eco-cultural History of the Nunu of Equatorial Africa. New York: Cambridge University Press.

Harris, Marvin
1968   The Rise of Anthropological Theory: A History of Theories of Culture. New York: Thomas Y. Crowell.
1985   Cows, Pigs, Wars, and Witches. New York: Random House.

Harvey, David
1973   Social Justice and the City. Baltimore: Johns Hopkins University Press.
1989   The Condition of Postmodernity: An Enquiry into the Origins of Cultural Change. Oxford: Basil Blackwell.

Hassan, Fekri A.
1974   The Archaeology of Dishna Plain: A Study of a Late Palaeolithic Settlement in Upper Egypt. Publication No. 59. Geological Survey of Egypt.
1978   Demographic Archaeology. In Advances in Archaeological Method and Theory, vol. 1, M. B. Schiffer, ed., pp. 49–103. New York: Academic Press.
1981a   Historical Nile Floods and Their Implications for Climatic Change. Science 212:1142–45.
1981b   Demographic Archaeology. New York: Academic Press.
1986   Holocene Lakes and Prehistoric Settlements of the Western Faiyum, Egypt. Journal of Archaeological Science 13:483–501.
1988   The Predynastic of Egypt. Journal of World Prehistory 2:135–85.
1990   Nile River Records as a Measure of North African Monsoon Fluctuations (Abstract). In Monsoons and Palaeomonsoons. Seattle: Quaternary Research Center.

Hassan, Fekri A., and Barbara R. Stucki
1987   Nile Floods and Climatic Change. In Climate: History, Periodicity, and Predictability, Michael R. Rampino, John E. Sanders, Walter S. Newman, and L. K. Königsson, eds., pp. 37–46. New York: Van Nostrand Reinhold.

Hastrup, Kirsten
1981   Cosmology and Society in Medieval Iceland: A Social Anthropological Perspective on World-View. Ethnologia Scandinavica, 63–78.
1985   Culture and History in Medieval Iceland: An Anthropological Analysis of Structure and Change. Oxford: Clarendon Press.
1989   Saeters in Iceland 900–1600: An Anthropological Analysis of Economy and Cosmology. Acta Borealia 6(1):72–85.

Hecht, Alan D., ed.
1985   Paleoclimate Analysis and Modeling. New York: John Wiley & Sons.
Heidenreich, Conrad
1971   Huronia: A History and Geography of the Huron Indians 1600–1650. Toronto: McClelland & Stewart.
Hempel, Carl G.
1966   Philosophy of Natural Science. Englewood Cliffs, NJ: Prentice-Hall.
Hill, John
1991   State's Tax Hikes Lag behind Growth. Gainesville Sun, 18 June, pp. 1A, 6A.
Hoffman, Michael A., H. A. Hamroush, and R. O. Allen
1986   A Model of Urban Development for the Hierakonopolis Region from Predynastic through Old Kingdom Times. Journal of American Research in Central Egypt 23:175–87.
Holling, C. S.
1973   Resilience and Stability of Ecological Systems. Annual Review of Ecology and Systematics 4:1–23.
1978   Overview and Conclusions. In Adaptive Environmental Assessment and Management, C. S. Holling, ed., pp. 1–37. Chichester: John Wiley and Sons.
1986   The Resilience of Terrestrial Ecosystems: Local Surprise and Global Change. In Sustainable Development of the Biosphere, W. C. Clark and R. E. Munn, eds., pp. 292–317. New Rochelle, NY: Cambridge University Press.
Holling, C. S., ed.
1978   Adaptive Environmental Assessment and Management. Chichister: John Wiley & Sons.
Holling, C. S., and M. A. Goldberg
1981   Ecology and Planning. In Contemporary Anthropology: An Anthology, D. G. Bates and S. H. Lees, eds., pp. 78–93. New York: Alfred A. Knopf.
Hollingsworth, T.
1969   Historical Demography. Ithaca: Cornell University Press.
Horn, H.
1974   The Ecology of Secondary Succession. Annual Review of Ecology and Systematics 5:25–37.
Houghton, J. T., G. J. Jenkins, and J. J. Ephraums
1990   Climatic Change: The IPCC Scientific Assessment. Cambridge: Cambridge University Press.
Hubert, Henri
1934   The Greatness and Decline of the Celts. London: Kegan Paul. Reprinted London: Constable, 1987.
Hugill, Peter J.
1988   Transport of Desires: Trade as the Engine of History. Paper presented at the conference "What Is the Engine of History?" at Texas A&M University, College Station.
Hull, David L.
1974   Philosophy of Biological Science. Englewood Cliffs, NJ: Prentice-Hall.
Hurst, H. E.
1957   The Nile. London: Constable.
Ingerson, Alice
1988   Methods and Morality: A Conference on Landscape History and Ecological Succession. Cruiser (newsletter of the Forest History Society) 11 (Spring):7.
1989   The Uses of History by Ecologists. Journal of Forest History 33 (July):114 (special issue).

Jäger, Klaus-Dieter, and Vojen Ložek
1982 Environmental Conditions and Land Cultivation during the Urnfield Bronze Age in Central Europe. *In* Climatic Change in Later Prehistory, A. F. Harding, ed., pp. 162–78. Edinburgh: Edinburgh University Press.

James, Ian N.
1988 Meteorology of a Flat Earth. Nature 333:118.

Jameson, Fredric
1981 The Political Unconscious: Narrative as a Socially Symbolic Act. Ithaca: Cornell University Press.

Jamieson, Neil L., and George W. Lovelace
1985 Cultural Values and Human Ecology. *In* Cultural Values and Human Ecology in Southeast Asia, Karl L. Hutterer, A. Terry Rambo, and George Lovelace, eds., pp. 27–54. Michigan Papers on South and Southeast Asia 277. Ann Arbor: Center for South and Southeast Asian Studies, University of Michigan.

Jansen, H. J.
1972 A Critical Account of the Written and Archaeological Sources' Evidence Concerning the Norse Settlements in Greenland. Meddelelser om Grønland 182(4).

Johnson, Gregory A.
1982 Organizational Structure and Scalar Stress. *In* Theory and Explanation in Archaeology, Colin Renfrew, Michael J. Rowlands, and Barbara Abbott Segraves, eds., pp. 389–421. New York: Academic Press.

Jones, Gwyn
1985 The Norse Atlantic Saga. 2d ed. Oxford: Oxford University Press.

Jones, Philip D., and Tom M. L. Wigley
1990 Global Warming Trends. Scientific American 263:84–91.

Journal of American History
1990 Round Table: Environmental History, vol. 76 (March). Includes Donald Worster, "Transformations of the Earth: Toward an Agroecological Perspective in History"; Alfred W. Crosby, "An Enthusiastic Second"; Richard White, "Environmental History, Ecology, and Meaning"; Carolyn Merchant, "Gender and Environmental History"; William Cronon, "Modes of Prophecy and Production: Placing Nature in History"; Stephen J. Pyne, "Firestick History"; and Donald Worster, "Seeing beyond Culture."

Judd, Alan
1991a Florida's Water Systematically Mismanaged. Gainesville Sun (3 March):1A, 4A.
1991b In Oregon, Water Comes First. Gainesville Sun (7 March): 1A, 8A–9A.
1991c Loopholes, or Reforms, Drain Taxes. Gainesville Sun (19 June):1A, 7A.

Kahn, Herbert
1979 World Economic Development: 1979 and Beyond. Boulder, CO: Westview Press.

Kaijage, Frederick
1989 The AIDS Crisis in Kagera Region, Tanzania, in Historical Perspective. Paper presented at the Workshop on Behavioral and Epidemiological Aspects of AIDS Research in Tanzania, 6–8 December, Dar es Salaam.
1990 AIDS Control and the Burden of History in Northwestern Tanzania. Paper presented at the annual meeting of the American Association for the Advancement of Science, 14–19 February, Washington, D.C.

Kees, H.
1961 Ancient Egypt: A Cultural Geography. Chicago: University of Chicago Press.

Keller, Christian
1991 Vikings in the West Atlantic: A Model for Norse Greenland Medieval Society. *In*

The Norse of the North Atlantic, G. F. Bigelow, ed., pp. 126–41. Acta Archaeological (Copenhagen) 61 (special issue).

In press The Eastern Settlement Reconsidered: Some Analyses of Norse Medieval Greenland. Glasgow: University of Glasgow Press.

Kelley, Klara B.
1985 Navajo Land Use: An Ethnoarchaeological Study. New York: Academic Press.

Kellner, Douglas
1989 Jameson, Marxism, and Postmodernism. In Postmodernism/Jameson/Critique, Douglas Kellner, ed., pp. 1–42. Washington, D.C.: Maisonneuve.

Kjekshus, Helge
1977 Ecology Control and Economic Development in East Africa: The Case of Tanganyika 1850–1950. London: Heinemann.

Kosík, Karel
1976 Dialectics of the Concrete: A Study on Problems of Man and World. Translated by Karel Kovanda with James Schmidt. Dordrecht, The Netherlands: D. Reidel. [First published in 1961]

Krantz, Grover S.
1980 Sapienization and Speech. Current Anthropology 21:773–79.

Krogh, K. J.
1982 Eirik den Rodes Grønland. Copenhagen: Nationalmuseet.

Kuhn, Thomas S.
1967 The Structure of Scientific Revolutions. Chicago: University of Chicago Press.

Kutzbach, John E.
1985 Modeling of Paleoclimates. In Advances in Geophysics 28A:159–96. New York: Academic Press.

Kutzbach, John E., and R. A. Bryson
1974 Variance Spectrum of Holocene Climatic Fluctuations in the North Atlantic Sector. Journal of Atmospheric Sciences 31:1958–63.

Kutzbach, John E., and R. G. Gallimore
1989 Gangaean Climates: Megamonsoons of the Megacontinent. Journal of Geophysical Research 94(D3):3341–57.

Ladurie, Emmanuel LeRoy
1971 Times of Feast, Times of Famine: A History of Climate since the Year 1000. New York: Doubleday.

LaFontaine, C. Vada, Reid A. Bryson, and Wayne M. Wendland
1990 Airstream Regions of North Africa and the Mediterranean. Journal of Climate 3:366:72.

Lamb, H. H.
1977 Climate: Past, Present, and Future. 2 vols. London: Methuen.

Landscheidt, Theodor
1987 Long-range Forecasts of Solar Cycles and Climate Change. In Climate: History, Periodicity, and Predictability, Michael R. Rampino, John E. Sanders, Walter S. Newman, and L. K. Königsson, eds., pp. 421–45. New York: Van Nostrand Reinhold.
1988 Solar Rotation, Impulses of the Torque in the Sun's Motion, and Climatic Variation. Climatic Change 12:265–95.

Lane-Poole, Stanley
1901 A History of Egypt in the Middle Ages. London: Frank Cass. [Reprinted in 1961]

Langdale-Brown, I., H. A. Osmaston, and J. G. Wilson
1964 The Vegetation of Uganda and Its Bearing on Land Use. Entebbe: Government Printing Office.

Laseski, Ruth
 1983 Modern Pollen Data and Holocene Climate Change in Eastern Africa. Ph.D. dissertation, Brown University.
Laudonnière, René de
 1975 Three Voyages. Translated and edited by Charles E. Bennett. Gainesville: University Presses of Florida.
Lee, Douglas Bennett
 1992 America's Third Coast. National Geographic 182:2–37.
Leiss, William
 1976 The Limits to Satisfaction. Toronto: University of Toronto Press.
Lengeyel, Lancelot
 1969 Le secret des Celtes. Choisy-le-Roi: Robert Morel.
Levins, Richard, and Richard Lewontin
 1985 The Dialectical Biologist. Cambridge: Harvard University Press.
Lévi-Strauss, Claude
 1966 The Savage Mind. Chicago: University of Chicago Press.
Lewis, Naphtali
 1983 Life in Egypt under Roman Rule. Oxford: Clarendon Press.
Lewis, Robert
 1979 Science and Industrialisation in the USSR: Industrial Research and Development, 1917–1940. London: Macmillan.
Lewontin, R. C.
 1966 Is Nature Probable or Capricious? BioScience 16:25–27.
 1967 The Principle of Historicity in Evolution. In Mathematical Challenges to the Neo-Darwinian Interpretation of Evolution, P. S. Moorhead and M. M. Kaplan, eds., pp. 81–88. Philadelphia: Wistar Institute Press.
 1969 The Meaning of Stability. Brookhaven Symposia in Biology 22:13–24.
 1974 The Analysis of Variance and the Analysis of Causes. American Journal of Human Genetics 26:400–11.
Lindeman, R. L.
 1942 The Trophic-Dynamic Aspect of Ecology. Ecology 23:399–418.
Lovelock, James
 1979 Gaia: A New Look at Life on Earth. Oxford: Oxford University Press.
Lukács, Georg
 1967 History and Class Consciousness: Studies in Marxist Dialectics. Cambridge: MIT Press.
Lukes, Steven
 1974 Power: A Radical View. London: Macmillan.
 1986 Introduction. In Power, Steven Lukes, ed., pp. 1–18. Oxford: Basil Blackwell.
Lwihura, M.
 1988 Seroprevalence: HIV Infection in Kagera Region, Tanzania: A Population-Based Study. Abstract no. 5034, International Conference on AIDS, Stockholm.
McCulloch, Warren S.
 1945 A Heterarchy of Values Determined by the Topology of Nervous Nets. Bulletin of Mathematical Biophysics 7:89–93.
McGhee, Robert
 1984 Contact between Native North Americans and the Medieval Norse: A Review of the Evidence. American Antiquity 49:12–29.
McGovern, T. H.
 1979 Thule-Norse Interaction in Southwest Greenland: A Speculative Model. In The Thule Eskimo Culture: An Anthropological Retrospective, pp. 171–89. National

Museum of Man Mercury Series no. 88. Ottawa: National Museum of Man.

1980   Site Catchment and Maritime Adaptation in Norse Greenland. *In* Site Catchment Analysis: Essays on Prehistoric Resource Space, F. Findlow and J. Eriksson, eds., pp. 193–209. Los Angeles: University of California at Los Angeles.

1980   The Vinland Adventure: A North Atlantic Perspective. North American Archae-
–81   ologist 2:285–308.

1981   The Economics of Extinction in Norse Greenland. *In* Climate and History, T. M. L. Wigley et al., eds., pp. 404–34. Cambridge: Cambridge University Press.

1985a The Arctic Frontier of Norse Greenland. *In* The Archaeology of Frontiers and Boundaries, S. Green and S. Perlman, eds., pp. 275–323. New York: Academic Press.

1985b Contributions to the Paleoeconomy of Norse Greenland. Acta Archaeologica 54:73–122.

1986   Climate, Correlation, and Causation in Norse Greenland. Paper presented at the meeting of the Society for American Anthropology, Philadelphia.

1988   Bones, Buildings, and Boundaries: Patterns in Greenlandic Paleoeconomy. Paper presented at the Bowdoin Conference on Norse Archaeology of the North Atlantic, April.

1990   The Archaeology of the Norse North Atlantic. Annual Review of Anthropology 19:331–51.

1992   Bones, Buildings, and Boundaries: Palaeoeconomic Approaches to Norse Greenland. *In* Norse and Later Settlement and Subsistence in the North Atlantic, C. D. Morris and D. J. Rackham, eds., pp. 193–230. Glasgow: University of Glasgow Press, Archetype Publications.

McGovern, T. H., and R. H. Jordan
1982   Settlement and Land Use in the Inner Fjords of Godthaab District, West Greenland. Arctic Anthropology 19(1):63–80.

McGovern, T. H., G. F. Bigelow, T. Amorosi, and D. Russell
1988   Northern Islands, Human Error, and Environmental Degradation: A View of Social and Ecological Change in the Medieval North Atlantic. Human Ecology 16(3):176–221.

McGuire, Randall H.
1983   Breaking down Cultural Complexity: Inequality and Heterogeneity. *In* Advances in Archaeological Method and Theory, vol. 6, Michael B. Schiffer, ed., pp. 91–142. New York: Academic Press.

McIntosh, R. P.
1976   Ecology since 1900. *In* Issues and Ideas in America, B. J. Taylor and T. J. White, eds., pp. 353–72. Norman: University of Oklahoma Press.

1985   The Background of Ecology: Concept and Theory. Cambridge: Cambridge University Press.

MacKendrick, Paul
1987   The Romans in Burgundy. *In* Regional Dynamics: Burgundian Landscapes in Historical Perspective, Carole L. Crumley and William H. Marquardt, eds., pp. 431–45. San Diego: Academic Press.

Margalef, R.
1969   Diversity and Stability: A Practical Proposal and a Model of Interdependence. Brookhaven Symposia in Biology 22:25–37.

Margulis, Lynn
1970   Origin of Eukaryotic Cells: Evidence and Research Implications for a Theory of the Origin and Evolution of Microbial, Plant, and Animal Cells on the Precambrian Earth. New Haven: Yale University Press.

Margulis, Lynn, and David Bermudes
1985   Symbiosis as a Mechanism of Evolution. Philadelphia: Balaban.
Markaz el-Bihouth el-Arabia
1988   Azmatt Miah en-Nil [The Nilewater crisis]. Cairo: Dar el-thakaffa al-Gadida.
Marquardt, William H.
    1984   The Josslyn Island Mound and Its Role in the Investigation of Southwest Florida's
            Past. Miscellaneous Project Report Series no. 22. Gainesville: Florida State
            Museum, Department of Anthropology.
    1985   Complexity and Scale in the Study of Fisher-Gatherer-Hunters: An Example
            from the Eastern United States. In Prehistoric Hunter-Gatherers: The Emergence
            of Cultural Complexity, T. Douglas Price and James A. Brown, eds., pp. 59–98.
            Orlando, Fla.: Academic Press.
    1987a   The Calusa Social Formation in Protohistoric South Florida. In Power Rela-
            tions and State Formation, Thomas C. Patterson and Christine W. Gailey, eds.,
            pp. 98–116. Washington, D.C.: Archeology Section, American Anthropological
            Association.
    1987b   Calusa News 1. Gainesville: Institute of Archaeology and Paleoenvironmental
            Studies, Florida Museum of Natural History, University of Florida.
    1988a   Calusa News 2. Gainesville: Institute of Archaeology and Paleoenvironmental
            Studies, Florida Museum of Natural History, University of Florida.
    1988b   Politics and Production among the Calusa of South Florida. In Hunters and
            Gatherers, vol. 1: History, Environment, and Social Change among Hunting
            and Gathering Societies, David Riches, Tim Ingold, and James Woodburn, eds.,
            pp. 161–88. London: Berg.
    1991   Introduction. In Missions to the Calusa, by John H. Hann. Gainesville: Univer-
            sity Presses of Florida.
    1992a   Dialectical Archaeology. In Archaeological Method and Theory, vol. 4,
            Michael B. Schiffer, ed., pp. 101–40. Tucson: University of Arizona Press.
    1992b   Recent Archaeological and Paleoenvironmental Investigations in Southwest
            Florida. In Culture and Environment in the Domain of the Calusa, William H.
            Marquardt, ed., pp. 9–57. Monograph 1. Gainesville: University of Florida, In-
            stitute of Archaeology and Paleoenvironmental Studies.
Marquardt, William H., ed.
    1992   Culture and Environment in the Domain of the Calusa. Monograph 1. Gaines-
            ville: University of Florida, Institute of Archaeology and Paleoenvironmental
            Studies.
Marquardt, William H., and Charles Blanchard
    1989   Calusa News 3. Gainesville: Institute of Archaeology and Paleoenvironmental
            Studies, Florida Museum of Natural History, University of Florida.
    1990   Calusa News 5. Gainesville: Institute of Archaeology and Paleoenvironmental
            Studies, Florida Museum of Natural History, University of Florida.
Marquardt, William H., and Carole L. Crumley
    1987   Theoretical Issues in the Analysis of Spatial Patterning. In Regional Dynam-
            ics: Burgundian Landscapes in Historical Perspective, Carole L. Crumley and
            William H. Marquardt, eds., pp. 1–18. San Diego: Academic Press.
Marx, Karl, and Frederick Engels
1970   Selected Works in Three Volumes. Moscow: Progress Publishers.
Mayr, Ernst
    1982   The Growth of Biological Thought: Diversity, Evolution, and Inheritance. Cam-
            bridge: Harvard University Press.

1988 Is Biology an Autonomous Science? *In* Toward a New Philosophy of Biology: Observations of an Evolutionist. Cambridge: Harvard University Press.

Megaw, J. V. S.
1970 Art of the European Iron Age. New York: Harper & Row.

Melko, Matthew, and Leighton R. Scott
1987 The Boundaries of Civilizations in Space and Time. Lanham, MD: University Press of America.

Mellos, Koula
1988 Perspectives in Ecology: A Critical Essay. New York: St. Martin's Press.

Mészáros, István
1972 Lukács' Concept of the Dialectic. London: Merlin Press.
1983 Totality. *In* A Dictionary of Marxist Thought, Tom Bottomore, ed., pp. 479–81. Cambridge: Harvard University Press.

Miller, W. I.
1986 Dreams, Prophecy, and Sorcery: Blaming the Secret Offender in Medieval Iceland. Scandinavian Studies 58:101–23.

Minsky, M., and S. Papert
1972 Artificial Intelligence Progress Report. AI Memo no. 252. Cambridge: MIT Artificial Intelligence Laboratory.

Mitchell, J. Murray, Jr., Charles W. Stockton, and David M. Meko
1979 Evidence of a 22-Year Rhythm of Drought in the Western United States Related to the Hale Solar Cycle since the 17th Century. *In* Solar-Terrestrial Influences on Weather and Climate, B. McCormac and T. Seliga, eds. Dordrecht, The Netherlands: Reidel.

Moran, E. F., ed.
1984 The Ecosystem Concept in Anthropology. Boulder, CO: Westview Press.

Morris, Chris
1985 Viking Orkney: A Survey. *In* The Prehistory of Orkney, Colin Renfrew, ed., pp. 210–42. Edinburgh: Edinburgh University Press.

Nash, Gerald D.
1989 Eden or Armageddon? Recent Studies of Water in the Twentieth-Century West. Journal of Forest History 33 (October):197–200.

National Academy of Sciences
1975 Understanding Climatic Change: A Program for Action. Washington, D.C.: National Academy of Sciences.

Naveh, Zev, and Arthur S. Lieberman
1990 Landscape Ecology: Theory and Application. Student edition. New York: Springer-Verlag.

Nelson, Richard K.
1969 Hunters of the Northern Ice. Chicago: University of Chicago Press.
1983 Make Prayers to the Raven: A Koyukon View of the Northern Forest. Chicago: University of Chicago Press. Paperback edition, 1986.

Netting, Robert McC.
1981 Balancing on an Alp: Ecological Change and Continuity in a Swiss Mountain Community. New York: Cambridge University Press.

Nisbet, Robert
1980 History of the Idea of Progress. New York: Basic Books.

Nørlund, P., and Martin Stenberger
1934 Brattablid. Meddelelser om Grønland 88(1).

Nove, Alec
1969 An Economic History of the USSR. Harmondsworth: Penguin Books.

Oaks, Laura S.
  1987   Epona in the Aeduan Landscape: Transfunctional Deity under Changing Rule. *In* Regional Dynamics: Burgundian Landscapes in Historical Perspective, Carole L. Crumley and William H. Marquardt, eds., pp. 295–333. San Diego: Academic Press.

O'Connor, D.
  1972   A Regional Population in Egypt to circa 600 B.C. *In* Population Growth: Anthropological Implications, B. J. Spooner, ed., pp. 78–100. Cambridge: MIT Press.

Odum, E. P.
  1964   The New Ecology. BioScience 14:14–16.
  1969   The Strategy of Ecosystem Development. Science 164:262–70.

Ogilvie, Astrid
  1985   The Past Climate and Sea-Ice Record from Iceland, Part I: Data to A.D. 1780. Climatic Change 6:131–52.

Ollman, Bertell
  1976   Alienation: Marx's Conception of Man in Capitalist Society. New York: Cambridge University Press.

O'Neill, R. V., D. L. DeAngelis, J. B. Walde, and T. F. H. Allen
  1986   A Hierarchical Concept of Ecosystems. Princeton: Princeton University Press.

Ophuls, William
  1977   Ecology and the Politics of Scarcity: Prologue to a Political Theory of the Steady State. San Francisco: W. H. Freeman.

Padoch, Christine, and Wil de Jong
  1991   The House Gardens of Santa Rosa: Diversity and Variability in an Amazonian Agricultural System. Economic Botany 45:166–75.

Palsson, Gisli
  1991   The Name of the Witch: Sagas, Sorcery, and Social Context. *In* Oromo Studies and Other Essays in Honor of Paul Baxter, David Brookenshaw, ed. Syracuse, NY: FACS Publications.

Parker, D. E., and C. K. Folland
  1989   Worldwide Surface Temperature Trends since the Mid-Nineteenth Century. *In* Proceedings of the US DOE Workshop on Greenhouse Gas Induced Climatic Change (Amherst, MA, 8–12 May).

Parks, Arva Moore
  1985   Where the River Found the Bay: Historical Study of the Granada Site, John W. Griffin, ed. Archaeology and History of the Granada Site, vol. 2. Tallahassee: Florida Division of Archives, History, and Records Management.

Pattee, Howard H., ed.
  1973   Hierarchy Theory: The Challenge of Complex Systems. New York: George Braziller.

Patten, B. C.
  1975   Ecosystem as a Coevolutionary Unit: A Theme for Teaching Systems Ecology. *In* New Directions in the Analysis of Ecological Systems, G. S. Innis, ed., pp. 1–8. Simulation Council Proceedings, vol. 5, no. 1. La Jolla, CA: Society for Computer Simulation.

Patten, B. C., and E. P. Odum
  1981   The Cybernetic Nature of Ecosystems. American Naturalist 118:886–95.

Patterson, Thomas C.
  1990   Archaeology, History and the Concept of Totality. Manuscript in possession of the author.

Patterson, William A. III, and Kenneth E. Sassaman
 1988   Indian Fires in the Prehistory of New England. *In* Holocene Human Ecology in Northeastern North America, G. Nicholas, ed., pp. 107–31. New York: Plenum.
Paynter, Robert
 1989   The Archaeology of Equality and Inequality. Annual Review of Anthropology 18:369–99.
Pepper, David M.
 1984   The Roots of Modern Environmentalism. London: Croom Helm.
Perdue, Peter C.
 1987   Exhausting the Earth: State and Peasant in Hunan, 1500–1850. Cambridge: Harvard University Press.
Pfister, Christian
 1988   Short-term Variations in the Spring-Summer Climate of Central Europe from the High Middle Ages to 1850. *In* Lecture Notes in Earth Sciences, 1–14. Unpublished typescript.
Pickett, S. T. A., and P. S. White, eds.
 1985   The Ecology of Natural Disturbance and Patch Dynamics. Orlando, FL: Academic Press.
Pisani, Donald J.
 1985   Forests and Conservation, 1865–1890. Journal of American History 72 (September):340–59.
Pitkin, Hannah Fennichel
 1974   Wittgenstein and Social Justice. Berkeley: University of California Press.
Pope, Geoffrey G.
 1989   Bamboo in Human Evolution. Natural History (October):49–56.
Posey, Darrell
 1988   Kayapó Indian Natural-Resource Management. *In* People of the Tropical Rain Forest, Julie Sloan Denslow and Christine Padoch, eds., pp. 89–90. Berkeley and Los Angeles: University of California Press.
Powell, T. G. E.
 1966   Prehistoric Art. London: Thames & Hudson.
Prigogine, Ilya, and Isabelle Stengers
 1984   Order out of Chaos: Man's New Dialogue with Nature. Boulder, CO: Shambala/New Science Library.
Pyne, Stephen J.
 1982   Fire in America: A Cultural History of Wildland and Rural Fire. Princeton: Princeton University Press.
 1991   Burning Bush: A Fire History of Australia. New York: Holt.
Radcliffe-Brown, A. R.
 1957   A Natural Science of Society. Glencoe, IL: Free Press.
Rampino, Michael R., and Stephen Self
 1984   The Atmospheric Effects of El Chicón. Scientific American 251(1):48–57.
Rampino, Michael R., John E. Sanders, Walter S. Newman, and L. K. Königsson
 1987   Climate: History, Periodicity, and Predictability. New York: Van Nostrand Reinhold.
Reinhold, Brian
 1987   Weather Regimes: The Challenge in Extended-Range Forecasting. Science 235:437–41.
Reining, Priscilla
 1967   The Haya: The Agrarian System of a Sedentary People. Ph.D. dissertation, University of Chicago.

Renfrew, Colin, and John F. Cherry, eds.
  1986   Peer Polity Interaction and Socio-Political Change. Cambridge and New York: Cambridge University Press.
Richter, Hauptmann
  1900   Notizen über Lebensweise, Zeitrechnung, Industrie und Handwerk der Bewohner des Bezirk Bukoba. Mittheilungen aus dem Deutschen Schutzgebieten 13:115–26.
Ricklefs, Robert E.
  1987   Structural Ecology: A Review of "A Hierarchical Concept of Ecosystems." Science 236:206–7.
Rieter, E. R.
  1961   Jetstream Meteorology. Chicago: University of Chicago Press.
Rigler, F. H.
  1975   The Concept of Energy Flow and Nutrient Flow between Trophic Levels. In Unifying Concepts in Ecology, W. H. van Dobben and R. H. Lowe-McConnell, eds., pp. 15–26. The Hague: Dr. W. Junk B.V.
Roberts, John M., Chien Chiao, and Triloki N. Pandey
  1975   Meaningful God Sets from a Chinese Personal Pantheon and a Hindu Personal Pantheon. Ethnology 14:121–48.
Rossi-Landi, Ferruccio
  1983   Toward a Marxian Use of Wittgenstein. In Language as Work and Trade: A Semiotic Homology for Linguistics and Economics, Martha Adams, trans. South Hadley, MA: Bergin & Garvey.
Rotberg, R. I., and T. K. Rabb, eds.
  1981   Climate and History. Princeton: Princeton University Press.
Roussell, Aage
  1936   Sandnes and the Neighboring Farms. Meddelelser om Gronland 88(3).
Russell, J. C.
  1966   The Population of Medieval Egypt. Journal of the American Research Center in Egypt 5:69–82.
Sadler, Jon
  1991   Beetles, Boats, and Biogeography: Insect Invaders of the North Atlantic. In The Norse of the North Atlantic, G. F. Bigelow, ed., pp. 199–211. Acta Archaeological (Copenhagen) 61 (special issue).
Salmon, Merrilee H.
  1982   Philosophy of Archaeology. New York: Academic Press.
Schledermann, Peter
  1990   Crossroads to Greenland: 3000 Years of Prehistory in the High Arctic. In Komatik, no. 2. Calgary: Arctic Institute of North America.
Schleffer, Israel
  1967   Science and Subjectivity. Indianapolis: Bobbs-Merrill.
Schmidt, Peter R.
  1978   Historical Archaeology: A Structural Approach in an African Culture. Westport, Conn.: Greenwood Press.
  1980   Early Iron Age Settlements and Industrial Locales in West Lake. Tanzania Notes and Records 84–85:325–40.
  1983   Cultural Meaning and History in African Myth. International Journal of Oral History 4(3):165–83.
  1989   Early Exploitation and Settlement in the Usambara Mountains. In Forest Conservation in the East Usambara Mountains, Tanzania, A. C. Hamilton and R. Bensted-Smith, eds., pp. 75–78. Gland, Switzerland: IUCN.

Schmidt, Peter R., and D. H. Avery
1978   Complex Iron Smelting and Prehistoric Culture in Tanzania. Science 201:1085–89.
Schneider, Stephen H.
1987   Climate Modeling. Scientific American 256(5):72–80.
Schumacher, E. F.
1973   Small Is Beautiful: Economics as if People Mattered. New York: Harper & Row.
Selim, Hussein Kamel
1940   Twenty Years of Agricultural Development in Egypt (1919–1939). Cairo: Government Press.
Shepard, Paul
1973   The Tender Carnivore and the Sacred Game. New York: Scribner's.
Simenstad, C. A., J. A. Estes, and K. W. Kenyon
1978   Aleuts, Sea Otters, and Alternate Stable-State Communities. Science 200:403–11.
Simonsen, J. N., D. Cameron, and M. Gakinya
1988   Human Immunodeficiency Virus Infection among Men with Sexually Transmitted Diseases. New England Journal of Medicine 319:274.
Simpson, G. G.
1970   Uniformitarianism: An Inquiry into Principle, Theory, and Method in Geohistory and Biohistory. In Essays in Evolution and Genetics in Honor of Theodosius Dobzhansky, M. K. Hecht and W. C. Steere, eds., pp. 43–96. New York: Appleton-Century-Crofts.
Snow, C. P.
1959   The Two Cultures and the Scientific Revolution. New York: Cambridge University Press.
Soja, Edward W.
1985   The Spatiality of Social Life: Towards a Transformative Retheorisation. In Social Relations and Spatial Structures, Derek Gregory and John Urry, eds., pp. 90–127. New York: St. Martin's Press.
Solís de Merás, Gonzalo
1964   Pedro Menéndez de Avilés: Memorial. Translated by Jeannette Thurber Conner. Facsimile reproduction of the 1923 edition, with Introduction by Lyle N. McAlister. Gainesville: University of Florida Press.
Southwood, T. R. E.
1977   Habitat, the Templet for Ecological Strategies? Journal of Animal Ecology 46:337–65.
Stahle, David W., Edward R. Cook, and James W. C. Hehr
1985   Tree-ring Dating of Bald Cypress and the Potential for Millennia-long Chronologies in the Southeast. American Antiquity 50:796–802.
Stanley, Steven M.
1984   The New Evolutionary Timetable. New York: Basic Books.
Stapor, Frank W., Jr., Thomas D. Mathews, and Fonda E. Lindfors-Kearns
1991   Barrier Island Progradation and Holocene Sea-Level History in Southwest Florida. Journal of Coastal Research 7:815–38.
Steward, Julian
1949   Cultural Causality and Law: A Trial Formulation of Early Civilization. American Anthropologist 51:1–27.
Stockton, Charles W., William R. Boggess, and David M. Meko
1985   Climate and Tree Rings. In Paleoclimate Analysis and Modeling, Alan D. Hecht, ed., pp. 71–150. New York: John Wiley & Sons.

Stommel, Henry, and Elizabeth Stommel
    1979   The Year without a Summer. Scientific American 240(6):176–86.
    1983   Volcano Weather: The Story of 1816, the Year without Summer. Newport, RI:
            Seven Seas Press.
Straus, Lawrence Guy
    1991   Southwestern Europe at the Last Glacial Maximum. Current Anthropology
            32:189–99.
Sturtevant, William C.
    1978   The Last of the South Florida Aborigines. In Tacachale: Essays on the Indians of
            Florida and Southeastern Georgia during the Historic Period, Jerald T. Milanich
            and Samuel Proctor, eds., pp. 141–62. Gainesville: University Presses of Florida.
Taylor, Lily Ross
    1966   Party Politics in the Age of Caesar. Berkeley and Los Angeles: University of Cali-
            fornia Press.
Thomas, David
    1979   Naturalism and Social Science. Cambridge: Cambridge University Press.
Thomas, Elizabeth Marshall
    1990   The Old Way (Lions). New Yorker, 15 October, pp. 78–110.
Tobey, Ronald C.
    1981   Saving the Prairies: The Life Cycle of the Founding School of American Plant
            Ecology, 1895–1955. Berkeley: University of California Press.
Toulmin, Stephen
    1953   The Philosophy of Science. New York: Harper & Row.
Trewartha, Glenn T.
    1961   The Earth's Problem Climates. Madison: University of Wisconsin Press.
Trigger, Bruce G.
    1969   The Huron Farmers of the North. New York: Holt, Rinehart & Winston.
Trigger, Bruce G., B. J. Kemp, D. O'Connor, and A. B. Lloyd
    1983   Ancient Egypt: A Social History. Cambridge: Cambridge University Press.
Turpin, Solveig A.
    1987   Ethnohistorical Observations of Bison in the Lower Pecos River Region: Impli-
            cations for Environmental Change. Plains Anthropologist 32(118):424–29.
United States Conference of Mayors, Special Committee on Historic Preservation
    1966   With Heritage So Rich: A Report. New York: Random House.
Vargas Ugarte, Rubén
    1935   The First Jesuit Mission in Florida. United States Catholic Historical Society,
            Historical Records and Studies 25:59–148.
Viazzo, Pier Paolo
    1989   Upland Communities: Environment, Population and Social Structure in the
            Alps since the Sixteenth Century. New York: Cambridge University Press.
Vibe, Chr.
    1967   Arctic Animals in Relation to Climatic Fluctuations. Meddelelser om Grønland
            170(5).
Walker, Karen Jo
    1992   The Zooarchaeology of Charlotte Harbor's Prehistoric Maritime Adaptation:
            Spatial and Temporal Perspectives. In Culture and Environment in the Domain
            of the Calusa, William H. Marquardt, ed., pp. 265–366. Monograph 1. Gaines-
            ville: University of Florida, Institute of Archaeology and Paleoenvironmental
            Studies.

Wallace, Birgitta
1991   L'Anse aux Meadows: Gateway to Vinland. *In* The Norse of the North Atlantic, G. F. Bigelow, ed., pp. 166–198. Acta Archaeological (Copenhagen) 61 (special issue).
Wallace, S. L.
1938   Taxation in Egypt from Augustus to Diocletian. Princeton University Studies in Papyrology, no. 2. Princeton: Princeton University Press.
Waterbury, John
1982   Riverines and Lacustrines: Toward International Cooperation in the Nile Basin. Discussion Papers, no. 107. Princeton: Woodrow Wilson School of Public and International Affairs, Princeton University.
Weber, David J.
1986   Turner, the Boltonians, and the Borderlands. American Historical Review 91 (February):66–81.
Webster, Peter J.
1981   Monsoons. Scientific American 245(2):108–18.
Wells, Peter S.
1984   Farms, Villages, and Cities: Commerce and Urban Origins in Late Prehistoric Europe. Ithaca: Cornell University Press.
Wendland, W. M., and Reid A. Bryson
1974   Dating Climatic Episodes of the Holocene. Quaternary Research 4:9–24.
Wenke, Robert J.
1989   Egypt: Origins of Complex Societies. Annual Review of Anthropology 18:129–55.
White, Leslie A.
1949   The Science of Culture. New York: Grove Press.
1959   The Evolution of Culture. New York: McGraw-Hill.
White, Luise
1990   The Comforts of Home: Prostitution in Colonial Nairobi. Chicago: University of Chicago Press.
White, Richard
1983   The Roots of Dependency: Subsistence, Environment, and Social Change among the Choctaws, Pawnees, and Navajos. Lincoln: University of Nebraska Press.
1985   American Environmental History: The Development of a New Historical Field. Pacific Historical Review 54:297–335.
Whittaker, R. H., and G. M. Woodwell
1972   Evolution of Natural Communities. *In* Ecosystem Structure and Function, J. A. Wiens, ed., pp. 137–59. Corvallis: Oregon State University Press.
Whorf, Benjamin Lee
1978   The Relation of Habitual Thought and Behavior to Language. *In* Language, Thought, and Reality, by Benjamin Lee Whorf, pp. 134–59. Cambridge: MIT Press. [First published in 1956]
Widmer, Randolph J.
1988   The Evolution of the Calusa: A Non-Agricultural Chiefdom on the Southwest Florida Coast. Tuscaloosa: University of Alabama Press.
Wiens, J. A.
1976   Population Responses to Patchy Environments. Annual Review of Ecology and Systematics 7:81–120.
1985   Vertebrate Responses to Environmental Patchiness in Arid and Semiarid Ecosystems. *In* The Ecology of Natural Disturbance and Patch Dynamics, S. T. A. Picket and P. S. White, eds., pp. 169–93. Orlando, FL: Academic Press.

Wilkie, David S.
 1988   Hunters and Farmers of the African Forest. *In* People of the Tropical Rain For-
        est, Julie Sloan Denslow and Christine Padoch, eds., pp. 111–26. Berkeley and
        Los Angeles: University of California Press.
Will, Pierre-Etienne
 1980   Bureaucratie et famine en Chine au 18e siècle. Paris: Mouton.
Willcocks, W.
 1899   Egyptian Irrigation. London: Spon.
Willcocks, W., and J. I. Craig
 1913   Egyptian Irrigation. 2 vols. London: Spon.
Willey, Gordon R., and Philip Phillips
 1958   Method and Theory in American Archaeology. Chicago: University of Chi-
        cago Press.
Williams, L. D., and T. M. L. Wigley
 1983   A Comparison of Evidence for Late Holocene Summer Temperature Variations
        in the Northern Hemisphere. Quaternary Research 20(3):286–307.
Williams, Raymond
 1977   Marxism and Literature. Oxford: Oxford University Press.
Wilson, J. A.
 1955   Buto and Hierakonpolis in the Geography of Egypt. Journal of Near Eastern
        Studies 14:209–36.
Winch, Peter
 1976   The Idea of a Social Science and Its Relation to Philosophy. New York: Humani-
        ties Press.
Winterhalder, Bruce
 1980   Environmental Analysis in Human Evolution and Adaptation Research. Human
        Ecology 8:135–70.
 1983a History and Ecology of the Boreal Zone in Ontario. *In* Boreal Forest Adapta-
        tions: The Northern Algonkians, A. T. Steegmann, Jr., ed., pp. 9–54. New York:
        Plenum Press.
 1983b Boreal Foraging Strategies. *In* Boreal Forest Adaptations: The Northern
        Algonkians, A. T. Steegmann, Jr., ed., pp. 201–41. New York: Plenum Press.
 1984   Reconsidering the Ecosystem Concept. Reviews in Anthropology 12:301–13.
 In press   Rainfall and Temperature Patterning and Predictability with Respect to Water
        Management in the Central Andes of Southern Peru. *In* Irrigation at High
        Altitudes: The Social Organization of Water Control Systems in the Andes,
        W. Mitchell and D. Guillet, eds. Washington, D.C.: Society for Latin American
        Anthropology.
Winterhalder, Bruce, and E. A. Smith
 1992   Evolutionary Ecology and the Social Sciences: An Introduction. *In* Evolutionary
        Ecology and Human Behavior, E. A. Smith and B. Winterhalder, eds., pp. 3–23.
        New York: Aldine de Gruyter.
Wolf, Eric R.
 1982   Europe and the People without History. Berkeley and Los Angeles: University
        of California Press.
Wolpoff, Milford H.
 1989   The Place of Neanderthals in Human Evolution. *In* The Emergence of Mod-
        ern Humans: Biocultural Adaptations in the Late Pleistocene, E. Trinkaus, ed.
        A School of American Research Advanced Studies Seminar Publication. Cam-
        bridge: Cambridge University Press.

Woodwell, G. M., and D. B. Botkin
  1970   Metabolism of Terrestrial Ecosystems by Gas Exchange Techniques: The Brook-
          haven Approach. *In* Analysis of Temperate Forest Ecosystems, D. E. Reichle, ed.,
          pp. 73–85. New York: Springer-Verlag.
World Bank
  1972   The Limits of Growth. Report of the Club of Rome on the State of Mankind.
          London.
Worster, Donald
  1977   Nature's Economy: A History of Ecological Ideas. New York: Cambridge Uni-
          versity Press.
  1984   History as Natural History: An Essay on Theory and Method. Pacific Historical
          Review 53:1–19.
  1985   Rivers of Empire: Water, Aridity, and the Growth of the American West. New
          York: Pantheon Books.
  1986   Review of David Pepper, The Roots of Modern Environmentalism (Dover, NH:
          Croom Helm, 1984). Journal of Forest History 30(1):46–47.
  1988a Appendix: Doing Environmental History. *In* The Ends of the Earth: Perspec-
          tives on Modern Environmental History, D. Worster, ed., pp. 289–307. Cam-
          bridge: Cambridge University Press.
  1988b The Vulnerable Earth: Toward a Planetary History. *In* The Ends of the Earth:
          Perspectives on Modern Environmental History, D. Worster, ed., pp. 3–20.
          Cambridge: Cambridge University Press.
  1990   The Ecology of Order and Chaos. Environmental History Review 14 (Spring/
          Summer):1–18.
Zakry, Antoun
  1926   The Nile in Pharaonic and Arab Periods [in Arabic]. Cairo: Maarif.
Zubillaga, Felix, ed.
  1946   Monumenta Antiquae Floridae (1566–1572). Monumenta Missionum Societa-
          tis Iesu, 3. Rome.
Zubrow, Ezra
  1990   The Depopulation of Native America. Antiquity 64:754–65.

Index

SCHOOL OF AMERICAN RESEARCH ADVANCED SEMINAR SERIES

SCHOOL OF AMERICAN RESEARCH ADVANCED SEMINAR SERIES

Published by University of New Mexico Press

Director of Publications: Joan K. O'Donnell
Copy Editor: June-el Piper
Designer: Deborah Flynn Post
Indexer: Douglas J. Easton
Typographer: Tseng Information Systems, Inc.
Printer: Edwards Brothers, Inc.

This book was set in Linotron Sabon and Berkeley Old Style Book.
The book paper is made from acid-free, recycled fibers.

Participants in the advanced seminar *Historical Ecology*.

Left to right:

Joel D. Gunn

Fekri A. Hassan

Peter R. Schmidt

Bruce P. Winterhalder

William H. Marquardt

Carole L. Crumley

Thomas H. McGovern

Alice E. Ingerson

Thomas C. Patterson

Christine Padoch